Situating Women

Gender Politics and Circumstance in Fiji

Situating Women

Gender Politics and Circumstance in Fiji

Nicole George

Australian
National
University

E PRESS

ANU
E PRESS

Published by ANU E Press
The Australian National University
Canberra ACT 0200, Australia
Email: anuepress@anu.edu.au
This title is also available online at http://epress.anu.edu.au

National Library of Australia Cataloguing-in-Publication entry

Author: George, Nicole Louise, 1966-

Title: Situating women: gender politics and circumstance in Fiji /
               Nicole George.

ISBN: 9781922144140 (pbk.) 9781922144157 (ebook)

Notes: Includes bibliographical references.

Subjects: Women--Political activity--Fiji.
               Women in development--Fiji.
               Sex discrimination against women--Fiji.
               Women's rights--Fiji.
               Women--Government policy--Fiji.

Dewey Number: 305.4099611

Cover design and layout by ANU E Press

Contents

In memory of Amelia Rokotuivuna

Maps and Illustrations

Maps

Illustrations

Acknowledgements

The research presented in this book was shaped in profound ways by my discussions with the early generation of gender activists who worked in Fiji in the Independence era and by one woman in particular, Amelia Rokotuivuna. I encountered Amelia as I started out on this research journey. At that stage she was semi-retired. Her health was failing. But she still retained her reputation as a radical. Indeed I had seen a few instances of this as I moved around Suva in the preceding months. I was intrigued by her, but hesitant. When we finally met I was inspired by her commitment, her intellect and her warmth.

Amelia became a figure central to the story I was weaving. She did more than assist my work as an informant. She provided me with an anchor. From her recollections, and her later generosity in entrusting me with the entire Fiji YWCA archival record, I was able to develop an understanding of the motivations which underpinned women's advocacy in the period when things became 'political'. This allowed me to 'situate' my examination of gender advocacy in later periods as the motivations of activist women shifted both in response to Fiji's tumultuous post-colonial history and the changing geopolitics of the region. Amelia's influence on the story I develop in these pages has been profound. I was fortunate to meet her and to be trusted by her. I profoundly regret that she did not see the first completed draft of this book before she passed away in 2005. I am sure there are things in it that would have made her unhappy. Nonetheless, the joy of 'giving back' my manuscript would have been worth opening up my work to her piercing critique.

I am thankful, however, that with publication comes the opportunity to 'give back', if only a little, to the many others who have so kindly assisted the development of this book. The ranks of Pacific experts at The Australian National University are legendary and I was immensely fortunate to begin this research in their proximity. Two figures amongst that population, Margaret Jolly and Greg Fry deserve my greatest thanks. Their example as committed, honest and rigorous researchers has helped me to understand with clarity, what it means to be a scholar. In addition to their ongoing mentorship in career-related matters, I value knowing them both as dear and generous friends. As much as anything, this book is the product of their unwearying encouragement.

My colleagues within the field of international relations and political science both at the ANU and, since 2009, at the University of Queensland, have provided me with a strong basis of professional support. I have greatly valued their willingness to seriously engage with my work and to defend the importance of my research agenda. To this end I am profoundly indebted to Chris Reus-Smit, Heather Rae, Paul Keal, Jacinta O'Hagen, Katherine Morton and Gavin Mount with whom I worked at the ANU, and Richard Devetak, Roland Bleiker, Tim Dunne, Gillian Whitehouse, Andy Hindmoor, Melissa Curley and Frank Mols, at UQ. I have been privileged to work amongst such diligent and accomplished people who continually provide great inspiration to achieve. I am grateful to Ewan Maidment from the Pacific Manuscripts Bureau (ANU) for microfilming the YWCA archive originally in 2002, and to Kylie Moloney who later arranged to digitise this collection in 2012. Thanks are also due to the Education and Multimedia Services, College of Asia and the Pacific (ANU) for preparing the detailed maps which appear in the introductory chapter of this book.

This research would not have been possible without the cooperation of many women and men in Fiji who indulged my requests for interviews with great generosity and who frequently spent many hours explaining the local terrain of gender politics in great detail. Thanks in particular to Claire Slatter, Peni Moore, Sharon Bhagwan Rolls, Dianne Goodwillie, Ruth Lechte, Tupou Vere, Nisha Buksh, Peter Sipeli, Carlos Perera, Gina Houng Lee, Viri Buadromo and Luisa Tora for their eagerness to assist during field work and the interest they have shown in my research. In addition, I am profoundly grateful to those in Fiji who in the ten years since I began my work in the country have become research collaborators and friends. My heart skips a beat when I now disembark from my plane at Nausori Airport and think about continuing discussions with my Suva-based colleagues: Sandra Tarte, Claire Slatter, Ashwin Raj, Peni Moore, Asenati Liki Chan Tung and Alumita Durutalo.

I am immensely grateful to Carolyn Brewer, described to me as the best copy-editor at the ANU, Mary Louise Hickey, also working at the ANU, and Sara Meger, currently located at the University of Melbourne, for helping me navigate all the technical issues that are involved when one turns a manuscript into a book. I thank those associated with the Pacific Studies series at ANU E Press and particularly Margaret Jolly and Stewart Firth for locating the financial resources to fund some of this work.

There is plenty to 'give back' when a project such as this is completed, and more than anything I feel indebted to my family. Without their practical and emotional support, my ability to complete this research and bring it to publication would have been seriously tested. My parents have shown unswerving faith in me and a pride in my achievements that inspires me to continue. My beautiful children, Angus and Olivia have endured my frequent field-work-related absences with stoicism beyond their years. My partner Gavin has continued to support my career even when our daily juggling routine becomes mired in complexity and competing obligations. His love, patience and continued encouragement have been invaluable and are never taken for granted.

Abbreviations and Acronyms

ACP-EU	African Caribbean Pacific-European Union Accord
ACS	Adi Cakobau School
ACWF	All China Women's Federation
ACWIN	Action Centre for Women in Need
AIDAB	Australian International Development Assistance Bureau (later AusAID)
ANU	Australian National University
ATOM	Against Testing on Muroroa
AusAID	Australian Agency for International Development
AWID	Association for Women's Rights in Development
BPA	Beijing Platform for Action
CCF	Citizens' Constitutional Forum
CEDAW	Convention For the Elimination of Discrimination Against Women
CSR	Colonial Sugar Refineries
CWGL	Center for Women's Global Leadership
DAWN	Development Alternatives with Women for a New Era
DFID	Department for International Development
ECREA	Ecumenical Centre for Research Education and Advocacy
ESCAP	Economic and Social Commission for Asia and the Pacific
FHRC	Fiji Human Rights Commission
FLRC	Fiji Law Reform Commission
FLS	Forward Looking Strategies
FTUC	Fiji Trade Union Council
FWCC	Fiji Women's Crisis Centre
FWRM	Fiji Women's Rights Movement
GPA	Global Platform for Action
IMF	International Monetary Fund
IWDA	International Women's Development Agency
IWTC	International Women's Tribune Centre
IWY	International Women's Year
NCW	National Council of Women
NGO	Non-governmental Organisation
NFP	National Federation Party
NIEO	New International Economic Order
PAC	Public Affairs Committee

PACER	Pacific Island Countries Agreement on Closer Economic Relations
PACER-PLUS	A regional structure for Pacific free trade
PAMBU	Pacific Manuscript Bureau
PANG	Pacific Network on Globalisation
PCP	Pacific Centre for Peacebuilding
PICTA	Pacific Island Countries Trade Agreement
PNG	Papua New Guinea
PPA	Pacific Platform for Action
PPSEAWA	Pan Pacific and Southeast Asian Women's Association
RTU	Reconciliation, Tolerance and Unity Bill
PWRB	Pacific Women's Resource Bureau
PWRC	Pacific Women's Resource Centre
RRRT	Regional Rights Resource Team
SCF	Save the Children Fiji
SDL	Soqosoqo Duavata ni Lawenivanua
SPC	South Pacific Commission
SSVM	Soqosoqo Vakamarama I Taukei
SVT	Soqosoqo ni Vakavulewa ni Taukei
UN	United Nations
UNCEDAW	United Nations Convention For the Elimination of Discrimination Against Women
UNDP	UN Development Programme
UNDP-RRRT	UN Development Programme-Regional Rights Resource Team
UNIFEM	United Nations Development Fund for Women
UNIWY	United Nations International Women's Year
UNESCAP	United Nations Economic and Social Commission for Asia and the Pacific
UNGASS	United Nations Generally Assembly Special Session
USP	University of the South Pacific
VAT	Value Added Tax
WAC	Women's Action for Change
WAC/SM	Women's Action for Change/Sexual Minorities Project
WAD'aP	Women's Action for Democracy and Peace
WID	Women in Development
WILPF	Women's International League for Peace and Freedom
WIP	Women In Politics
YWCA	Young Women's Christian Association

Introduction: Situating Women

'A 'ohe o kahi nana o luna o ka pali; iho mai a lalo nei; 'ike I ke au nui ke au iji he alo a he alo.

The top of the cliff isn't the place to look at us; come down here and learn of the big and little currents, face to face (Pukui 1983: 24).[1]

Feminist international relations and political science scholarship has, in the last two decades, demonstrated an increasing interest in the political agency of women's organisations. The claim that the institutions of global governance— the state, multilateral organisations and financial institutions—are 'gendered, and gendered male' (Pettman 1996: vii),[2] has underpinned this scholarship. As a result, feminist scholars have turned their attention to alternative spheres of political engagement which have allowed women to have a global political voice. From this perspective, women's organising is recognised as a significant realm of collective political activity with the capacity to challenge or initiate change within the structures of global governance.

Scholarship on this subject can easily incite controversy, as Peggy Antrobus notes in the opening lines of her book *The Global Women's Movement* (Antrobus 2004: 1). Some studies have avoided this by emphasising the celebratory aspects of women's activism and the many gains that women's organisations have achieved in making 'gender matter'[3] within formal political institutions (Reilly 2009; Brown Thompson 2002; Keck and Sikkink 1998; Joachim 1999, 2003; True and Mintrom 2001; Stephenson 1995). This work amasses a strong body of evidence to support the claim that women's organisations have been local *and* global drivers of political reform. The reforms are charted in a relatively uncomplicated manner, and the final analysis is, presumably, pleasing to all those who read it.

---

1   This quote, drawn from a collection of Hawaiian language proverbs edited by Mary Kawena Pukui, is originally cited by Teresia Teaiwa in her article tracing the evolution of Pacific native cultural studies entitled 'Lo(o)sing the edge,' which appeared in *The Contemporary Pacific* in 2001. Teaiwa's discussion of academic frames of reference and analytical perspectives is particularly relevant to the methodological approaches adopted in this book (Teaiwa 2001: 343).

2   Jindy Pettman has made this claim primarily in relation to states; however, a wide range of feminist scholarship demonstrates that this claim can be extended to also include international multilateral organisations. A contemporary diffusion of gender equity norms may be apparent within the rhetoric of global governance, yet, as this scholarship attests, formal political institutions continue to function in ways which contribute to women's political and economic subordination (Pettman 1996; Elshtain 1981; Grant 1991; Peterson 1992; Goetz 1997; Tinker 1999; Rankin 2002; Peterson and Runyan 2010; Parpart and Zalewski 2008).

3   A conscious play on the title of the book *Making Women Matter* by Hilkka Pietilä and Jeanne Vickers (1996) which discusses how women have shaped gender policy within the United Nations.

But others have told this story in a different way. Adopting an alternative structure which emphasises a counter-politics of resistance rather than reform, these studies give closer critical attention to the challenges which have been unmet by the women's movement. They consider the institutional obstacles which have impeded women's progress, even the movement's unresolved internal tensions as activist agendas come to more closely resemble rather than challenge the conservative discourses on women promoted by a range of contemporary institutional actors. This work generates findings that are more uncomfortable and raises questions about the costs that women's movements incur as they become 'professionalised' through their engagement with formal political institutions (Yuval-Davis 2006: 288; Kahn 2002; Tobar 2003; Alvarez 1999; Lang 1997; Antrobus 1984).

It could be argued that these contending evaluations of women's organisations are underpinned by interesting 'ideal-typical' understandings of how women's movements should operate (Marx-Ferree 2006: 10). Both seem to offer compelling, if opposing, illustrations of women's capacities for political agency. But could they also be criticised for making their assessments from an analytical 'cliff-top'? Each portrait seems to easily privilege identifiable forms of reform- or resistance-oriented organisational activity and its alignment with pre-established ideals dictating the 'right' type of behavior for women's groups. Yet such assessments may simultaneously ignore the flux and contradiction that are an inherent part of everyday political life and how these too shape women's movements. Might we gain a different perspective of women's organising if a greater effort was made to understand the 'currents' which shape gender activists' own understandings of what has resulted locally, and globally, from their political activity, and equally, what courses of action they have judged to be politically viable at particular historical moments?

In this study, I develop a different analytical approach to the study of women's organising. My aim is develop a method of enquiry which goes beyond ideal-type assessments of organisational behaviour and the resultant narratives which often appear to map a linear trajectory of women's waxing or waning political influence over time. My own study of women's organising and gender politics in Fiji, and the broader Pacific region, gives extended consideration to the prevailing currents—socio-cultural, political, economic, religious, domestic and global—that have shaped the political landscapes negotiated by women activists across the past forty years. Importantly, I show how these broader factors influence the decisions women activists make about the appropriateness of their various advocacy strategies. Like many studies of gender politics conducted in other settings, this book therefore examines the emergence of evident trends in women's advocacy conducted on the local, regional and international stage since the 1960s. What makes this study distinctive, however, is the effort made to situate this activity within a global and local political context. In short, this investigation is driven by a preliminary question: How is women's political agency shaped by broader political contingencies?

The importance of such an approach was brought home to me with some urgency in the early stages of researching this project. Working as a volunteer with a Suva-based women's organisation in early 2002, I attended a forum hosted by the Fiji government's Ministry of Women on public policy approaches to gender mainstreaming in the convivial setting of Suva's Tradewinds Hotel. Participants at this meeting represented a diverse range of women's non-government organisations (NGOs), various aid organisations, a number of regional intergovernmental agencies, and members of Fiji's national government. Most of the forum's sessions involved presentations from a team of Asian Development Bank (ADB) consultants who had been coordinating a pilot gender mainstreaming project within two of Fiji's government ministries. On the whole, the forum's design afforded those assembled little opportunity for comment or feedback on presentations. The assembled audience of women's NGO representatives seemed to observe the proceedings quietly. At one point, however, a startling intervention took place as an older woman in the audience began to admonish the speakers for their prescriptive tone and their apparent disinterest in dialogue. 'NGOs want meaningful consultation,' she protested. She continued,

> This comes through a genesis of policy. Government wants the support of NGOs but the NGOs feel that they are not being consulted enough. They want to be part of the process. You talk about the need for NGOs to get on board. The government are [*sic*] the ones that don't understand the processes of gender mainstreaming not NGOs!

This blunt interjection and the woman's agitated demeanour contrasted dramatically with the general, more diplomatic tenor of the meeting. And while I imagined that many of the audience members may have agreed with the substance of the woman's comments, and particularly her dissatisfaction with the lack of opportunities for consultation, she received no audible signs of support from other women in the room. In fact, her interjection was greeted with silence.

The audacity of the woman's response immediately sparked my interest. I was later told that the meeting's heckler was Amelia Rokotuivuna, a figure who had played an important role within the Fiji Young Women's Christian Association (YWCA), and someone recognised throughout the Pacific as a major contributor to regional debate on the status of women. Before embarking on this research trip, I had been told about Amelia's radical political profile in the 1960s and

1970s and her courageous efforts to promote social justice. As I saw for myself, some forty years later, Amelia had lost none of her legendary capacity for forthrightness.

In the weeks and months which followed, and as a result of follow-up trips made to Suva in later periods, I came to know Amelia better. I spent many hours talking to her about her involvement in Fiji's YWCA, her efforts to realise the goals of equitable development and peace in the Pacific, and her views about the contemporary terrain of women's organising in Fiji. In all of these discussions, I found Amelia to be no less frank than on the day I first observed her addressing (or perhaps that should be 'dressing-down') the ADB consultants. She would answer my questions directly, let me know in unambiguous terms if she thought I was assuming something incorrect, and offer piercing assessments of current gender advocacy strategies.

Amelia described herself as an early pioneer of the women's movement in Fiji and, as part of the executive of the newly formed YWCA, she and her associates certainly developed a far more politicised style of advocacy than had previously been the norm for women's organisations. Thanks to this work, she has been recognised regionally and internationally for the role she played spearheading campaigns which promoted women's rights to birth control, opposed Fiji's institutionalised systems of race discrimination, and identified threats to regional peace and security posed by powers outside the Pacific Islands.

However, as a result of discussions conducted with many other women activists in Fiji, I also came to understand that Amelia's uncompromising style reflected a trend in gender politics that was often criticised as outmoded and no longer appropriate. And this, in part, explained the silence which greeted her outburst at the forum described above. For some, the tone and substance of Amelia's brand of advocacy was deemed counterproductive for women's organisations in Fiji in this particular period because it too easily encouraged hostility and negative responses from a conservative and politically dominant section of Fijian society. Activist women therefore voiced the opinion that, if real gains for women were to be secured in the current context, strategies of engagement rather than confrontation were required.

How were these shifts in the tenor of women's advocacy to be understood? When asked about this, many of my interlocutors pointed out that although activists had adopted a more moderate political tone, their efforts to challenge women's subordination continued to be viewed in controversial terms by many of Fiji's political and religious leaders. The suggestion here was that radicalism was not absent from Fiji's women's movement, but simply present in ways that were different from the radicalism of the past. While such scenarios alerted me to the importance of understanding the shifts which take place within the realm of gender advocacy over time, they also highlighted the need for careful examination of the prevailing political circumstances in which advocacy takes place, with attention paid to how these circumstances alter and perhaps necessitate the formulation of new political strategies and agendas.

This book, therefore seeks to contribute to broader scholarship on women's political agency by examining changing political contexts and considering how these shape the political agendas pursued by women's organisations. In focusing upon the shifting currents of political life, at the local, regional and international levels across the previous four decades, this book demonstrates the 'complexities' of women's political agency (Leckie 2002: 156). My aim here is to examine how particular trends evident in women's political advocacy emerge at particular historical junctures and can be explained by shifts in the prevailing global and local political environment.

Fiji provides an important site for study of this type. The women's movement in this setting is generally viewed as one of the strongest and most successful in the Pacific Island region (Jolly 2005a: 153), thanks to the intensity of activists' political engagement and their increasing national, regional and international influence. Through a range of sustained campaigns they have raised the profile of issues such as women's legal status, gender violence, women's media presence and women's rights to fair wages. They have won important government reforms for women in areas such as ministerial representation and law reform.

Fiji's women activists have also been active participants on the regional and international political stage. Their efforts to focus international attention on the specific phenomena disadvantaging women in Pacific contexts have won global recognition and demonstrated the transnational reach of their advocacy (Keck and Sikkink 1998: 185; Merry 2006a and 2006b; Riles 2001; Fraser 1987).

Yet developments within the realm of gender politics in Fiji cannot simply be mapped in a way which suggests a linear trajectory of increasing political influence. As will be demonstrated, Fiji's women activists have, since decolonisation, also worked within a volatile local political environment and negotiated serious challenges to national stability. The ramifications of the four coups that have taken place in Fiji since 1987, the development crises and communal tensions that these events have triggered, and the ensuing political struggles that have been waged over Fiji's governance structures have had important impacts within the realm of women's organising and have tended to shape women's political agency in complex ways.

Authoritarianism has generally been the counterpart of coup-making in Fiji and this has made the operations of some women's organisations precarious in certain instances. Post-coup political elites have frequently favoured restrictive interpretations of cultural and religious mores in an effort to protect indigenous political privilege (Lawson 1996). This has constrained the political role of women and often helped to de-legitimise the views of those female critics who have challenged Fiji's self-imposed regimes. This has discouraged some women activists from articulating overtly politicised or highly partisan agendas but the trend has not been universal. Other women have taken active and often conflicting roles in the ongoing debate which rages in Fiji about how the country should be governed. They have linked efforts to promote women's status with more broadly held concerns about appropriate models of governance and development for the country overall. For all activists, however, the impact of changing local political circumstances, in combination with shifting international norms influencing the directions of global political debate on questions of governance and development, has been profound. These changing circumstances have shaped activists' understandings of their political capacity at various points in time, and ultimately influenced the way they have articulated and pursued political goals within local and international arenas.

Demonstrating the impact of these broader political contingencies and how they have shaped women's political agency is, therefore, a key objective of this study. Yet my use of the term contingency should not be confused with those modes of critical academic enquiry which aim to 'disassemble' universal claims through the demonstration of 'radical historical contingency and modes of construction for everything' (Haraway 1991). Rather, I use the term contingency to examine the relationship between political agency and political context. In this sense, contingency is understood as a broadly encompassing term. It signifies the conjuncture of events and political circumstances which influence the political strategies employed by Fiji-based women's organisations at particular points in time, and within particular arenas of political activity—local, regional or international. Through the use of the term contingency, I seek to explain how historical legacies, socio-cultural influences, sites of local political contestation, and broader international norms relating to governance and development shape the terrain of gender advocacy in Fiji. Ultimately, this enables me to develop a situated account of the local and global political agency of Fiji's women's organisations in the previous four decades.

These insights are further extended through close attention to gender activists' own understandings of what has been achieved and what is possible in particular contexts. From this perspective, agency is not only considered in terms of outcome or influence, but also 'situated' through an added consideration of the meanings which actors themselves ascribe to the events under consideration. As such, I borrow from Donna Haraway's (1991) concept of 'situated knowledge' and construct a 'situated' history of women's organising which employs participant observation and textual and archival analysis as investigative tools while also drawing heavily from gender advocates' oral histories, gathered through 'face-to-face' conversations. This approach allows for greater reflection upon the ways politically active women have appraised the events under consideration (a more precise elaboration of this study's methodology follows in a later section of this chapter).

Examining gender politics in Fiji in a way which employs a situated perspective and is sensitive to activists' own perceptions and evaluations of their political actions will ultimately enable a more nuanced understanding of women's political agency. Chiefly, it will enable me to demonstrate how, at each level of political engagement—domestic, regional and international—the activity of Fiji's women's organisations has been shaped by interplaying global and local factors. By focusing upon activists' own understandings of these influences, I will show how they shape organisational activity, opening up some avenues of institutional engagement and closing off others. The result is a study which emphasises 'face-to-face' learning and an understanding of how Fiji's women activists have navigated the 'big and little' currents which shape their political environment. This approach differs in important respects from more conventional academic approaches to the study of women's movements in other contexts.

Conceptual framework

Scholarly examinations of women's organising generally tend to be oriented in two ways. Either they emphasise the reform capacities of women's organisations and their institutional agency, or they demonstrate these groups' capacity to act as sites of resistance to the formalised realm of politics. Across both perspectives, there tends to be a similar interest in establishing a conceptual distance between the organisational and institutional realms. This is done by highlighting particular features and approaches to the exercise of power which are said to be distinctive to the domain of women's organising and by contrasting these with the more formal, institutional sphere. This sees a heavy emphasis placed upon collectivity, progressive ideas and transnationalism as characteristic features of women's organising. These features are routinely contrasted with those said to define institutional politics and which are alternatively construed as hierarchical, conservative and governed internationally by state interest (Lang 1997; Alvarez 1999; Joachim 1999, 2003; True and Mintrom 2001; Walker 1984; Stephenson 1995; Ferguson 1984). It has been common for feminist researchers to therefore assert that the features of collectivity, progressive ideas and transnationalism define the realm of women's organising *and* enhance the political agency of women's groups in national and international politics.

Feminist researchers employing a reform-oriented perspective have frequently described the collective basis of women's approach to power as a characteristic style of political engagement which differentiates this realm from the more hierarchical and individually competitive institutional political sphere (Reilly 2009; Marques-Pereira and Siim 2002; Stephenson 1995; Ferguson 1984). Emphasis is placed upon the horizontal and collective organisational structures of women's groups, said to enable a distinctive, fluid and participatory style of political engagement (Walker 1984; Goetz 1997; Lang 1997; Alvarez 1999; Friedman 1999). Those working from a resistance orientation also privilege the collective and 'transversal' aspect of women's organising as distinctive and enabling a 'politics of dialogue and communication' (Yuval-Davis 2006: 281). This is viewed as challenging 'assimilationist universalism' on the one hand and the reification of difference to the point of exclusion on the other (Yuval-Davis 2006: 281). Yet the integrity of this transversal politics is said to be threatened when women's organisations engage with institutional actors, be they state-based bureaucracies or multilateral organisations. These are often judged to interfere with the collective structure of women's groups and encourage the emergence of hierarchies within and between organisations (Yuval-Davis 2006; Riles 2001; Lang 1997; Alvarez 1999; Friedman 1999).

The idea that women's organising is a realm of progressive ideas also features in a great deal of feminist literature on women's organising. Within reform-oriented studies, women's organisations are seen to respond to the needs of grass-roots women in ways which are more innovative and progressive than gendered (masculine dominated) institutions (Joachim 1999, 2003; True and Mintrom 2001; Walker 1984; Karl 1995; Kaplan 1997). Within resistance-oriented perspectives this innovative potential is celebrated but also seen to be stifled as a result of institutional engagement (Rankin 2002; Bergeron 2003; Steinstra 1994; Tinker 1999; Lang 1997; Alvarez 1999).

References to transnationalism constitute a third important feature of feminist research on women's organising. In this context, transnationalism is generally defined loosely, taken to signify 'any actor, organisation, or issue that could be either international or global in orientation' (Booth 1998: 120). Within studies of women's organising, utilisation of this concept draws attention to the international correspondence between women's struggles in localised settings, and emphasises the broader global frequency of women's movements (Al-Ali 2003; Alvarez 1999). At the same time, the notion of transnationalism is felt to enable a more flexible approach to comparative appraisals of feminist politics at the global level. This term is used to avoid questions of gender subordination being articulated in ways which reference hegemonic universalising ideals (Ackerly 2001; Reilly 2009) or romantic, yet essentialising images of 'global sisterhood' (Alexander and Mohanty 1997; Grewal and Kaplan 1994). Transnationalism therefore enables consideration to be given to the common feminist perspectives which link the efforts of advocates while simultaneously acknowledging the specific circumstances which contribute to gender subordination in particular settings. This 'principled' transnationalism is contrasted with the more self-interested international relations that occur within the realm of state-centric institutional politics (True and Mintrom 2001; Keck and Sikkink 1998).

Transnationalism within the sphere of women's organising is viewed as facilitating the emergence of consensual norms (Jaquette 2003) which allow for a 'more internationalised and multilayered feminist politics' attentive to the intersectional influences—class, age, religion, ethnicity—that contribute to women's disadvantage (Pettman 1996, 212; Reilly 2009: 14–15; Ackerly 2001). Conversely, resistance-oriented accounts have suggested that over-emphasising transnationalism can distract women's organisations from responding to urgent issues of concern to women at the local level (Friedman 1999; Riles 2001; Spivak 1996; Oloka-Onyango and Tamale 1995). Others have been sceptical of the extent to which feminist transnationalism is truly participatory. They argue that a sense of superiority amongst western feminists often combined with a misplaced 'saviour' narrative, alienated women from the global South in the 1970s and has continued to negatively mark encounters between women from the west and non-west today (Tripp 2006).

This study addresses the same aspects of organisational activity—collectivity, progressive ideas and transnationalism—which feature in the accounts described above. My objective here, however, is to describe these features in a way which is sensitive to the changing contingencies—local and global—which shape political life in Fiji. In this way, I avoid privileging assumptions about organisational structures, ambitions or transnational engagements in ways that reinforce the idea of distance between women's organising and a monolithic institutional politics. To do this, I place a heavy emphasis upon 'situated' understandings of these aspects of organisational behaviour and examine gender activists' own appraisals of how they contribute to women's political agency. To this end, I aim to construct a 'situated' history of women's organising in Fiji which examines how gender advocates have themselves understood the significance of, and possibilities for, collectivity, progressive ideas and transnationalism at particular historical junctures.

'Situating' method

The utility of developing a 'situated history' of women's organising is beneficial in two key respects. First, it allows a comparison of organisational activities across time, *as well as* a comparative discussion of gender activists' motivations.

As such, the history recounted in these pages becomes not simply a story of women's campaigning towards achieved political outcomes, but instead, a nuanced and contextualised reflection upon women's political ambition and the factors which account for shifts in that ambition over time. This study provides an important counter narrative to a great deal of the feminist research into women's organising which tends to map political 'achievement' in ways that suggest either a teleology of increasing institutional agency or a negative teleology of increasing institutional cooptation. Instead, this study is inspired by a more limited body of work on women's organising which emphasises greater attention paid to political agency in context (outlined in greater detail in the following chapter). It therefore examines how activists' understandings of prevailing political circumstance have shaped their political ambitions and, in turn, how this translates into political achievement.

Second, this approach allows for Pacific women to feature as differentiated agents of history, rather than homogenous and passive observers (or even victims) of history. My historical account of campaigns undertaken by Fiji's activists to advance the status of women locally, and across the region generally, provides important insights into how Pacific women have contributed to projects of social and political change. This activity was certainly not uniform, and did not always achieve its intended aims. Yet scrutiny of women activists' personal explanations of how and why this activity evolved at a particular moment, provides an important means by which to reorient the 'content and purpose' (Thompson 1998: 22, cited in D'Costa 2006) of dominant masculinist narratives of struggle within contemporary Pacific history. While these have tended to emphasise a region sliding into post-colonial crisis (Reilly 2000: 261, 2004; Henderson 2005; Borgu 2002),[4] such assessments have frequently made the grave error of discounting the political agency and capacities of Pacific women and relegating them to the margins of Pacific history (Douglas 1999).[5]

While these methodological choices contribute an innovative dimension to this study, my efforts to situate history are also subject to some limitations. These relate to my own subjectivity as a researcher and the particular positioning of my investigative lens. These considerations will be developed as I describe in more detail the research practicalities of this project.

Research for this book involved two long field-work trips to Suva which were taken in 2002 (together lasting roughly six months), and many follow-up trips conducted in later years. During this time, my position as an outsider connected

---

4   This perspective of regional Pacific Island affairs, although largely persuasive in Australian and New Zealand policy-making circles, has been roundly critiqued by eminent regional scholars such as David Chappell 2005: 290; Greg Fry 1997, 2000; and Jon Fraenkel 2004.

5   For a critique of this scenario and a discussion of the constructive role women can and should play in the achievement of regional security see George 2011.

to, but not of, the Pacific Island region, was something which I recognised would potentially interfere with my ambition to 'learn face to face' about the history of women's organising in this setting. My status as an Australian during this period played heavily on my mind given my own government's tendency towards heavy-handed engagement in the Pacific Island region and my knowledge that Fiji-based activists had unhesitatingly decried Australian industry and government 'neo-colonialism' in the past.[6] Additionally, preparatory research also indicated that the Australian government's policies towards its indigenous peoples were frequently viewed in gender activist circles as an issue which undermined the regional credibility of Australian aid and development objectives in the Pacific Islands.

While sensitivity to these issues was important, my increasing awareness of the history of transnational collaboration between local gender activists and women in my own country also suggested that contact between the Pacific Island region and 'outside' did not necessarily have to be negatively construed. Many representatives from women's organisations described to me the important support they had received from partner non-government organisations in Australia, or from Australian government sources. Others described to me the regional importance of 1970s Australian feminist figures such as Germaine Greer or Elizabeth Reid and the inspiration they had provided for early local feminist struggles for gender equality or for higher levels of female representation within government.[7]

My decision to work on a voluntary basis with one local women's organisation during both my field trips in 2002 also helped to reduce the weight of my outsider status. Through this work, I was able to build a close relationship with the group's coordinator and a number of other staff members, as well as engage in participatory observation of the daily operations of a key women's group. This work was highly beneficial to my research but also gave me entrée into the broader sphere of women's organising in Fiji. This allowed me to conduct over sixty interviews with representatives from a wide range of women's organisations ranging from faith-based groups, to secular, union-based and

---

6   In 2001, these issues had again been brought to a head as Pacific Islands activists voiced strong opposition to the Australian government's 'Pacific Solution' to illegal immigration which involved transferring over 800 asylum seekers entering Australia to neighbouring Pacific Islands states. These states were then paid by the Australian government to house, clothe and feed the deported asylum seekers, and process their claims for refugee status. These policies were identified by critics in the region as reflecting a coercive and opportunistic approach to regional security issues in Australia and were intensely debated amongst many activists when I visited Fiji in 2002. I was left with little to say in response to the accusation I faced from one young NGO representative that these events were indicative of an Australian tendency to engage with the Pacific Islands region only in a self-serving manner.

7   In 1973, Elizabeth Reid was appointed as advisor on women's affairs to the Australian Prime Minister, Gough Whitlam. It was the first bureaucratic position of this type created in the world. Reid presided over government events to mark International Women's Year in 1975 and also led the Australian Delegation to the UN Women's conference of that year staged in Mexico City (Caine *et al.* 1998: 481).

welfare-oriented women's organisations. I also conducted in-depth interviews with long-time Fiji-based activists who had been connected with the women's movement for a number of decades and who were able to comment upon the local evolution of gender politics. Through these contacts, I was given access to organisational archives, and given advice about where other organisational publications might be located.

In addition to my interviews with gender activists, I also interviewed local religious leaders, government bureaucrats, parliamentarians, representatives of Fiji's law and justice sector, local and foreign-based aid industry participants, and local academics, in order to gain a closer appreciation of the contours of the local political environment in which gender advocates operated. I also found daily newspapers a valuable resource which allowed me to follow the strands of current political debate in Fiji, while also providing some insights into how women's organisations use the print media to promote discussion on women's issues in the public domain.[8]

Although my outsider status sometimes made the task of discussing Fiji's gender politics with my interlocutors difficult, it was, at times, also beneficial. Often I became a confidante, with interlocutors divulging sensitive information in a way which suggested that amongst the relatively small circle of gender activists in Suva, the outside ear could be privy to information, opinions or concerns that might not be raised amongst associates. In this vein, I had discussions with gender activists regarding intimate aspects of family life and their own experiences of subordination, their misgivings regarding perceived failures in local gender advocacy and their disappointments when internal organisational trust was broken. On many occasions, I was surprised by the open and frank accounts of this type offered by some of my interlocutors and the extent to which they appeared to contradict the more generally accepted representations of gender politics in Fiji, especially with regard to the effectiveness of policy gains, or the extent of NGOs' political influence.

At the same time, my efforts to construct this 'situated' history were limited by my geographic location during much of this research and my decision to focus upon women's organisations operating out of Fiji's capital, Suva. The emphasis placed upon transnationalism within this study made Suva an obvious choice since it is a key site for transnational engagement beyond the Pacific Island region, as well as an important site for women's organising at the national and regional level. The fact that many national, regional and international organisations concerned

---

8   This situation altered in April 2009 when the Bainimarama-led military government placed its own officials inside the country's newsrooms to monitor reporting of national issues. This policy of news censorship has shut down public political debate in the mainstream media with the result that newspaper reporting has become much 'safer' and less critical in the intervening years.

with gender and development are headquartered or have representation in this city, made Fiji's capital an obvious site for researching the transnational aspects of women's organising.[9]

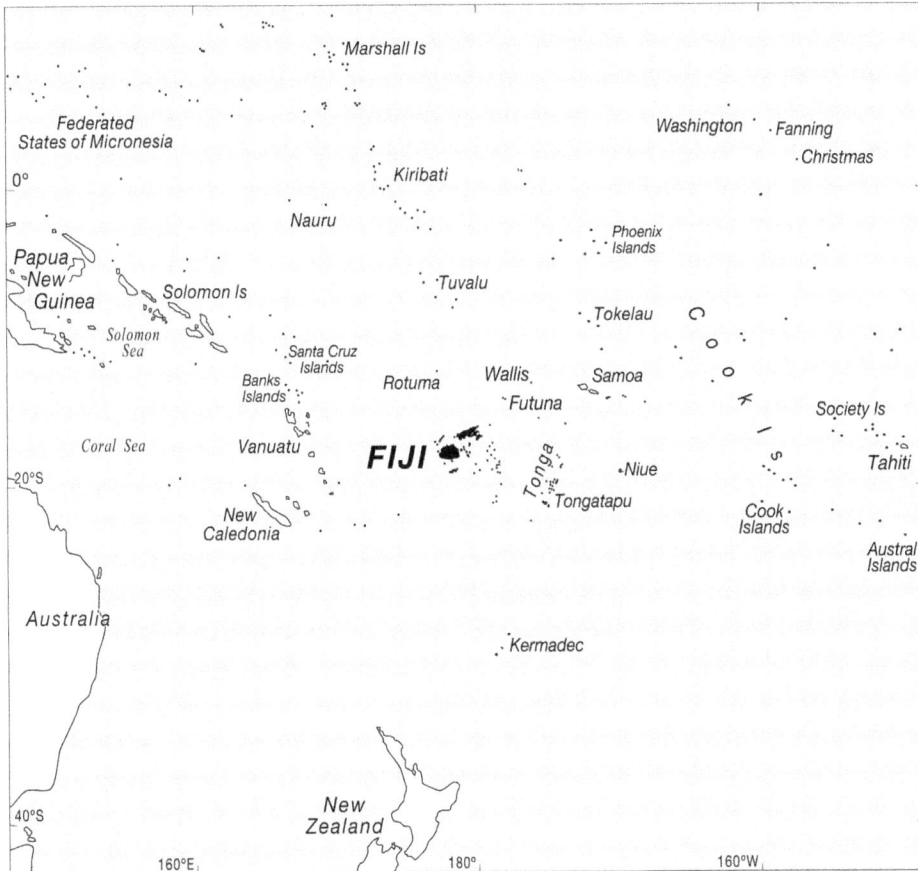

Map 1. Map of the Pacific Islands.

Source: Map production by Education and Multimedia Services, College of Asia and the Pacific, The Australian National University.

---

9   A large number of regional institutions are located in Suva which brings together representatives from Pacific Islands communities across the region. The city's central location within the Pacific Islands region has made it home to the Pacific Islands Forum Secretariat, the Community Education and Training Centre which provides training in development to Pacific Islanders, the University of the South Pacific, the Pacific Theological College and the Pacific Regional Seminary of the Roman Catholic Church. In addition, the regional importance of Suva has also been noted by international agencies such as the International Labour Office (ILO), the United Nations Development Program (UNDP), and the United Nations Development Fund for Women (UNIFEM), all of which have regional offices established in Fiji's capital. Likewise influential regional non-government organisations such as the Pacific Concerns Resource Centre (PCRC), the Regional Rights Resource Team (RRRT), Pacific Islands Network on Globalization (PANG), and the Foundation of the Peoples of the South Pacific, also use Suva as their base.

But this choice also limited the scope of my work in another sense. My concentration upon the urban setting meant that I was in contact with women's groups who travelled to rural settings for consultations, network meetings, or for performances of drama and film, but ultimately I had limited engagement with women's organisations located outside Fiji's principle urban areas or the on the country's remote islands.[10] The scope of the study was also limited by my conscious decision not to consider in detail the activities of women's unions. In certain instances, I give consideration to the activities of the Fiji Nursing Association in order to demonstrate how questions of women's labour rights are dealt with in a particular political context and what that might suggest about how women's rights claims are received at the institutional level and amongst policy elites. For the most part, however, I have considered the activities of women's labour associations only when they have intersected with women's organisations promoting women's rights more generally, a research strategy which, in part, reflects a decision not to duplicate the efforts of researchers who have already done important work on the issue of women and labour in Fiji such as Jacqueline Leckie (2002, 2000a, 2000b, 1997), Claire Slatter (1987), 'Atu Emberson-Bain (1992, 2001) and Christy Harrington (2000, 2004).

In addition to these general research limitations, the act of authorship means that, in the final instance, this 'situated history' of Fiji's gender politics reflects my own 'face to face' learning choices regarding the ordering of information, and privileging of testimonies. The admission of limitations within this 'situated' history should not be viewed as a claim to historical relativism, which as Donna Haraway argues, implies a promise of vision from 'everywhere and nowhere' and a 'denial of responsibility and of critical enquiry' (Haraway 1991: 191). Situating this history does not preclude the construction of broader conclusions, nor does it detract from their critical value; it simply acknowledges the partial quality of these claims (Haraway 1991). As a result, the final conclusions I draw should be read in this vein, for they are tendered not as reductionist, absolute or verifiable truths, but as critical contributions to an ongoing conversation about women's political agency in the Pacific Islands and beyond them. To this end, I also envisage that this is a cross-disciplinary contribution reflecting the fact that the construction of this 'situated history' has required close consideration of factors such as Fiji's geopolitical location, colonial legacies, and socio-cultural environment. In addition it has drawn upon a diverse range of academic literatures which span international relations, political science, development studies, gender studies, Pacific history and Pacific anthropology.

---

10   My research did take me to the South of Vanua Levu (Fiji's 'second' island) and the neighbouring island of Taveuni.

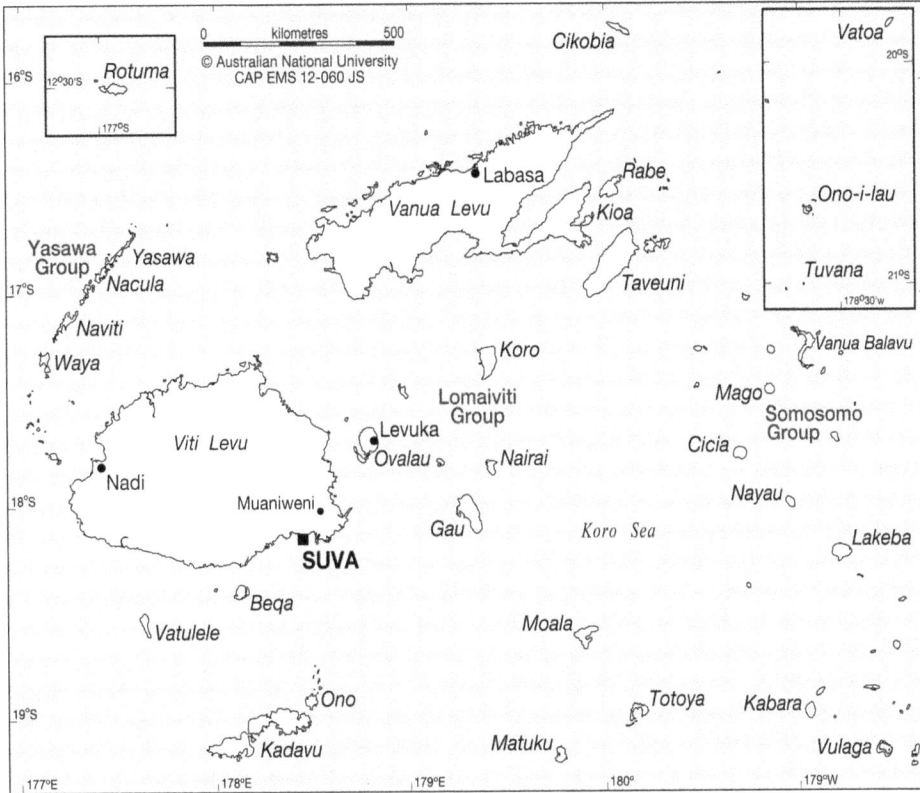

Map 2. Map of the Fiji Islands.

Source: Map production by Education and Multimedia Services, College of Asia and the Pacific, The Australian National University.

Conclusion

This book provides an account of the history of women's organising in Fiji. It pays particular attention to the ways that global and local political influences contour the spaces for gender advocacy and, consequently, activists' negotiations of collectivity, progress and transnationalism. Detailed consideration is given to the interactions that take place amongst women's organisations and between this sphere of political activity and the broader institutional realm, with ongoing attention paid to the prevailing political conditions which shape these interactions. Through examination of the varying trends that have been evident in women's organisational activity in this setting since the 1960s, this study provides a clear indication of the ways that domestic and international contingencies can shape the political space available to women's organisations and the implications this can have for their political agency.

The following chapter provides a more detailed theoretical discussion of women's political agency and the relationship between political capacity and contingency. It provides a critical reading of reform- and resistance-oriented accounts of women's organising. From here, it draws upon a smaller body of work undertaken by scholars such as Jude Howell in China, Aili Mari Tripp in Africa and Nadje Al-Ali in the Middle East, to demonstrate the analytical gains which occur when women's advocacy is assessed in ways that eschew 'ideal-types' and pays more attention to context. Again the themes of collectivity, progressive ideas and transnationalism provide the conceptual framework for this discussion. I show why it is important to develop a 'situated' understanding of the presumed 'standard features' of women's organising and how they may in fact broaden the contours of varied socio-political environments. At various points in this discussion, I relate these points back to the Pacific Island context. Here I demonstrate how and why a focus on contingency is vital to understanding the organisational terrain of gender politics in Fiji and the broader Oceanic Region.

Chapters 2 to 6 provide an empirically focused investigation of the terrain of gender politics in Fiji since the 1960s, with each roughly structured to reflect a ten-year period. Discussion in the first part of each chapter examines how women's organisations have negotiated prevailing domestic, regional and international political influences during this period. Each chapter concludes with a more thematically driven analysis of women's organisations' negotiations of collectivity, progressive ideas and transnationalism and draws attention to the impact of prevailing contextual factors in each of these regards.

Chapter 2 describes the early work of women's community development organisations and the important leadership role for women played by the Fiji YWCA in the 1960s to the mid-1970s. Here I also describe how women's organisations were able to articulate locally provocative agendas of reform in the immediate pre- and post-independence political environment. Chapter 3 is devoted to developments occurring within the sphere of women's organising at the local, regional and international levels during the United Nations Decade for Women and describes how the initial importance of redistributive issues in local gender politics began to give way to a new style of gender advocacy organisation which was more issue-focused. Chapter 4 concentrates upon the period 1985–1995 when issue-focused women's organisations flourished but also struggled for formal recognition in a local political environment which was less receptive to provocative articulations of gender advancement than was evident in earlier periods. Chapter 5 examines the situation from 1995 until 2003. Here I describe how the initial period of domestic political reform in the mid-1990s appeared to provide great scope for gender advocacy but ultimately dissipated in the wake of the 2000 coup. The ensuing rise of ethno-national allegiance which followed locally in the wake of this event was coupled with the regional and global predominance of neoliberal approaches to development which together created a restricted environment for activists aiming to promote reform agendas. Chapter 6 examines how the realm of women's advocacy fared in the political environment leading up to, and following, Fiji's 2006 coup. While it describes the civil society divisions which have again challenged the women's movement locally in the wake of the coup, it also discusses the emergence of an introspective and self-reflexive mood amongst women advocates. This has led to the broadening of formerly narrow issue-specific advocacy agendas and new interest shown in the promotion of peace and global economic justice. In the conclusion, I reiterate some of this study's most important findings and demonstrate the gains in understanding which have resulted from taking a situated approach to the study of women's political agency in Fiji. I also consider how these findings contribute new insights into broader academic debate taking place on the place of civil society in global politics.

1. A Feel for Context: Contingency and Women's Collective Agency

What is a contingent approach to women's collective political agency and why is it valuable? This chapter offers answers to these questions by surveying existing approaches to the study of women's organising and considering where and how these approaches might be usefully expanded. The conceptual framework I develop here foregrounds the importance of contextual factors when seeking to understand women's political agency. This framework is then deployed in the following chapters to investigate the ways in which circumstance has shaped the political ambitions articulated by women's organisation in Fiji over the past four decades.

As I have established, feminist analysis of women's organising has generally been oriented in ways which avoid these considerations. In the main, emphasis has been placed upon the distance separating the sphere of formal institutional politics from the sphere of women's organising, and the outcomes which result when the two spheres engage. These accounts have provided important insights into the ways that women's collective political agency is manifest in domestic and international politics. Yet as I have shown, this approach allows limited emphasis to be placed upon the broader contingencies which shape this type of political activity.

Feminist research into women's organising is vast and demonstrates a diverse range of opinions and perspectives that are not always in harmony. Yet, at the risk of reductionism, I contend that two predominant orientations can be found in this literature. The first emphasises reform and the extent to which women's organisations are responsible for promoting gender-sensitive change within formal political institutions (Stephenson 1995; Keck and Sikkink 1998; Joachim 1999, 2003; True and Mintrom 2001; Brown-Thompson 2002; Reilly 2009). The second emphasises a feminist counter-politics of resistance and gives closer attention to the challenges which have been unmet by the women's movement. This type of research examines the increasingly 'professionalised' processes of political negotiation occurring amongst women's organisations and asks if women's capacities to challenge conservative and gender-discriminatory institutional agendas are diminished in the process (Yuval-Davis 2006: 288; Antrobus 1984; Lang 1997; Alvarez 1999; Kahn 2002; Tobar 2003).

Each of these perspectives offers compelling, if opposing, illustrations of women's capacities for political agency. But could they also be criticised for making their assessments from an analytical 'cliff-top'? Are these contending evaluations of women's organisations underpinned by '"ideal-typical" understandings of how women's movements should operate in the broader political terrain' (Marx-Ferree 2006: 10)? Both approaches privilege easily identifiable forms of reform-or resistance-oriented organisational activity but they also seem to assess how this behaviour aligns with pre-established ideals dictating the 'right' type of behaviour for women's groups.

Such ideal-type understandings of organisational integrity help to reinforce the conceptual distance which many see as separating the domains of women's organising and institutional politics. This is done by highlighting particular organisational features and approaches to the exercise of power which are said to be distinctive to women's organisations and which facilitate their reform- or resistance-oriented political activity. This type of analysis heavily emphasises collectivity, progressive ideas and transnationalism within the realm of women's organising and routine contrasts are drawn with formal models of institutional politics which are alternatively construed as hierarchical, conservative and ultimately governed by state interest (Walker 1984; Ferguson 1984; Stephenson 1995; Lang 1997; Alvarez 1999; Joachim 1999, 2003; True and Mintrom 2001). What seems to be missing from these accounts is a consideration of the way that contingent factors in the shape of historical legacies, socio-cultural influences, faith-based allegiances, class affinity, local political identification and broader trends in global governance and development all influence women activists' negotiations of these privileged aspects of organisational activity in specific settings.

This study of the women's movement in Fiji addresses the same aspects of organisational activity—collectivity, progressive ideas and transnationalism—which feature as key themes in the research described above. My objective here, however, is to describe these features in a way which is sensitive to the types of interplaying contingent factors previously noted as they have emerged locally in Fiji and shaped the regional and international political terrain.

In this way, I avoid privileging assumptions about organisational structures, ambitions or transnational engagements in ways which reinforce the idea of an obligatory distance between women's organising and a monolithic institutional politics operating locally or globally. Rather, the aim is to develop a 'situated' appraisal of these aspects of organisational behaviour, showing how they are shaped by prevailing local and global factors and forecasting what this might mean for assessments of women's political agency more generally. In the following discussion, therefore, I describe the conventional ways in which collectivity, progressive ideas and transnationalism are described in literature on women's organising and then draw on a smaller body of research conducted in this area which eschews ideal-typical assessments of organisational agency in favour of greater attention to 'agency in context' (Howell 2003; Al-Ali 2003; Tripp 2003; see also Howell and Mulligan 2005). I conclude each section of this discussion with a consideration of how and why this focus on contingency is vital to understanding the history of women's organising in Fiji and the broader Pacific Island region.

Collectivity

Within both reform- and resistance-oriented studies of women's political activity, a strong emphasis is placed upon collectivity as a defining feature of women's organising. This is routinely contrasted with the individually competitive realm of formal institutional politics. Women's capacity to work together to achieve political goals is seen as a strength of the women's movement and something distinctive within the broader realm of political behaviour (Ferguson 1984: 217; Stephenson 1995; Marques-Pereira and Siim 2002; Jaquette 2003: 340). Much is made of the absence of hierarchy both within and between women's organisations and invidious contrasts are drawn with the rigid and competitive realm of formal political institutions which is deemed to be more 'hostile to women' (Ferguson cited in Jaquette 2003: 339; see also Walker 1984; Goetz 1997; Lang 1997; Alvarez 1999; Friedman 1999). Therefore, across both reform- and resistance-oriented literatures, a strong degree of emphasis is placed upon the horizontal and fluid nature of relationships amongst and within women's organisations and the extent to which this enables collective political agency to be maintained (Stienstra 1994: 146; Jaquette 2003: 340).

For scholars who take a reform-oriented view of women's organising, the collective and non-hierarchical aspects of women's political activity are viewed as unconventional and yet influential. These ideas are particularly evident in work which focuses upon political engagement between women's organisations and the United Nations (UN), and most significantly, in studies which describe the participation of women's organisations in the UN World Conferences for Women in Mexico City (1975), Copenhagen (1980), Nairobi (1985) and Beijing (1995). These events are understood to have set the stage for the emergence of a 'new feminist movement' which was flamboyant, participatory, spontaneous, even chaotic, but also influential (Stephenson 1995: 136; also Stienstra 1995; West 1999; UNIWY Secretariat 1975: 38). Lois West (1999: 178) argues, for example, that as the profile of women's organisations rose through participation at these types of events, increased recognition was given to 'non-institutionalized efforts … to change national and international processes.'

When these questions are examined from a resistance-oriented perspective, assessments of organisational capacities to sustain horizontal models of collectivity are less optimistic. From this vantage point, there is a strong suggestion that engagement with formal institutions both at state and international levels tends to stifle organisational capacities for fluidity and makes the maintenance of horizontal relationships within and between organisations more difficult. Even when organisations have an ideological commitment towards collective horizontality, evidenced by efforts to foster voluntarism and collaboration, interaction with the institutional realm is seen to mitigate against this lasting. The idea here is that institutional influence encourages women's groups to become more professionalised, adapt their operations to the more vertical structures of formal politics, and act less cooperatively as they compete for institutional largesse (Lang 1997; Alvarez 1999; Tobar 2003).

This privileging of fluid and horizontal collectivity is an important feature of research into women's organising, yet it has also been challenged by a smaller body of research conducted in settings as diverse as China, sub-Saharan Africa and the Middle East which offers a more contextualised perspective of how women's organisations operate (Howell 2003; Al-Ali 2003; Tripp 2003; see also Howell and Mulligan 2005). In these studies, the broader protocols that regulate social and political life also appear within organisational structures, influencing how models of collectivity are negotiated. This research shows how state-authority structures, religious-belief systems and socio-political influences have an impact on conduct within women's organisations.

For example, where the state is a dominant presence in economic, social and political life, mass women's organisations have been a common feature of the political landscape. These organisations may define themselves as NGOs but they often retain close links with the state and operate along similarly hierarchical lines. Jude Howell's description of the structures which regulate Chinese mass organisations, in particular, the All China Women's Federation (ACWF) is one powerful example of this tendency (Howell 2003: 205–08). Although the dominance of the ACWF in China has made it more difficult for newer women's organisations to establish their own credentials, the ACWF's close and often 'porous' relationships with the Chinese state has also provided some of these groups with an 'institutional structure with inroads into the system already in place' (Howell 2003: 205, 206).

Howell's account suggests that in state-dominant contexts, women's organisations can position themselves to draw political advantage by adopting similarly vertical structures. Aili Mari Tripp's descriptions of the position of mass women's organisations in post-independence Africa are more pessimistic about the scope for political agency that results from such tactics. In the immediate post-independence context, where many African countries were ruled by single-party regimes, mass organisations for women were also common and, as in China, mirrored the hierarchical structures of ruling parties (2003: 235–38). But as funding for these organisations often came from ruling political parties, women's organisations were, for the most part, following 'party-dictated agendas' which offered limited avenues for challenging the 'status quo when it came to pushing for women's advancement' (Tripp 2003: 237).

Discussing the Middle Eastern context, Nadje Al-Ali has also argued that women's organisations reflect the broader 'hierarchical and authoritarian' nature of political life (2003: 226). While some organisations have attempted to create more participatory organisational structures, they have encountered opposition from the state, from Islamists and also from 'other activists within civil society who follow more traditional patterns of political and social engagement' (Al-Ali 2003: 228). Moreover, even in organisations that take a strong stance against such pressures there is a tendency for 'charismatic activists to frequently take over leadership' and direct operations according to their own vision (Al-Ali 2003: 226). Al-Ali's account of women's organising in the Middle East suggests that with the increasing politicisation of Islam, and a 'lack of existing democratic models and experiences in democratic political structures,' the scope for organisations to manifest the type of informal, non-hierarchical structure conventionally understood to enhance women's political agency is extremely limited (2003: 228). Nevertheless, she also contends that although collective horizontality may be less evident amongst women's organisations in the Middle East than elsewhere, these groups continue to bring difficult and confronting aspects of gender disadvantage into the public domain (2003).

Similar considerations need to be taken into account when examining the nature of collectivity within women's movements in the Pacific. In this context, personal understandings of social location are shaped by prevailing cultural and political imperatives and these have a profound influence upon the ways that individual members within women's organisations, and indeed entire organisations, tend to conduct themselves.

The impact of Christianity is significant in this regard. Christianity may be an imported institution, but it is also important to appreciate how Christianity has been 'indigenised' in the Pacific (Jolly and MacIntyre 1989; Jolly 1996, 1997, 2003; Tuwere 1997; Douglas 2000b; Ryle 2005; Tomlinson 2009), how it influences the conduct of women's groups generally in this setting (Douglas 2003: 7; see also Jolly 1996, 1997, 2000, 2003; Douglas 1998, 2002; Boseto 2000) and how it can 'normalise' hierarchical structures of authority even within entities which adopt a more secular identity.[1] For example, Anna Paini's (2003: 88–90) study of the Drueulu Women's Group in Lifou, New Caledonia, shows how broader social hierarchies were reflected within this organisation and

---

[1] The Church's strong community-level presence in the Pacific is such that it is often only faith-based women's organisations which have the network capacity to 'reach down and to make links between village women' (Scheyvens 2003: 29).

linked to women's participation in faith-based communities. She argues that the membership of a local high chief's wife, other elderly women married into high-ranking families, and the wives of two local catechists, provided leadership for a local women's group with the added benefit of enhancing its credibility within the community when it tackled difficult social questions.

Other considerations about social location are pertinent to understanding the way relationships are formed and how they structure women's groups. This is particularly evident if we consider the influence of communalism and its impact on women's organisation in Fiji. Communalism is a contemporary legacy of the roughly one- hundred-year period of British colonial rule on this island territory which ended officially in 1970 (Sutherland 1992; Denoon 1997; Firth 1997; Robertson and Sutherland 2001; Kelly and Kaplan 2001). While it has been common to examine the potency of ethnic politics, or the 'race' question as it is defined in the local idiom, in ways which concentrate upon formalised sites of political contestation between the country's indigenous and Indian population (primarily descended from a colonially imported, indentured labour-force) less attention has been focused upon the communalism prevalent within Fiji's civil society. Today the make-up of many sporting associations, youth groups, cultural organisations and even some trade unions is defined on the basis of ethnicity. In addition religious affiliations within both the Indo-Fijian (Moslem and Hindu) and Fijian (Christian, primarily Methodist) communities also reinforce this communal aspect within Fiji's civil society. The profile of many associations pursuing interests in policy, welfare, advocacy or education tends to emphasise an overarching, faith-based orientation. The make-up of many women's organisations has reflected this broader communalist trend and in important instances has seen groups coalesce around sites of religious, cultural or ethnic identity.

Of course, neither of Fiji's two principal ethnic communities is homogeneous. Within the indigenous population particularly, intra-communal rivalries over control of the country's political and economic resources, have also contributed to political instability in Fiji as a narrow chiefly elite, endowed with political privilege during the colonial period, has sought to protect its status since decolonisation (Durutalo 1985; Sutherland 1992; Robertson and Sutherland 2001; Fraenkel 2000). This group has sought to legitimise a hierarchical, clan-based vision of political leadership in Fiji through appeals to the cultural authenticity of such a model and its effectiveness in safeguarding broader aspects of indigenous paramountcy, such as the preservation of land tenure.[2]

---

2 Indigenous protocols generally promote hierarchical and patriarchal social structures as the norm, although, as Christian Toren (1999: 163–81) suggests, these structures may also be balanced by ideas about reciprocity and competitive equality.

This emphasis upon the appropriateness of hierarchy again spills over into civil society. The leadership structures of some important civil society groups tend to invest authority in those members who have a high social rank or age seniority. Other organisations may have begun with flatter structures but over time produced personalities with a firmly established organisational authority. These figures neither voluntarily relinquish their positions nor are they likely to face challenges from their 'subordinates.' Again, this has ramifications for how questions of collectivity are negotiated amongst women's organisations. For example, Annelise Riles (2001: 51) described the importance of 'institutionalized expressions of Fijian norms of hierarchy' within women's organisations stating that older women and women with a higher chiefly rank assumed the right to speak first while younger women were given the opportunity to speak only when explicitly asked.

The strong cultural importance placed upon norms of quiet diplomacy, frequently described as the 'appropriate' means by which to articulate and mediate between political demands in the Pacific, also explains the presence of hierarchy within civil society. Within particular associations, interactions between 'superiors' and 'subordinates' are expected to take place in accordance with protocols which emphasise 'modesty,' 'self-effacement' and the good of the community (or organisation) rather than the promotion of individual will (Robertson and Sutherland 2001: 56).

Within the women's movement in Fiji, there have been activists who have sought to challenge the prevalence of social hierarchy and communalism both within individual organisations and as they shape community interaction and political engagement more generally. Since the 1960s, women's groups have formed which have challenged the racially segregated terrain of women's organising by promoting a multicultural identity and models of collectivity which are not defined by ethnic identity. However, as the following chapters will demonstrate, these organisations have not been immune to the communal tensions that have simmered more generally in Fiji across the previous decades. Their efforts to maintain a harmonious collective structure have often been imperilled when national political crises have threatened to fracture the country along its ethnic fault lines.

Likewise, there have been groups that have worked to promote ideas that are antithetical to notions of hierarchy but still culturally relevant—reciprocity, accountability and competitive equality (Toren 1999). Yet the repeated emergence of anti-democratic and authoritarian political forces has made this task increasingly difficult in Fiji.

These preliminary considerations demonstrate the importance of developing a contingent understanding of organisational collectivity and how this might be shaped by prevailing socio-cultural, political and religious values. As the following chapters of this book will make clear, this perspective challenges the more conventional idea of women's organising as a sphere in which hierarchy or division should be ideally absent, and produced only as a result of engagement with formal political institutions.

Progressive ideas

Women's organisations contribute to the 'conscience of the body politic,' argues Arvonne Fraser, for they have a political autonomy which allows them the 'freedom to test out and promote the adoption of new ideas, policies and programs' (cited in Karl 1995: 5). Such claims about the relative autonomy of these groups, and how this enhances their progressive political potential, feature heavily in research on women's organising. The idea here is that proximity to grassroots communities, rather than the more rigid realm of institutional politics, enables women's organisations to operate in a creative manner, enhancing their capacity to formulate innovative and progressive responses to the needs of women. As such, progress and innovation are seen to be the domain of women's organisations and to contrast with institutional political activity, viewed more negatively as 'out of touch' with community expectations and inclined to reinforce rather than challenge the (gender discriminatory and conservative) status quo.

Within reform-oriented accounts of women's organising there is a strong appreciation of the limitations that are placed upon organisational autonomy. Nonetheless, strong emphasis is placed upon the idea that organisations' normative legitimacy depends upon the maintenance of a certain degree of distance from institutional authority. This, it is assumed, will allow groups to at least function as creative issue framers or 'autonomous makers of meaning' (Khagram, Riker and Sikkink 2002: 11) and allow them to bring something innovative, and potentially progressive, to the negotiating table when attempts are made to reform the institutional realm.

The success of global campaigns waged in the early 1990s to make the issue of violence against women an international human rights concern have been widely analysed and celebrated from this perspective. This effort was led by an important coalition of women's organisations associated with the Center for Women's Global Leadership, headed by Charlotte Bunch, and is said to have been instrumental in bringing the issue of violence against women into international focus (Connors 1996; Otto 1996; Keck and Sikkink 1998; Joachim 1999, 2003; Brown Thompson 2002). This strategy saw women's organisations argue that gendered forms of violence should no longer be considered 'domestic' or 'private' phenomena. Rather, these acts of violence were presented as violations of international human rights law; a shift which threw both the perpetrators of the violence *and* the states condoning such violence into the international spotlight. Favourable UN responses to this argument at the end of 1993, and the incorporation of this position into a number of UN policy documents promoting human rights and gender equality in the ensuing years, are repeatedly cited as evidence of women's organisations' progressive and innovative potential as promoters of institutional reform at the international level (Keck and Sikkink 1998; Joachim 1999; Brown Thompson 2002).

In the field of international development, the progressive potential of women's organisations has been similarly acclaimed. Women's organisations are understood to be the drivers of innovation in development policy, assisting in the creation of 'new structures and organisational cultures' that are participatory and respond directly to 'women's needs, interests and behavioral preferences' (Goetz 1997: 7; see also Clark 1997; Hulme and Edwards 1997; Van Rooy 1998; Howell and Pearce 2001). The idea that women's organisations have the capacity to transform the development perspectives of institutional actors in ways which are appropriate to local settings has seen governments and aid agencies increasingly seek active partnership with local women's groups in many settings (Lang 1997; Alvarez 1999).

Resistance-oriented perspectives of women's organising tender alternative explanations for why institutions may be interested in developing closer relations with women's organisations. It is argued that increased emphasis upon the participation of non-state actors in development is consistent with neoliberal approaches to development economics which posit the importance of state streamlining and local entrepreneurship above state welfare support and other more literal forms of social provisioning (Hulme and Edwards 1997; Van Rooy 1998; Howell and Pearce 2001; Schild 2002). The outsourcing of government services to the private and non-government sector has become an important aspect of this policy platform and further opened the way for women's organisations to play a role in institutional efforts to promote women in development. Yet, although development institutions tend to describe their working relationships with women's organisations as 'partnerships,' the degree to which organisations can maintain their autonomy while accessing institutional funding and other forms of benevolence comes into question. Observers in a number of settings have noted that as organisations are pressured to assume aspects of service provision that have previously been undertaken by the state, they begin to emulate the normative vocabulary of formal institutions, and in so doing, tend to reinforce rather than challenge the status quo (Lang 1997; Alvarez 1999; Rankin 2002; Schild 2002; Bergeron 2003;). Such assessments suggest a stifling of organisations' progressive capacities through institutional engagement.

This privileging of autonomy as the key to innovative potential within women's organisations is challenged, however, by accounts that examine how these groups operate in authoritarian political contexts, or developing states (Friedman 1999; Howell 2003; Al-Ali 2003). Here, they are seen to interact with formal or more informal sites of political authority in complex and fluid ways. Less emphasis is placed upon the supposed links between organisational autonomy and progressive potential, and greater attention is paid to the ways in which women's organisations negotiate the space to articulate agendas of reform while operating in close proximity to institutionalised sites of political power.

For example, in authoritarian contexts the relationship between organisational autonomy and progressive capacity is less clear than in more conventionally framed accounts of women's political agency. Jude Howell suggests that while a degree of autonomy may be conventionally understood, 'axiomatically,' as a 'measure of the strength and validity of civil society,' the dynamics of relationships between women's organisations and the state in China are far more complex (2003: 205). She observes that in China: '[n]ot only are the boundaries porous and blurred,… but civil society organizations often, but not always, positively seek a relationship with the state so as to seek access to resources, legitimacy and authority' (2003: 205).

Many women's organisations have close links with the communist state, through the organisational involvement of state officials, and the corresponding determination shown by many groups to access the 'funds, contracts and protection' that the state can provide (Howell 2003: 205). Since the state remains a dominant presence in economic and social life, many women's organisations choose to 'work with or keep a quiet distance from the party-state rather than directly oppose it' (Howell 2003: 206). The important point Howell makes in this analysis, however, is that progressive potential and a capacity for innovation does not necessarily rely upon organisational autonomy from the state.

Al-Ali makes some similar observations in relation to the Middle Eastern context (2003: 222). In many cases, women's non-government organisations were actually the result of initiatives begun by women located within state bureaucracies. In Iran the relationship between the two spheres is such that women's groups are often labelled as governmental non-government organisations. Such seeming contradictions are indicative of how state-civil-society relations operate within the Middle Eastern political environment, where repressive measures have often been put in place to curb critical political activity. Yet as Al-Ali maintains, within the realm of institutional politics, individual government officials often voice support for participatory models of governance and a stronger 'commitment to democratic principles' than is evident in official institutional rhetoric (2003: 231). Al-Ali's reflections suggest that while the state may maintain a strong degree of control over civil-society activity in certain settings, at the level of individual agency there can still be some convergence of political agendas, and recognition of the need for reform of the status quo. Such views challenge the idea of a monolithic institutional politic, necessarily hostile to those promoting gender-sensitive reform.

Elisabeth Friedman's (1999) research on women's organisation in Venezuela also reflects this idea as she describes how innovative reforms for women have at times also been negotiated through close cooperation with state authorities. Through the creation of a women's non-government coordinating body named CONG, women's groups in cooperation with state authorities, were able to push for wider public recognition of gender issues and to lead important campaigns for legal reform and the creation of institutional machineries for women. Although she is critical of the ways in which the engagement between CONG and the Venezuelan government has played out in more recent times, Friedman claims that in the early years CONG maintained a strong cooperative relationship with the state. She argues that this productive engagement was made possible due to the fact that both within CONG and within the state, a diversity of political interests were represented and no one voice was in a position to dominate (1999: 366–68).[3] Together, these discussions indicate that in settings where women's political autonomy is limited, the capacity to promote progressive agendas of reform may remain.

Likewise, existing research on women's organising in the Pacific Islands suggests the need for a more nuanced understanding of the relationship between autonomy and progress and, in particular, an understanding of how the region's women activists negotiate the social importance of prevailing systems of cultural and religious belief. From a western secular standpoint, cultural and religious influences are often viewed as an obstacle to women's advancement (Merry 2003a, 2006b). Yet in the context of the Pacific Islands, these influences are evident within civil society and have important impacts upon the ways women's organisations promote feminist goals. While it might be assumed that this scenario indicates the reduced autonomy of women's organisations operating in the Pacific, provocative challenges to the prevailing status quo remain possible in these circumstances.

For example, gender activists frequently make reference to local systems of religious and customary belief in their efforts to promote women's advancement. In so doing, they attempt to navigate local resistance which dismisses ideas associated with 'women's liberation or feminism' as 'European, colonial

---

3   While this scenario helped CONG to preserve its autonomy in the short term, Friedman argues that in the longer term, the organisation became increasingly dependent upon state funding and that this climate encouraged women to think of their own projects first rather than broader goals that might require greater collaboration between organisations. Friedman argues that as a result of 'near-clientelism' projects were tailored to the priorities of government and 'radicality' was lost in the process (Friedman 1999: 370–71).

or alien' to local patterns of social life (Douglas 2003: 8). This sees women activists make reference to the customary significance of women's roles as they promote challenging messages of social or political reform. Affirmation of women's customary authority—within the family, within the realm of cultural production, and within some systems of social hierarchy—are all seen as important strategies which imbue Pacific women activists' political demands with a cultural legitimation and local authenticity (Jolly 2000: 132; Tariseisei 2000; Paini 2003).

References to Christianity function in the same way. Commentaries upon campaigns led by Pacific women to challenge the pervasiveness of gender-based violence, for example, have described how activists combine references to Christian teachings on the respectful and just treatment of women with appeals to more secularised rights-based agendas prevailing within transnational advocacy communities (Jolly 1997, Douglas 2003;). Again, such strategies are seen to lend a local authenticity to activity which is often viewed in a contentious frame by those who brand feminism as harmful to traditions and local value systems.

While these challenges to gender discrimination are promoted in ways which have correspondence with the cultural and religious institutions of the Pacific Islands, they also indicate how prevailing values and belief systems shape the public space in which women's organisations operate. Certainly these strategies can be viewed as 'creative' (Jolly 2005a: 154) forms of advocacy which draw upon local cultural and religious values as 'resources'. Yet it also needs to be recognised that this type of activity references social norms and values which have not always been empowering for women (see Stivens 2000: 22).

For example, invocation of women's maternal roles may well provide campaigns led by women's groups with a politically powerful communal reference point and lend local legitimacy to advocacy efforts. Nonetheless, this positive emphasis also tends to gloss over the fact that rates of maternal mortality in some Pacific countries are amongst the highest in the world and that for many women of the region, motherhood has a 'considerable physical and mental cost' (Douglas 2003: 10).[4]

In a similar vein, the articulation of women's human rights messages with Christianity also tends to downplay patriarchy in the Church. Women have minimal representation within the authority structures of Pacific mainline churches and biblical texts are frequently used selectively by religious leaders to legitimate women's subordinate status in society more generally. Women may be recognised as the 'backbone of the church' in many Pacific contexts

---

4 In her examination of women's roles in Simbo, Western Solomon Islands, Christine Dureau (1993: 18, 20–22) argued that despite women's maternal roles being viewed as central to their gender identity, Simbo women also equated motherhood with 'exhaustion, illness and decrepitude.'

(Varani-Norton 2005: 223), however the expectation that their Church duties will involve participation in fundraising activities and practical support for Church meetings and social occasions generally results in increased demands made upon 'women's time, material wealth and energy' and little else (Varani-Norton 2005: 240). Emphasising the emancipatory aspects of Christian faith in the Pacific also downplays the historical influence of the Christian missions which, in combination with colonial influences, frequently deprived Pacific Island women of their customary and traditional status (Jolly and MacIntyre 1989; Ralston 1989; Meggitt 1989).

Promoting women's rights in ways which reference customary values may also entail some risk. In many post-independence contexts, local political elites within the Pacific region have frequently made reference to customary values in ways that aim to restrict women or sabotage the political ambitions of those committed to gender equality (Jolly 1997: 155). Such tendencies are particularly pertinent to analysis of gender politics in Fiji where selective discourses of 'indigeneity' have been used by successive nationalist-dominated political regimes to justify women's minimal representation in formal politics (Cretton 2004: 4). In recent decades, Fijian nationalists have also issued increasingly vocal demands that Fiji declare itself a Christian state, thus reinforcing the close links between state authority and the Church in this context, and further legitimising patriarchal systems of social and political regulation.

When appraised in this light, it is clear that gender advocates' references to systems of religious belief or customary value can be politically enabling and constraining. These strategies may open the way for women activists to broach difficult questions in Pacific societies. Yet they may also reflect underlying currents that restrict the ways local actors understand their place in Fiji's broader politics. Contending scenarios of this type demonstrate why a contingent appraisal of women's organisations' progressive potential is warranted. In this study, I avoid overemphasising the supposed benefits of organisational autonomy, and instead provide a more situated account of the varying ways Fiji's women activists have themselves understood their capacity to negotiate progressive solutions for women in shifting political circumstances. Such an approach provides insight into the benefits *and* risks that have accrued from activists' efforts to work within and respect prevailing socio-cultural systems.

Transnationalism

References to transnationalism constitute a third important theme in feminist research on women's organising, with attention frequently drawn to the local and international 'frequency' of gender advocacy efforts (Al-Ali 2003:

224; Alvarez 1999). In these discussions, transnationalism is defined loosely, signifying 'any actor, organization, or issue that could be either international or global in orientation' (Booth 1998: 120). This allows researchers to consider how women's organisations use transnational networks to make local questions of gender subordination resonate at the international level (Joachim 1999, 2003; Brown Thompson 2002; True and Mintrom 2001). Reversing this lens, they also focus upon the 'significance of transnational advocacy and activist networks' at the local level, describing how international discourses are employed by women's organisations in the community context (Naples and Desai 2002: 34–41; Bickham Mendez 2002; Wells 2002; Karides 2002; Wing 2002; Friedman 1999).

The term transnationalism is used to examine the corresponding political agendas taken up by women's organisations from different locations. It is viewed as enabling a more flexible approach to comparative appraisals of feminist politics at the global level. This terminology is often invoked to avoid questions of gender subordination being articulated in ways which reference hegemonic, universalising ideals (Reilly 2009; Ackerly 2001) or romantic, yet essentialising images of 'global sisterhood' (Alexander and Mohanty 1997; Grewal and Kaplan 1994). Transnationalism, therefore, enables consideration to be given to common feminist perspectives which link the efforts of women advocates around the globe, while simultaneously acknowledging the specific circumstances which contribute to gender subordination in particular settings. This type of 'principled' transnationalism is contrasted with the more self-interested, international engagement which takes place within the institutional political realm (True and Mintrom 2001; c.f. Keck and Sikkink 1998).

Reform-oriented perspectives of women's organising generally describe a flourishing of feminist transnationalism which challenges 'business-as-usual,' state-centric international politics (True and Mintrom 2001: 27). From this perspective, the United Nations Declaration of the Decade for Women and the subsequent four conferences and non-governmental forums that were held in the period from 1975 to 1995 are viewed as events which have strengthened the transnational dimensions of women's political agency.[5]

---

5 While there has been great interest in documenting the recent history of transnational connection between women's organisations and the implications for global governance, scholars such as Nina Berkovitch, Margaret Galey and Deborah Stienstra have suggested that the procedural authority of these transnational networks has a long, if largely unrecognised, pedigree outside feminist circles that stretches back to the late 1800s. They discuss the emergence of early international women's organisations such as the International Congress of Women, the Socialist Women's International, the World Young Women's Christian Movement, the World Women's Christian Temperance Union and the General Federation of Women's Clubs (Berkovitch 1999; Stienstra 1994; Galey 1995b). They also note early attempts to stage international congresses for women, listing events such as an International Women's Rights Conference held in Paris in the 1870s (Galey 1995b: 22), and the 1915 International Congress for Women held in The Hague which brought together 2,800 women from fifteen, mainly European countries (Stienstra 1994: 51).

Writing in 2003, Jane Jaquette cites statistics which show a significant increase in NGO participation at the parallel forums from Mexico City in 1975 to Beijing in 1995. These developments, she argues, are indicators that transnational women's organising 'over the past three decades has been a feminist success story' (Jaquette 2003: 336). Moreover, the significant increase in the numbers of women's organisations and their participation in policy debates taking place at the international level is viewed by Riles as an exercise in legitimation, not only of transnational women's organising, but also of the international institutions responsible for these events: 'NGOs contribute to the "success" of the conferences, but the conferences … are claimed in retrospect by the NGO community as a validation of the significance of NGOs and their causes domestically and internationally' (Riles 2001: 10).

Women's organisations are also seen to gain from their participation in transnational networks that facilitate the flow of information and knowledge, allowing them to 'break their isolation' and 'exchange … ideas and experience' (Karl 1995: 38). In this way they are seen to benefit from the transfer of information and knowledge 'concerning alternative political strategies and how they may be applied to further promote policy change' (True and Mintrom 2001: 29). Hence transnational connection is seen as an important asset for women's organisations and something that can contribute to their capacity to promote institutional reform, particularly in the area of gender-mainstreaming (True and Mintrom 2001).

Transnationalism is also viewed as enabling the emergence of consensual norms (Jaquette 2003) within the realm of women's organising. This is particularly evident in research that emphasises how women's organisations have taken up human rights advocacy frameworks in their efforts to promote gender equality. Although human rights concepts are 'contested' for their presumed incompatibility with 'non-Western traditions of thought' (Nussbaum 2002: 48), reform-oriented accounts of women's organising have frequently celebrated gender advocates' efforts to 'forcibly' reshape these concepts so that they resonate in ways which are appropriate to local contexts (Stivens 2000: 18–24) and are taken up as issues of concern with policy-making elites (Reilly 2009; Bunch 1990; Brown Thompson 2002; Keck and Sikkink 1998; Joachim 1999, 2003). This may see advocates align their human rights frameworks with broader nation-building goals (Wing 2002), or with locally prevailing social or cultural practices that reflect principles of equality and inclusiveness (Ackerly 2001). In this way, contemporary feminist transnationalism is seen to accommodate local diversity and demonstrate a multilayered, multicentric potential (Reilly 2009; Ackerly 2001; Pettman 1996; Antrobus 2004; Ruppert 2002).

Resistance-oriented critiques of women's organising tend to view such evaluations of women's transnational activity with a greater level of scepticism, however.

On the one hand, they are cautious about the extent to which transnationalism is empowering for women's groups, finding instead that transnational influences can be a distraction, which 'skews' organisations' efforts away from the needs of local communities in times of crisis (Friedman 1999: 375). On the other hand, it has been argued that the procedures of information exchange and the 'drafting and redrafting' of documentation to be shared amongst transnational organisational networks tend to become the priority of many organisations such that they become bogged down in the procedural aspects of their work and lose sight of the broader normative political goals that provided the original motivation (Riles 2001: xvi, 174).

Some Third World feminists have also been highly critical of the extent to which transnationalism contributes to a 'multilayered' and 'dialogic' feminist politics (Pettman 1996: 212). Rather than focusing upon the benefits of transnational processes of information and knowledge exchange, consideration is given to the relative power of contending discourses within the realm of women's transnational organising and the mechanics of representation. Questions are duly asked about which views are given the greatest exposure within transnational feminist networks and which tend to be obscured (Tripp 2006). The contention here is that southern women find themselves continually co-opted into a transnational realm of political engagement where western, learned and elite women are dominant (Spivak 1996; Mohanty 1984). This strand of argument calls attention, in particular, to the limitations of contemporary trends in gender advocacy which are framed in human rights terms and their incapacity to address the 'multiple dimensions of gender oppression .... set in motion by global forces' (Oloka-Onyango and Tamale 1995: 702; see also Mackie 2001). Such frameworks have been decried for their heavy reliance upon activists' technical and professionalised socio-legal expertise, a development which is said to undermine the mass-movement orientation of women's activism (Yuval-Davis 2006: 288). Kahn perhaps best summarises this thinking when she condemns activism oriented towards human rights as 'abstracted, unlocated and apolitical' in manner (Khan 2002: 41).

Yet such assessments tend not to consider how interplaying global and local political influences shape the transnational advocacy agendas promoted by women's organisational networks. These processes are made more clearly apparent when a situated appraisal of women's transnational engagement is undertaken.

Sally Engle Merry adopts such a perspective when she offers her unconventional critique of the gains for women supposedly made through the utilisation of human rights advocacy frameworks. Merry (2003a: 62) argues that these frameworks are frequently deployed in ways which reinforce the idea that it is 'culture that is subordinating women' and universal concepts of 'modernity' which will 'free them'. Such strategies are seen to encourage activists to take a localised view of gender disadvantage while diverting their attention away from global phenomena such as 'expansive capitalism' or violent conflict and how these might also impact seriously on women's well-being. The 'culturing' of the debate surrounding women's human rights is seen to allegedly absolve 'rich countries of responsibility for the suffering caused by these processes' (Merry 2003a: 64). According to Merry developed countries have political and economic 'vested interests' in seeing human rights perspectives of gender disadvantage legitimised globally. In this process, local culture rather than western models of development becomes 'demonised' as the cause of women's subordination (2003a: 64).

Others argue that the utilisation of human rights advocacy frameworks places a heavy emphasis upon the juridical rights of the subordinated and can over-emphasise the role of the state, as the 'critical agent for improving women's lives' (Brown Thompson 2002: 114). This liberal view again diverts attention away from the socio-economic disadvantage endured by women all over the world, and particularly in the global South, by emphasising the 'law and order' dimension of women's subordination. Moreover, such views suppose that victims of subordination enjoy a level of 'capability' which gives them access to the legal instruments and infrastructure allowing them to redeem 'state-protected' rights (Nussbaum 2002). Karen Brown Thompson argues that while rights frameworks are commonly articulated at the local level via 'legalistic discourse,' this is 'at the least, not empowering, and at the worst, disempowering for … some, depending on their social context' (Brown Thompson 2002: 116; see also Merry 2003b).

Research into the prevalence and reporting of gender violence in Fiji supports such findings. It has been shown that socio-cultural factors help to make all forms of violence against women hidden phenomena in Fiji, with a strong stigma attached in particular to crimes such as rape, and rape victims are frequently blamed for inciting their attackers (Adinkrah 1995: 79). Within the Indian community, the high value placed on notions of *izzat* (honour) and *sharm* (shame) mean that victims of sexual violence face pressure from clan members or relatives not to report attacks to state authorities to avoid bringing disrepute upon the family (Lateef 1990: 45). Within Fijian communities, women victims of violence face similar pressures. Rather than reporting such incidents to state authorities, they are encouraged to see ceremonies of ritual apology (*i soro*) as the more appropriate avenue for redress.[6] These tendencies help to explain why

---

6   Ceremonies of ritual apology (*i soro*) are an important part of indigenous custom in Fiji and used within communities to reconcile a range of grievances (Kelly and Kaplan 2001: 144). The practice of *bulubulu* is a ceremony of pardon used in cases of injury, particularly in cases of rape or domestic violence. However, in recent times, gender activists have also argued that this practice has been subject to abuse, used within

only between 5–10 ten per cent of women victims of rape report these incidents to the police (Adinkrah 1995: 75–79), a statistic which indicates the limited effectiveness of 'law and order' approaches to combating gender violence.

The subordinate economic circumstances of a large proportion of Fiji's women also throw into doubt the extent to which the legalistic aspects of human rights advocacy can be considered to be universally empowering for women. Fiji's women are disproportionately affected by poverty (Narsey 2007: 106–08). In part, this reflects the fact that women shoulder the chief responsibilities for domestic care-giving within Fiji's households (Chattier 2005). In part, this situation is explained by women's involvement in subsistence agriculture and fishing work and their over-representation in low-wage, low-skilled, non-unionised industries, many of which are sustained by foreign capital, such as Fiji's garment manufacturing industry (United Nations Convention For the Elimination of Discrimination Against Women (UN CEDAW) 2000). Women are also further disadvantaged by a state welfare system which is limited, inadequately publicised and difficult to access (Harrington 2004). This suggests that, like women in many other parts of the developing world, global and local factors have combined to compound the economic vulnerability of Fiji's women (Slatter 1994, 2006; Elson 1995; Marchand and Runyan 2000; Firth 2000; Rai 2002; Steans 2003;). And this can jeopardise their ability to achieve the type of financial autonomy needed to access the legal mechanisms enacted to protect their human rights should they become victims of gender-based violence (Chattier 2005: 267, 270–71).

Despite the fact that many of Fiji's women live in precarious circumstances, activists in this setting have frequently sought to emulate the more general trend in transnational gender advocacy by increasingly seeking to frame their demands for women's advancement in human rights terms. This development would seem to support the idea of a growing transnational consensus within the realm of women's organising regarding the utility of such advocacy frameworks (Yuval-Davis 2006; Reilly 2009). Yet, as the considerations raised previously suggest, a 'situated' assessment of the political environment—local and global—exposes some difficulties with this advocacy pathway. On the one hand it seems to reflect activists' underestimation of the depths of economic and social vulnerability borne by women in Fiji and the broader Pacific Islands. On the other hand it perhaps also reflects activists' overestimation of how women can effectively mobilise human rights frameworks to resist disadvantage. In broader terms, such strategies might also be seen as ultimately serving the

indigenous communities to absolve perpetrators of gender violence from responsibility for their actions, and to dissuade women from reporting acts of violence perpetrated against them to state authorities (Cretton 2004: 5; Emberson-Bain 1992).

interests of domestic and international policy-making elites whose activities are not adequately scrutinised for the extent to which they contribute in direct terms to the perpetuation of women's disadvantage.[7]

For these reasons, this study gives critical consideration to the varying ways in which Fiji-based activists have participated in transnational advocacy networks. I consider how these activists have sought to raise global awareness of women's disadvantage in the Pacific context, and also how developments within transnational gender advocacy realms have been translated in the local context. Most significantly, however, I consider the ways that interplaying global and local political influences have shaped the transnational dimensions of this activity in particular instances. This enables a more nuanced and contextualised appreciation of the transnational 'frequency' of women's political agency than has often been provided in accounts of women's organising which take a reform- or resistance-oriented perspective of this terrain.

Conclusion

The previous discussion has demonstrated the importance of developing an analytical approach to women's organising which departs from the more conventional reform- or resistance-oriented narratives. As I have shown, analysis of women's political agency in Pacific Island contexts demands an in-depth consideration of prevailing historical legacies, socio-cultural factors and religious influences, broader international orthodoxies dictating policy on governance and development and how such influences shape women's political ambitions and achievements. In the chapters which follow I will build upon the insights developed in this chapter and demonstrate how activists' 'situated' understandings of these various currents influence advocacy decisions. I will show how they opened up some avenues of organisational activity and institutional engagement and closed down others.

While each of the subsequent chapters will conclude with a more analytically focused discussion of the ways in which collectivity, progressive ideas and transnationalism have featured as aspects of organisational behaviour, the emphasis will not be upon understanding how these characteristics define the sphere of women's organising as distinct from formal institutional politics in Fiji, or how they work to enhance women's political agency. Rather, by emphasising activists' 'situated' discussions of how these features were negotiated at particular historical junctures, I will show how collectivity, progressive ideas

---

7   There is some evidence to suggest, however, that this trend may be changing as some women's groups in Fiji have begun to examine in greater detail the local implications of Pacific Island accession to a range of international free trade agreements. See Chapter 5.

and transnationalism were manifest within the realm of women's organising in ways which reflect the broader trends shaping the prevailing political environment at that point in time.

The following chapters provide a detailed empirical defence of this argument. The next chapter begins with a discussion of women's organising in colonial Fiji and then documents the growing politicisation of this field in the period during which Fiji negotiated its independence. Fiji's women activists viewed this era as one of national and international transition. This inspired them to 'pioneer' an activist model that linked concerns about the advancement of women with a provocatively defined political agenda calling attention to inequities in the global distribution of political and economic power and how this compounded disadvantage in the Pacific Islands. Their efforts sought to make the concerns of Pacific women resonate in local and international political contexts and provided a critical momentum for gender-focussed advocacy, which is remembered with gratitude by local activists to this day. However, as later chapters of this book will demonstrate, the particular orientation of this type of activity was very much in keeping with the thinking of the times. As I will make clear, such challenging political agendas became much harder to sustain in later decades as local politics became more unsettled and authoritarian, and international institutional actors became less willing to indulge Third World efforts to promote global economic and political structural reform.

2. 'A New Frontier': Pioneering Gender Politics in Fiji's Independence Era

Up until the early 1960s, women's organisations in Fiji were generally disengaged from national political debate. This changed in the decade leading up to Fiji's independence in 1970, as newly formed national women's organisations began to articulate their concerns through practical programs and more politically oriented activities. This chapter examines how this political dimension to women's organising gathered strength in the 1960s and early 1970s. As the following pages will demonstrate, local women became increasingly involved in provocative political activity in these years, their focus of engagement moving from a narrow articulation of 'women's issues' to a series of campaigns that challenged prevailing community values at the local and national level, as well as the broader structures of international political and economic power. In many respects, this activity appears to be highly radical. When closer concentration is given to the situated experience of those involved, however, other considerations come to light. It becomes possible to appreciate how trends within the broader political environment influenced activists' assessments of their own political capacities in this setting and seemed to enable this provocatively styled behaviour. The personal reminiscences of those close to these events demonstrate that this type of political engagement was felt to be allowed within an independence era environment where the possibilities for political action appeared expansive. New futures for Fiji, Fiji's women, and Pacific peoples more generally, were highly anticipated in this period. Women's activism at this time reflects this general sense of optimism.

This chapter begins with an examination of the existing terrain of women's organising prior to the emergence of the more politically oriented groups in the early 1960s. Consideration is given to the position occupied by older, well-established women's cultural and religious organisations, and the role played by the colonial Fiji Women's Interest Office in the early 1960s in encouraging the formation of new women's voluntary associations.

The next section of the chapter examines the role of one prominent women's voluntary organisation in Fiji, the Young Women's Christian Association (YWCA). This organisation, like many others formed in the early 1960s, began life with a strong commitment to the participatory ethos of 'community development' and the presumed benefits of organisational membership for young women. In only a few years, however, the YWCA program challenged conventional approaches to the women and community development agenda which tended to define women's responsibilities in purely domestic and familial terms. On the one hand, it promoted a multicultural approach to women's advocacy. This was a significant departure from the more usual communal focus of women's organising in Fiji which had tended to emphasise women's interests as shaped by their location within particular ethnically defined or faith-based populations. On the other hand, the YWCA also sought to challenge the idea that women's interests were somehow distinct from broader sites of community and international debate, and hence 'non-political' in content.

As this chapter goes on to demonstrate, such thinking saw YWCA members articulate a vision of gender equality on the local, regional and international stage, which was closely articulated with broader, internationalised perspectives of social justice. Such agendas contrasted dramatically with conventional styles of political dialogue in Fiji which tended to identify sources of local inequality in racialised rather than internationalised terms. It also contrasted with the more moderate political stance adopted by other women's organisations operating in Fiji in the lead up to independence.

The final section of this chapter offers a more personalised perspective of how activists in Fiji understood their capacity to expand the space made available to women's organisations within civil society during this period. I show why YWCA members judged the possibilities for provocative political activity to be expansive and explain how this influenced their negotiation of collectivity, progressive ideas and transnationalism. These are aspects of women's political agency which are generally assumed to be distinctive to the terrain of women's organising but, as the preceding chapters have demonstrated, they need also to be examined in ways which recognise their contingent nature.

Women and community development

Fiji's YWCA was formed in the early 1960s, the final decade of British colonial rule in this island territory. Throughout the preceding colonial period, few development initiatives had been put in place for women. Those that did exist were geared around the conviction that the lives of local women required 'improvement' and 'uplifting' (Leckie 2002: 161). As such, colonial programs aimed to instruct Fiji's women in European child-rearing and housekeeping techniques in the 'earnest belief' that this would set them on the 'path of progress and social evolution' (Schoeffel 1986: 42; see also Knapman 1986: 20–28; Lukere 1997; Jolly 1998: 191–99).

In the final decades of Fiji's colonial history, government medical and education departments continued to run women's programs that retained this educative orientation but also incorporated a community development approach which aimed to encourage greater local level participation (Sue 1982: 63).[1] This shift was introduced by Marjorie Stewart, a development specialist with experience in East Africa and the West Indies who was posted to Fiji in the late 1950s by the British Colonial Office's Ministry of Overseas Development. Stewart was instrumental in creating a more structured development program for women within the colonial administration and she encouraged Fiji's women to form their own voluntary associations. By 1960 she had established a national Women's Interest Office in Suva which came formally under the jurisdiction of Fiji's Education Department (SPC 1976: 31). The programs administered by this office were chiefly concerned with the non-formal education of women and included such themes as 'The Woman in Her Home and Village' which provided instruction in areas such as home gardening, home beautification and improvement, cooking and sewing, hygiene, handicraft production and the use of 'appropriate technologies' in the home (Stewart 1960a: 45, 1962: 42). While Stewart moved on from this post in a short space of time, taking up the position of Women's Interest Officer for the regional South Pacific Commission (SPC), the work of the Fiji-based Women's Interest Office continued with great energy throughout the 1960s.

Frequent articles on the operations of Fiji's Women's Interest Office appearing in the *South Pacific Bulletin* during these years attest to the vibrancy of these efforts and report a flourishing of women's organisations around Fiji. The newly formed groups were seen to provide women with the opportunity to exchange ideas and experiences (Stewart 1960a: 44), while also developing their 'initiative and leadership' skills (Parkinson 1961: 63).

Of course, there were many well-established women's organisations operating in Fiji at this time, with some in existence for decades prior to the initiatives undertaken by the Women's Interest Office in the 1960s. One of the earliest of these was the *Soqosoqo Vakamarama I Taukei* (SSVM), a Methodist organisation for indigenous Fijian women, which was founded in 1924 and known initially as *Qele ni Ruve* (Leckie 2002: 161). The organisation was headed by Rene Derrick, the wife of a colonial missionary. During this early colonial period, the majority of initiatives for women were only able to gain legitimacy if European or expatriate women were involved. A long-time Australian expatriate with close connections to the women's movement in Fiji, Ruth Lechte, argued for example that 'if a white woman didn't head something up, it simply didn't

---

1   During this period, community development approaches were viewed as a remedy to correct the shortcomings of conventional 'trickle down' development programs by encouraging what today might be termed a more 'participatory' style of development. In a UN report which examined women's roles in community development, the term was defined as 'the processes by which the efforts of people themselves are united with those of government authorities to improve the economic, social and cultural conditions of communities, to integrate these communities into the life of the nation, and to enable them to contribute fully to national progress' (UN 1972: 5).

happen' (2005). This meant that white women frequently held privileged positions within women's organisations as leaders, and mentors. While this was certainly the case with *Ruve*, the efforts of local indigenous women of the Davuilevu region of Viti Levu and, in particular, the work done by the *Ruve's* Vice-President, Lolohea Waqairawai, contributed greatly to the early strength of the organisation (Lechte 2005).

The domestic orientation of the programs favoured by the *Soqosoqo Vakamarama* (Schoeffel 1988: 35) is described by Eta Baro who recounts how, in the early days, the organisation would send 'sewing patterns and cooking recipes … from Davuilevu' to clubs all over Fiji. According to Baro, these efforts instructed 'Fijian women … how to sew, cook using new recipes, keep their homes and villages clean and generally bring up healthy families' (Baro 1975: 34).

However, as Penelope Schoeffel has argued, the indigenous imprint upon the organisation was strongly evident. The income-generating activities women were encouraged to take up, for example, were generally in the area of traditional Fijian arts and crafts (1988: 35). And, with the Derricks' departure from Fiji in the 1940s, the whole leadership structure of the organisation began to more closely reflect the social structures that traditionally regulated Fijian social life. The importance of Fijian cultural protocols within this organisation is clearly evidenced by Waqairawai's decision at this time to turn down requests that she assume the role of national president. Although she had been one of the longest serving members of the SSVM, she maintained that her lack of chiefly status precluded her from leading a Fijian organisation (Baro 1975: 35).

In addition to the SSVM, women's associations were also formed within Fiji's faith communities. According to their religious affiliation, women in Fiji might belong to the Methodist Women's Fellowship, the Catholic Women's League, or the Fiji Moslem Zenana League. However, the potential for these groups to develop programs solely for women was often limited by gendered expectations which defined their role primarily in terms of serving and supporting the needs of the broader community (see chapter 1; Griffen 1984: 517; Varani-Norton 2005).

The Women's Interest Office in Suva was instrumental in creating enthusiasm for the establishment of secular women's clubs which were more primarily focused upon addressing the needs of local women in their community. By 1962, the Office had over 410 women's clubs registered on its books (Stewart 1962: 42) and had begun publishing a newsletter that went out to clubs keeping them informed of training courses and new network opportunities. Yet the precedent for interventions designed to 'improve' women's lives remained. The domestic orientation of these programs saw a heavy emphasis placed upon aspects of maternal life such as improving family nutrition, domestic hygiene and home improvement. While these programs also encouraged women to participate in civic duties outside the home and develop local leadership skills, it is also clear that within the rubric of community development, 'women's interests' were defined as 'separate from those of men' and oriented towards women's familial responsibilities (Schoeffel 1982: 60).[2]

YWCA programs

By the end of the 1960s, one women's organisation had begun formulating programs which challenged the narrower conceptualisation of women's interests evident in the community development approach. This organisation was the Fiji YWCA. It had begun life in 1961 as a body with fairly moderate aims, offering a range of programs for young women that were entirely in keeping with the thinking of the times. However, a remarkable transition took place within this organisation in the space of a few years.

Beyond her responsibilities to the colonial government, Marjorie Stewart played an important role in the establishment of the YWCA in Fiji and acted as the organisation's founding president.[3] A close association developed between this organisation in its early days and the prestigious girls' college, Adi Cakobau School (ACS),[4] located in the Suva-Nausori corridor. Through her personal friendship with the principal of this school, Stewart was able to use the school's networks to raise funds for the organisation and also to recruit YWCA members from its student population.

Amelia Rokotuivuna was the head prefect of ACS, and a personality well known to Stewart. Upon leaving school, Rokotuivuna was encouraged to apply for a paid position within the YWCA. Her long career with this organisation began with her employment as a receptionist and coordinator of the YWCA's Girls Clubs. Taufa Vakatale, who went on to become president of the YWCA, was a teacher at the ACS in these years and also became involved in the organisation through this connection.

---

2 Although, as Bronwen Douglas has argued, these types of programs also provided local women with the opportunity for socialisation beyond the more laborious tasks that they undertook in the domestic environment. While Douglas acknowledges the fact that these programs contributed to a widespread promotion of European gender stereotypes, she also contends that blanket dismissal of these types of projects as old-fashioned, or outmoded, tends to overlook the extent to which they also provided a source of collective social empowerment for local women (1999, 2003).

3 The YWCA began as a Suva-based organisation and was initially affiliated with the New Zealand YWCA. In 1965, the Fiji YWCA was formed as a national organisation. Even so, the majority of the organisation's activities were located in Suva. By 1970, the Fiji YWCA had also established a branch in Lautoka.

4 *Adi* is a chiefly title for indigenous women in Fiji.

As previously noted, during Fiji's colonial period, it was almost mandatory for women's organisations to include the presence of European women if they were to gain any type of legitimate recognition within the community, and there was certainly a strong expatriate presence within the YWCA in its early years. Nonetheless, the local women who were actively involved in the YWCA at this time described this expatriate presence in generous terms. Stewart herself was remembered as a personality whose Quaker faith was underpinned by a commitment to 'social service.' Rokotuivuna argued that her capacity for both organisation and intellectual thought were highly beneficial to the YWCA in its early years (2002b). The 1962 appointment of two professional, salaried women, both expatriate Australians, to run the day-to-day activities of the organisation was also seen as contributing positively to the YWCA's development. Ruth Lechte was appointed as the organisation's General Secretary and Anne Walker was made Program Secretary. Vakatale argued that it was the presence of these two figures that 'basically ... made the Y go.' She stated that they were personalities of the 'right caliber' to deal with the varied membership that the organisation attracted in ensuing years (2002).

While expatriate women contributed the types of skills and experience that would be beneficial to the day-to-day operations of the YWCA, they also fostered a vibrant intellectual profile within the organisation and an encompassing leadership philosophy (Rokotuivuna 2002a, 2002b; Vakatale 2002). Rokotuivuna argued that from the time of the YWCA's establishment, there existed a 'serious intellectual group that talked about issues.' Many of the early members of the organisation argued that unlike the older and more well-established women's organisations whose leadership structures generally reflected age or social status hierarchies, the founding members of the YWCA encouraged young, educated, community-minded local women with an interest in social and political change to assume positions of authority.

In addition, the participation of local women university graduates was a benefit to the YWCA. In 1968, the University of the South Pacific (USP) was founded and figures such as Rokotuivuna worked hard to forge strong relationships between the YWCA and the local student community, particularly through links with the USP campus chapter of the Christian Student Association.[5] Whereas the strong proportion of overseas, tertiary-educated women within the local YWCA community contributed initially to the organisation's intellectual profile, in later periods increasing numbers of local university students coming into the YWCA contributed to the emerging activist profile of this organisation.[6]

---

5   Before this time, women pursuing higher education were required to travel to New Zealand, Australia or England. Vakatale, Siwatibau, Esiteri Kamikamica and Rokotuivuna completed university studies overseas, and returned to Suva prior to the establishment of USP.

6   According to Vanessa Griffen, Rokotuivuna was particularly instrumental in forging strong links with the local student population, women and men, and 'pulled them into the activities of the YWCA' (Griffen 2005).

YWCA activities at this time tended to reflect a philosophy of inclusiveness which stood in contrast to the communalist tendencies that structured the sphere of women's organising and the existing terrain of civil society more generally in Fiji. This was evident from the outset, as indicated by Stewart, herself (1962: 44) when she described her vision for the newly formed YWCA, as being able to: 'unite in its membership women and girls, irrespective of race or creed, in a programme devoted to spiritual, physical, cultural and social development and through that membership group to take action within the community on questions relating to women and girls' (1962: 44).

Figure 2.1. Cooking classes held at the YWCA.

Source: Photograph YWCA press cutting archive. Courtesy Pacific Manuscript Bureau (PAMBU), The Australian National University (ANU).

The ecumenical and multicultural focus was evident in the range of YWCA activities offered from its headquarters situated, at this time, on the first floor of the Suva Town Hall, and from various other sites around Suva. Classes were offered in English, Fijian and Hindi language, typing, public speaking, fabric printing, bag-making and sewing. While organised sport had, up until this point, been the principal domain of the colonial establishment and the indigenous elite (Goodwillie 2005), the YWCA promoted a multicultural approach to sporting activities and included programs for athletics, badminton, hockey, softball, swimming and tennis (Fiji YWCA 1965a, 1965b, 1970b; 1965–1970 Program Committee Record Books). Blue Circle Clubs catered for teenage girls and offered instruction in arts and crafts, sewing and cooking as well as local outings.

In addition, the YWCA ran Neighbourhood Clubs which offered activities on a weekly basis for young married women in various locations around Suva. These groups offered instruction in areas such as sewing, cooking, carpentry, inter-club sports and Red Cross first-aid training. In 1967, the YWCA also introduced a program of Housegirls Clubs. These were designed to provide a social outlet for household workers whose opportunities for socialising and learning new skills were limited by their 'live-in' employment situation (*Fiji Times* 22 April 1970).[7] In all of these activities, a strong emphasis was placed upon intercommunalism, something which contrasted with the more generally prevailing norm of ethnically segregated women's groups.

By the late 1960s, the YWCA had begun to broaden the focus of its activities further, developing activities not just for women and girls but for Fiji's youth more generally. A Home Industries program was established to enhance the earning capacity of early school leavers. In addition, a youth drop-in centre was created and a youth counsellor appointed (Fiji YWCA 1970b; *Fiji Times* 1 March 1973; Vakatale 2002).

In 1973, the YWCA moved to a new, purpose-built, five-storey headquarters in central Suva. In its public report released in 1969, the YWCA building committee was eager to point out that the new headquarters would not be 'a static monument' but instead 'a home for a living and growing program among the people of these islands—a contribution to the Fiji of the future' (*Fiji Times* 29 December 1969). These new premises allowed the YWCA's program to expand significantly. The existing curriculum was expanded to include vocational courses aimed at meeting the needs of early school leavers and enhancing their job prospects (*The Post* 27 March 1973).

In this capacity, Rokotuivuna argued that the YWCA was an early precursor to the modern day Fiji Institute of Technology (Rokotuivuna 2002b). YWCA records show that enrolments for the vocational courses totalled 220 in this period and in later years were to reach 500 with students receiving instruction in typing, book-keeping, English language, office work, shop assistants' work, household workers' training, hospitality work and commercial cleaning (Fiji YWCA 1973; Rokotuivuna 2002b).

---

7   The issue of household workers' free time was crucial to the Housegirls Clubs' success. Therefore in 1967, the YWCA's General Secretary wrote to the employers of household workers around Suva informing them of the YWCA's programs for their employees and urging them to allow the girls enough time off to attend club activities (Fiji YWCA 30 January 1967, Programme Committee Record Book).

Figure 2.2. Building plans for the YWCA showing the external design.

Source: Image YWCA press cutting archives. Courtesy of PAMBU, ANU.

The widely expanded focus of the YWCA's educative and social programs indicates that by the early 1970s, it had evolved as an organisation with a broad commitment not simply to the welfare of women and girls but to urban youth more generally. In this role, it clearly aimed to act as an adjunct to the state in the area of training and welfare provision, something no doubt encouraged through Stewart's earlier organisational mentorship and her dual roles as a YWCA member and colonial women's development officer. In a paper published by the organisation in 1967, and entitled 'The Role of Voluntary Services in Social Welfare,' the YWCA acknowledged the lack of state resources in developing countries and the complementary role that the non-government sector could play in social service provision. This paper argued that cooperative ventures between government and voluntary bodies could create a 'very adequate framework' for the provision of social services (Fiji YWCA 1967b).

However, in these years the 'Y' also assumed an important role as a public advocacy body and, in this function, it often emerged as a critic of state activity. From the moment of foundation, YWCA leaders had urged members to 'take action in the community'. In later years, the idea that the organisation should develop an 'active concern for human community' became a guiding principle (Fiji YWCA 1973), albeit one which led to frequent involvement in highly politicised and provocative public debate.

Public advocacy

Parliamentary representation

To begin with, the YWCA's local public advocacy occurred in a fairly ad hoc manner, with strategies limited to letter-writing campaigns or lobbying activities targeting local parliamentary representatives or civil servants (Rokotuivuna 2002b). However, in the lead-up to independence, one event in 1965 helped establish the YWCA's profile as an organisation that aimed to promote an increasingly radicalised political agenda.

With national debate raging over the contentious issue of political representation in the country's new parliament, and the likely number of communal seats reserved for each of Fiji's ethnic communities, YWCA members Suliana Siwatibau, Vakatale and Rokotuivuna, took part in a public forum convened to hear women's views on the future shape of Fiji's constitution and electoral system. The YWCA women used this occasion to articulate a vision for the future of Fiji that challenged in unambiguous terms the existing communal system of electoral representation. In front of the British Parliamentary Under-Secretary for the Colonies, Eirene White, delegates from other women's organisations, and the media, each of these YWCA speakers called attention to the unjust structures of administrative and political rule that had come into existence during colonial rule in Fiji, and argued for their abolition. Vakatale branded the denial of political representation to Fiji's Chinese community a violation of 'rights'. Siwatibau argued that the communal electoral system more generally had potentially harmful consequences for an independent Fiji. She remarked that 'protecting Fijians and having only what is good for Fijians, means that other races are not treated justly and injustice leads to strife' (*Fiji Times* 29 April 1965). The most contentious proposition of the meeting was offered by YWCA secretary Rokotuivuna, who voiced strong criticism of the hierarchical nature of indigenous political leadership and the longstanding practice of reserving Legislative Council positions for members of the Great Council of Chiefs. She argued that 'Fijians should vote as they like, for whom they like,' and that there should be a 'common roll worked in conjunction with the communal roll.' Further to this, she stated that she would like to see the Council of Chiefs 'wiped out' and ordinary Fijians begin to 'think for themselves' (*Fiji Times* 29 April 1965).

As news of the YWCA speakers' claims filtered through the media, their stand was widely interpreted as a betrayal of Fijian interests. Of all the submissions made by women's groups to the meeting, including the Fijian women's association *Soqosoqo Vakamara*, the Fiji Women's Club and the local branch of the Pan Pacific and Southeast Asian Women's Association (PPSEAWA), the YWCA members attracted national attention for their strong criticism of Fiji's governance structures.

This early challenge to colonial manipulations of race relations in Fiji reflected longstanding principles within the Fiji YWCA but they were also ideas that had been discussed within World YWCA conferences during this period. Indeed World YWCA conference resolutions from 1963 and 1967 had urged women within local YWCA associations to challenge institutionalised systems of racial discrimination and social and political injustice (World YWCA 1995: 131, 142; Lechte 2005). Fiji's YWCA members were fully apprised of this and determined to act on these issues when opportunities presented. This international mandate did not lessen the controversy surrounding the three women speakers' actions, however. The fallout from this event was significant. The YWCA came to be seen as a local centre for radical political thought. As Vakatale explains, 'we were branded as anti-chiefs, anti-tradition. So it started from there. The radicalism of the YWCA started from there' (2002).

Nuclear testing

One of the most significant campaigns run by the YWCA from the early 1970s onwards was in relation to nuclear testing in the Pacific region. Civil society organising around this issue was beginning to intensify at this time, as the YWCA, along with the USP Student Christian Association, and the Fiji Council of Churches, sought to organise protest activities and educate the public as to why continued tests should be opposed. A newly formed group, the Against Testing on Muroroa committee (ATOM), played a significant role in raising public awareness on nuclear testing in the Pacific and drew some of its most active members from YWCA ranks. However, in its own capacity, the YWCA also sought to raise local women's awareness of the threats a nuclearised Pacific posed to the long-term health of local populations and the environment.

Figure 2.3. Amelia Rokotuivuna and fellow ATOM member Akuila Yabaki sorting letters that were protesting about nuclear testing.

Source: Photograph YWCA press cuttings archive. Courtesy PAMBU, ANU.

Here again, YWCA activities on this question had a transnational currency and reflected concerns raised by the World YWCA in relation to warfare issues, the uses of nuclear energy, and the global proliferation of nuclear weapons (1995: 140). At the local level, however, there was some resistance to this radical expansion of 'women's interests'. A level of community scepticism and apathy saw comments such as 'Why can't they just concentrate on being young women rather than doing the anti-nuclear campaign?' directed at the YWCA (Rokotuivuna 2002b). This meant that the YWCA, along with the other civil society partners involved in this movement, had to work creatively to foster local interest in this issue. The YWCA used public education campaigns to turn community attitudes around and often relied on small theatre performances to encourage people to identify with this issue. As Slatter demonstrates, these types of advocacy methodologies could change attitudes. In a review of the YWCA's work in this area, she cites one observer's reaction to a critical account of nuclear testing in the Pacific:

Now (we) know, from what was presented today, what can happen as a result of such explosions. We admit our ignorance and lack of knowledge. We criticised the stand that the 'Y' and the USP students took in the past but we did not understand. We want a Fiji-wide march to be planned for all women in Fiji to witness (1976: 47).

The activities of Fiji YWCA members on this issue were also persuasive within the World YWCA Council, which in 1971, adopted a resolution that urged associations to express their concern to national governments over nuclear testing in the Pacific, and to also voice these protests within relevant agencies of the United Nations.[8] The world YWCA's recognition of the detrimental aspects of 'persistent nuclear testing in the Pacific Area' (World YWCA 1995: 148) was viewed as a win for Fiji YWCA members and reinforced the idea that they had an international mandate to undertake advocacy on these issues both at the local level, and when opportunities later arose, on the international stage (Vakatale 2002).

For the most part, however, the YWCA's activities on the anti-nuclear issue were aimed at building local-level support amongst the general public and within government. In the latter aim, the YWCA, in coalition with other organisations had some success. In the months leading up to Fiji's independence in October 1970, there was an increase in public demonstrations of opposition to French and US nuclear testing in the Pacific.[9] Responding to this pressure, government representatives began to take up this issue within regional forums such as the SPC, and after independence, within the United Nations and the Commonwealth (Ogashiwa 1991).

In the following years, YWCA members acting within the broader ATOM coalition continued their campaigns and urged the Fiji government to support regional moves to have 'all or part' of the Pacific Ocean declared a nuclear free zone. In addition, Fiji's statesmen were urged to refer the French administration's activities in the Pacific Territories to the United Nations Committee on Decolonization, on the grounds that its regimes were 'oppressive' (Ogashiwa 1991: 48). These efforts to link issues relating to nuclear testing with the

---

8   As early as 1963, the World YWCA Council had passed resolutions condemning the further development of weapons of mass destruction and, in particular, nuclear weapons technology (World YWCA 1995: 131).

9   In May 1970, five months before Fiji's Independence, expatriate USP academic Dr Graeme Bains published an article in the *Fiji Times* designed to raise local consciousness of the negative consequences of French nuclear weapons testing on Mururoa Atoll (Ogashiwa 1991: 46). Bains' critical appraisal of the situation attracted interest from the Student Christian Movement and the YWCA Public Affairs Committee which, along with the USP Student Association and the Fiji Council of Churches, organised a public meeting on the issue. This event attracted five hundred people, including the Fiji Minister for Labour, Ratu Edward Cakobau, who attended as a representative of the Chief Minister, Ratu Sir Kamisese Mara. The meeting passed a series of resolutions protesting against further French testing programs and urging Ratu Mara to take the issue to the South Pacific Conference scheduled for September 1970 (*Fiji Times* 30 May 1970). Before the September meeting of the South Pacific Conference, ATOM members briefed the Fijian delegate, Jonati Mavoa, who then took up the anti-nuclear cause during the formal conference proceedings (Ogashiwa 1991).

enduring presence of the colonial powers in the Pacific became an important plank of regional civil society activity and inspired the foundation of the Nuclear Free and Independent Pacific Movement which continues as an active organisation to this day.[10]

While local and regional activity on the anti-nuclear issue clearly paid dividends in terms of winning support from Fiji's government for the YWCA's anti-nuclear cause, it is also worth noting that even the local churches acted in support of this position. In a country such as Fiji, where religious values are deeply held, it was highly significant that the burgeoning anti-nuclear movement was able to garner support from the churches. They had generally steered a conservative political path and avoided explicit engagement on foreign policy issues. The Pacific Conference of Churches, a relatively liberal organisation, had played an important role in promoting awareness of nuclear testing issues in the public domain and passed a range of resolutions at its annual General Assemblies calling for a nuclear-free Pacific. In Suva, the Pacific Theological College had also been active on this issue and had taken part in anti-nuclear protest marches in 1969 (Siwatibau and Williams 1982: 68). However, the fact that the highly conservative Methodist Church of Fiji also supported civil society actors promoting an anti-nuclear stance (*Fiji Times* 6 December 1972), and had stood alongside Archbishop George Pearce, the leader of the Catholic Church in Fiji on this question (Slatter 1976: 45), demonstrates both the breadth and the ecumenical reach of anti-nuclear advocacy during this period. It may have been a radical departure from the 'women's improvement' programs of earlier periods, but the YWCA's political activism on the anti-nuclear issue can be seen as both driving and reflecting prevailing political sentiments of the time.

Family planning

YWCA campaigns on anti-nuclear issues certainly struck a chord with influential political and religious actors in Fiji at this time, yet the organisation's activity in some other areas was of a far more controversial hue. This was most strikingly evident when the organisation became involved in advocacy around questions of sexual health, family planning and birth control. Here the YWCA pitted itself against opposition ranks which were in some ways no less formidable in the domestic context, than the French administration had proved to be on the international issue of nuclear testing. For in this debate, the YWCA placed itself in direct contradiction to the very public 'pro-life' platforms supported by both the Catholic and Methodist Churches of Fiji—religious institutions that exercised significant influence over sections of Fiji's population.

---

10   In 1974, ATOM organised a regional conference on the issue of nuclear testing with Rokotuivuna chairing the planning committee. Out of this conference, the regional body known as the Nuclear Free and Independent Pacific was founded, which would become highly influential in generating awareness of both nuclear testing and colonisation issues in the following decades.

In 1973, the YWCA had begun to make public calls for improved services in the area of family planning, a greater availability of contraception and the creation of an abortion counselling service (*Fiji Times* 6 March 1973). Rokotuivuna and Lechte drew on their experiences of dealing with young women coming into the YWCA as a basis for their claims that issues relating to sex education and family planning were being ignored by the government and that this situation was having serious ramifications for young women (*Fiji Times* 6 March 1973).[11] In 1974, the YWCA Public Affairs Committee (PAC) presented a submission to government calling for increased activity in the area of family planning and the legalisation of abortion. YWCA members were conscious of the potentially divisive nature of this action and attempted to defend the organisation's position in a way that made reference to Christian teachings. The PAC submission, therefore, contrasted religiously conservative arguments which viewed man as responsible to God in all areas of his life, with more contemporary views which saw 'procreation as one of the areas of life now under a person's own control' (Fiji YWCA 2 May 1974, Public Affairs Committee (PAC) Record Book). The submission stated: 'The woman now has the responsibility to decide what happens to her body. This approach, when moral authority resides with the person and not with external authorities, seems very much in line with the growth to maturity which is the goal of Christian living' (Fiji YWCA 2 May 1974, PAC Record Book).

At the same time, the global affiliation of Fiji YWCA members to a broader association again influenced how this issue was approached in the local context. In the late 1960s, the World YWCA had begun to consider various aspects of family planning in relation to its policy on the social, educational and economic ramifications of population growth. While World YWCA Council resolutions at this time did not call explicitly for the legalisation of abortion, they did urge local associations to support the creation of health, education and counselling services for family planning that would safeguard individual freedom but at the same time remain widely accessible (World YWCA 1995: 135).

In the local context, attempts to create a theological defence of abortion, or to justify this stand through reference to resolutions passed within the global YWCA body, did not help diffuse opposition to the YWCA's stand on this issue. Indeed the organisation's pro-abortion position forced some members to question their continuing involvement in the organisation (Slatter 1976: 49; Vakatale 2002).

---

11 An article in the *Fiji Times* (6 March 1973), cites both Rokotuivuna and Lechte as arguing that 'criminal abortions were a major problem in Fiji' with Lechte describing her personal knowledge of two cases where young women had died as a result of illegal 'back-street' abortions. For these reasons, the YWCA claimed the need for social services that could provide counselling for those who sought abortions and more broad-reaching programs of sex education and family planning.

However, when asked about the YWCA's loss of support on this issue, Rokotuivuna argued that the organisation did not lose 'kudos' for its pro-abortion stance, and that many Fijian women privately voiced support for the YWCA position, but did not dare to make public statements to that effect (2002b). She felt that despite the submission's controversial nature, the organisation's relationship with government and other non-government bodies was not unduly harmed and the organisation 'was not locked out by its radical stance' (2002b). Certainly the YWCA's proposals on this matter were considered provocative in policy-making circles and were not taken up by the government of the day. As later discussion will show, however, the fact that they were issued at all is striking and indicative of a particular type of conviction held within the YWCA regarding the expansive nature of political space within civil society and the organisation's capacity to challenge religious convictions so strongly held within the community.

Economic justice

Questions of economic justice were also a powerful concern within the YWCA in these years and saw organisation members engage in a critical examination of global and local economic structures and how these impacted upon the lives of Fiji's women. The organisation had initiated a number of studies on wealth and resource distribution in Fiji, prepared a report entitled *Conditions of Work for Women* on the roles of women in the public service (Fiji YWCA 23 July 1974, PAC Record Book), and made submissions to parliamentary sub-committees investigating counter-inflation legislation (Fiji YWCA 12 August 1974, PAC Record Book). Prominent members of the YWCA had also been involved in two independent publications examining how international factors influenced development outcomes in Fiji.

Once again, these were areas of concern that had begun to receive attention within the World Council of the YWCA. In 1971, the Council passed a series of resolutions on social and economic justice in which national associations were urged to 'work deliberately to make YWCA members and the community aware of the inequalities which exist in each society' (World YWCA 1995: 147). These resolutions also required national associations to lobby governments to ensure that foreign and domestic policy was 'directed towards the achievement of economic and social justice' (World YWCA 1995: 147). Resolutions in this area clearly provided local YWCA members in Fiji with an international mandate to resist the influences which were felt to produce economic injustice within Pacific communities.

In 1973, Claire Slatter and Rokotuivuna contributed chapters to a work entitled *Fiji: A Developing Australian Colony* which exposed the extent to which

Australian interests had allegedly compromised Fiji's economic sovereignty (Dakuvula 1973: 10). Rokotuivuna argued that Australia's position as a 'dominant economic power in Fiji' had a 'bearing on existing problems' and would contribute to their exacerbation 'in the future' particularly given the country's reliance upon a sugar industry which was largely controlled by the Australian company, Colonial Sugar Refineries (CSR) (Rokotuivuna et al. 1973: 9). Slatter's contribution to this work investigated the tourism industry and the assumption that increasing numbers of tourists visiting Fiji meant increasing levels of wealth and well-being for local people. Slatter found that the 'nature and scale' of the type of tourism industry that predominated in Fiji made it largely an export economy which favoured not Fiji's people, but the 'metropolitan powers, including Australia, Japan and the United States' (1973: 18–25).

In 1975, Rokotuivuna and Slatter were involved in a seminar that resulted in another published work, *The Pacific Way: Social Issues in National Development*. Here again, discussion centred upon the ability of local populations to have their interests represented in development processes. For example, Rokotuivuna argued for the formulation of development plans which were built around 'quality of life' or 'style of life issues' rather than formal development 'growth' targets, which assume that quality of life improvement will occur as a by-product of national economic progress (Rokotuivuna 1975: 7).

For Rokotuivuna, Slatter and other YWCA members, strong grassroots and activist connections ensured that these types of deliberations were not simply an academic exercise in 'what ought to be', but firmly grounded in local concerns. For example, in this period, the YWCA made strenuous efforts to improve the working conditions and earning capacity of household workers. The organisation provided practical courses that aimed to improve the training of young women engaged in this industry and give it a more professional face (*Fiji Times* 17 December 1970). It also supported workers' efforts to create a household workers union, and made representations to government on this question (Fiji YWCA 9 October 1975, PAC Record Book).

And the Fiji government's responses to some aspects of this activity certainly appear to have been more lenient than in later periods. For example, the organisation's efforts to safeguard the earning potential and conditions of low-skilled, female, household workers appears to have won some sympathy from local policy makers. While the unionisation option was not taken up, the fact that government representatives were willing to consider a range of other state-initiated measures to protect these workers (Fiji YWCA 9 October 1975, PAC Record Book) indicates a prevailing liberal attitude within government towards the question of women's labour rights. This would become much harder to discern in ensuing decades. Therefore, while YWCA advocacy designed to create awareness of the international threats posed to Fiji's economic sovereignty, or more localised activity aimed to reduce the economic vulnerability of women workers, was both innovative and provocative to some extent, aspects of this activity also appear to have found favour with local political figures.

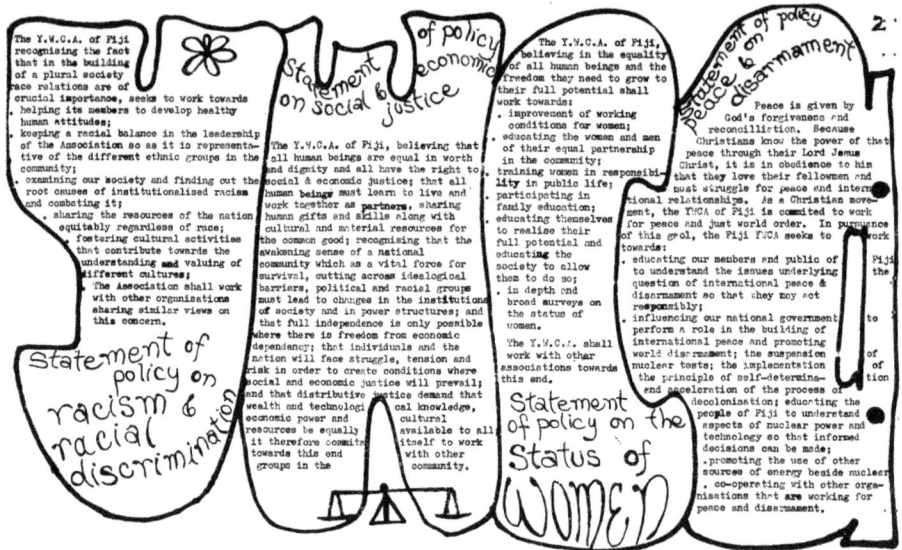

Figure 2.4. YCWA Platform for Public Affairs Advocacy. YWCA 3rd National Convention Report, 10–13 September 1976.

Source: Courtesy PAMBU, ANU.

International Women's Year: 1975

The independence era political environment seemed to provide an increased latitude for women's involvement in public debate, often in areas outside those more conventionally associated with women's advocacy. However, it is also clear that YWCA activity generally retained a distinctive quality and contrasted in significant ways with the public conduct of many other women's organisations. This included the recently established National Council of Women (NCW), formed in 1968 as a national peak body to represent women's organisations nationally, and act as a focal point for government liaison on women's issues. This entity enjoyed close government support and received a government grant of £40 to fund its establishment (Kamikamica 1982).

The NCW principally drew its membership from representatives of the older and more well-established women's groups in Fiji—faith-based organisations such as the Catholic Women's League or the Fiji Moslem Women's League, the mass organisation for indigenous women, the SSVM, organisations for Indo-

Fijian women and, in addition, some provincially based groups. While it has been argued that the NCW has followed a conservative political path thanks to its close relationship with the Fiji government (Jalal 1997), the fact that the NCW always aimed to speak for a range of women's organisations representing a broad span of interests also made the amalgamation of competing perspectives a difficult task (Goodwillie and Lechte 1985). This was particularly so given the influential presence of the SSVM within the NCW; a presence which tended to ensure that the organisation did not pursue political agendas deemed damaging to broader indigenous interests. To maintain a working relationship with its institutional benefactors and to avoid alienating important sections of its membership, the NCW therefore eschewed the YWCA's 'head-on' approach to questions of gender inequality or racial difference and assumed a more reserved political profile.

The divergent paths developed by the two organisations were clearly evident in the local activities undertaken by each association to mark International Women's Year (IWY), declared by the United Nations in 1975. This event was not accorded a high priority by the Fiji government or the local media and may have passed unnoticed were it not for the efforts of women's organisations and, in particular, the work of the Fiji YWCA and the NCW.[12] The NCW structured its IWY activities in ways that focused upon the unifying aspects of the broader national project in the post-independence context, and the need for greater recognition of women's contributions towards nation-building. On the other hand, the YWCA sought to use the IWY to focus attention upon the issue of race relations in Fiji, and the negative consequences for women of discriminatory political and social structures. The YWCA proposed a public affairs program which would examine negative racial stereotypes, structures of land access which were determined by race, and the preferential distribution of educational scholarships according to ethnic background in Fiji. In all these areas, YWCA activity threatened to challenge the doctrine of Fijian paramountcy, a concept fervently protected by the indigenous political establishment and either respected or negotiated with great caution by civil society actors at this time.

By focusing upon issues of race relations in Fiji, the YWCA was, again, clearly following an agenda that reflected World YWCA Council resolutions on questions of racial and ethnic discrimination. Yet, in the lead-up to the IWY, some within the local YWCA felt this to be an unnecessarily contentious course of action (Fiji YWCA 11 December 1974, PAC Record Book). Ultimately, the majority of the YWCA board voted in favour of a program devoted to a discussion of race relations in Fiji, persuaded by the view that the promotion of a multiracial

---

12 Reports on the subject in Fiji's newspapers, for example, were devoted to a discussion of local organisations' sale of promotional material featuring the symbol of the IWY dove rather than any clear consideration of what this development at the international level might mean in concrete terms for Fiji's women (*Fiji Times* 22 April 1975).

Fiji would be a positive activity for Fiji's women in general terms (Fiji YWCA 1974, PAC Record Book). The emergence of internal contestation within the organisation around this question is significant, however, and demonstrates the presence of rupture points within the association's collective structure which, in later more troubled political periods, would become significant.

Advocacy on the international stage

Given the quite different local political profiles of Fiji's two national women's organisations, it is perhaps not surprising that when the government named its delegation to attend the intergovernmental UN conference for women in Mexico City in 1975, it included a representative of the NCW. The low priority placed by the government on conference attendance is evidenced by the fact that the only government representative on the delegation was an assistant to the Minister of Social Welfare, Adi Losalini Dovi. The nomination of these two delegates was interpreted by YWCA members as an extremely conservative decision, and it was felt that neither woman would engage in any critical reflection upon women's status in Fiji (Rokotuivuna 2002b).

YWCA members therefore looked to the parallel NGO Tribune proposed for the Mexico City event as the type of venue which might more easily allow for critical deliberation. The World YWCA used its networks to recruit women to attend the Tribune,[13] and the Fiji YWCA was asked to suggest suitable participants from the Pacific Islands. This request came soon after the first Nuclear Free and Independent Pacific Conference that was held in Suva in April, 1975. Building upon the contacts forged by Fiji YWCA members at this event with critically minded civil society actors from a number of Pacific locations, a list of 'radical women', who were sure to pursue a provocative agenda in Mexico City, was presented to Tribune organisers (Rokotuivuna 2002b). For these reasons, the Pacific delegation sponsored by the World YWCA to attend the Mexico City Forum included independence and indigenous rights activists such as Déwé Gorodé from New Caledonia, Tea Hirshon from Tahiti, Hilda-Halkyard Harawira from Aotearoa New Zealand and Grace Mera Molisa from the New Hebrides (Rokotuivuna 2002b; personal communication Claire Slatter July 2005). These were personalities who shared the strong anti-nuclear stance of the Fiji YWCA members, and were emerging as important and radical political figures in their own countries. Rokotuivuna, Lechte, Vanessa Griffen and Slatter represented the Fiji YWCA in Mexico City.

Many delegates to the 1975 Mexico City Tribune found the event overwhelming, and the representatives from the Pacific Islands were no exception (McConaghy

---

13 This situation is undoubtedly explained by the fact that Mildred Persinger, head of the World YWCA during this period, was also one of the chief organisers of the Mexico City Forum (Fraser 1987).

1975).[14] The sheer scale of the event left some of the region's delegates with the impression that they gained little from their international participation (Siwatibau 2002). Rokotuivuna was one of the few delegates from the region who was given the opportunity to participate on a formal Tribune panel. She spoke on nuclear disarmament issues alongside Sean MacBride, winner of the 1974 Nobel Peace Prize, and a Jamaican-born representative, Noel Brown. While each of the male speakers outlined the dangers of nuclear weapons and the nuclear industry in general terms, Rokotuivuna emphasised the impact of nuclearisation in the Pacific Islands, and highlighted local women's perspectives on the continuing influence of colonial powers in the region (Moore 1975: 14). In addition to this formal appearance, Pacific delegates also released two joint statements calling for an end to nuclear testing in the region, and self-rule for the region's colonial territories.

Pacific women's contributions to this forum were designed to highlight the unique combination of local and international influences that contributed to the subordination of Pacific Island communities and, by extension, local women. According to Rokotuivuna, this was a framework that resonated strongly with some Tribune participants as closely resembling their own situation. For others, however, it presented a challenging perspective on gender inequality that was difficult to accept.

Certainly, pronouncements upon the international dimensions of women's disadvantage and, in particular, demands for a more equitable global redistribution of economic and political resources, were frequently evident within the official UN conference proceedings in Mexico City. Within the intergovernmental forum, G77 representatives described the impacts of local instances of poverty and racism in ways that consistently laid the blame for these conditions at the door of the western, industrialised nations. They described these phenomena as colonial legacies that developed states now had an obligation to rectify in order to stabilise the post-colonial world. They also argued that Third World economic dependency would only be eradicated when exploitative relationships between developed and developing regions were ended (Mair 1986; Tinker and Jaquette 1987; Fraser 1987).[15] These demands

---

14   While some Fiji members had experience of international forums for women through their participation at World YWCA conferences staged every four years, these affairs were hardly of the scale of the UN 1975 Tribune.

15   Such arguments had received broad international exposure during this period as G77 nations applied increasing pressure within the UN. In 1964, the General Assembly had been persuaded to support the formation of a Convention on Trade and Development (UNCTAD) which aimed to encourage a more equitable economic and trade environment internationally. In 1974, in large part due to G77 pressure, the General Assembly universally ratified a declaration for the Establishment of a New International Economic Order (NIEO), a policy which aimed to protect the economic sovereignty of all states and create the type of global economic environment which would promote trade and development in Third World countries and increase their economic participation at the international level (Bhagwati 1977; Gregg 1981; Labra *et al.* 1981; Hart 1983). It was hoped that these international mechanisms would encourage a more equitable global economic

caused great disquiet amongst delegates from industrialised nations, however. US Ambassador Barbara White argued that such tactics were designed to divert attention away from a closer consideration of 'women's issues and led to an unnecessary politicisation of conference debate' (UNIWY Secretariat 1975: 27).

The emergence of these same lines of division within the more informal Tribune proceedings (Fraser 1987: 62), tended to contradict the allegations of 'unnecessary' diversion made by White and others. As Mary-Jo McConaghy noted at the time, many of the NGO representatives from industrialised countries at the Tribune were 'uninformed' about Third World demands for a redistributive ethos to guide international policy-making generally and, in particular, G77 activity in support of the establishment of a New International Economic Order (NIEO). Determined to promote a feminist framework of 'solidarity between women', they were often bitterly disappointed when these ideas were rejected by activists from the South (McConaghy 1975: 104). Participants from the Third World, on the other hand, interpreted this determination to promote western-oriented feminist frameworks as an effort to cloister discussion of women's status in a way that was only relevant to developed regions. They argued that this was a strategy designed to focus attention away from the industrialised world's responsibilities to developing regions and tantamount to 'cultural imperialism' (Falk and Blasius 1976: 263; see also Mair 1986; Tinker and Jaquette 1987; Fraser 1987).

While both the official intergovernmental conference and the more informal NGO Tribune were sites of heated debate and serious division over these issues, the concerns of G77 states were ultimately reflected in the World Plan of Action, the official conference document. The introductory section of this text made specific reference to issues of colonial and neocolonial domination, racial discrimination and global inequality, describing these as impediments to the advancement of all peoples from the developing world. At the same time, G77 states also drafted a separate document to the Plan of Action, which became known as the Mexico Declaration. This document offered an even more critical perspective of the current practice of international political and economic relations, and their impact upon the lives of southern women. Here, calls were made for greater global economic equality, protection of state sovereignty over natural resources, and an end to the ongoing violence associated with practices of colonialism, neocolonialism, Zionism and apartheid (UNIWY Secretariat 1975: 52, 51–58).

environment by restructuring fiscal relations so that industrialised northern nations did not continue to benefit from their economic exploitation of disadvantaged southern states. During this period, G77 nations also demonstrated a strong sense of solidarity in relation to issues of apartheid in South Africa or the Israeli occupation of Palestinian territories in the Middle East. They frequently condemned international tolerance of these policies which, they claimed, amounted to the subordination of entire populations on the basis of ethnicity, denying them internationally accepted rights to political representation or self-determination.

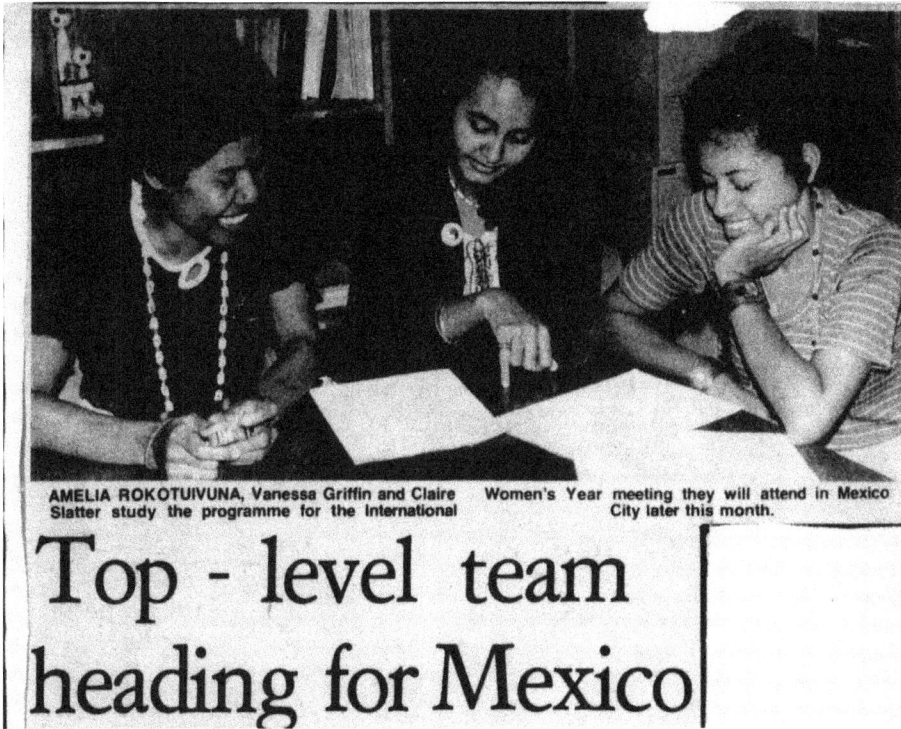

Figure 2.5. Fiji's NGO delegation examining the UN International Women's Year Conference Program before travelling to Mexico City.

Source: Photograph YWCA press cutting archive. Courtesy PAMBU, ANU.

When considered against these broader developments, it is clear that the position adopted by Pacific Island Tribune participants, and in particular that expressed by Rokotuivuna in her Tribune presentation, were entirely in keeping with broader themes frequently in evidence at the Mexico City conference. By drawing attention to the actions of the region's colonial powers and the alleged damage being done to the interests of Pacific Island peoples, Rokotuivuna and her fellow delegates articulated an analytical perspective on the status of women that was in keeping with the concerns raised by many other delegates from developing regions. For some present at Mexico City, this was a highly provocative strategy. For others, these actions were in keeping with broader currents shaping the political negotiations between developed and developing states during this period.

Regional developments

If the local resonance of the International Women's Year had been muted in Fiji before the Mexico City conference, the decision to stage a regional women's conference in Suva several months later stimulated interest in women's issues and simultaneously boosted the momentum of women's organising at both local and regional levels. This was a wholly NGO-organised affair with YWCA members in Papua New Guinea (PNG) and Fiji responsible for the conference organisation and the sourcing of sponsors to fund the event.[16] The 1975 Conference of Pacific Women in Suva attracted roughly eighty representatives from women's organisations across the Pacific Island states, and included women from non-independent territories of New Caledonia, New Hebrides, Hawaii and French Polynesia. Observers from Australia, New Zealand, Canada and the US were present, as was Jamaican-born Lucille Mair who had been a strong advocate for women from the developing world during the Mexico IWY event.[17]

Conference discussion revolved around the 'forces that shape women in society' (Slatter cited in Griffen 1975a: iv), and considered themes such as family and traditional culture, religion, education, the media, law and politics. In these presentations, it became apparent that two competing perspectives of women's disadvantage were employed. One was narrowly framed and examined women's customary and familial roles. The other 'reached far beyond' the conventional definition of 'women's issues', focusing more particularly upon the international factors that shaped the lives of Pacific women (Slatter in Griffen 1975a: iv). Melanesian delegates in particular were inclined to adopt this more broadly defined focus in their deliberations, examining how colonial interventions and modern ways of living had impacted upon traditional gender roles at the family level and encouraged a dissolution of traditional systems of knowledge and land tenure (Griffen 1975b: 15, 42–45, 70–77).

A speaker from PNG, for example, described how contact with European cultures had led to a diminishing of women's customary and familial status and an erosion of women's sites of traditional authority. Déwé Gorodé outlined the various ways in which continuing French rule in New Caledonia had destroyed Kanak traditions and social and cultural institutions. In the struggle to protect these things, Gorodé argued that the actions of the 'Kanak woman must be inseparable from the struggle for national liberation of the people' (cited in Griffen 1975b: 109).

---

16   Conference organisers relied upon a diverse range of international funding for the conference. Religious organisations such as the Board of Global Ministers of the United Methodist Church of the United States, the Australian Council of Churches and the Presbyterian Churches of the United States all donated money. The Canadian International Development Agency also provided significant financial support, as did the World YWCA and the Foundation for the Peoples of the South Pacific (Griffen 1975a).

17   In the lead-up to the 1980 UN Mid-Decade Conference for Women, Mair was made conference Secretary-General.

These were not perspectives shared by all, however. In particular, women from the Polynesian islands of Samoa, Tonga and the Cook Islands argued that the radicalism that defined the statements to the conference made by Melanesian delegates from Fiji, New Caledonia or the New Hebrides should not be considered applicable to Pacific women across the board.[18] These participants tended to argue that European interventions in the region should not be wholly criticised and had offered some positive benefits to local women, such as greater access to means of economic independence (Griffen 1975a: 11). Nevertheless, even where conference themes seemed to lend themselves to a more localised examination of patriarchal structures such as the role played by women in domestic life, this discussion invariably became infused with broader considerations of how Pacific Island social and cultural institutions were subverted or manipulated by influences emanating from outside the region (Griffen 1975a).

The foregrounding of Pacific experience in these discussions and the final conference declarations formulated in Suva which concentrated upon issues such as nuclear disarmament and decolonisation can be viewed as characteristic features of the advocacy of the women of the Pacific Islands during this period. Indeed, they continue the distinct trend towards a provocative and structurally inclined form of advocacy that first emerged within the Fiji YWCA in the mid-1960s. While statements made by many of the most radical participants at this event echoed themes that had been taken up by post-colonial leaders in other settings in the preceding years, it is important to note that the issues raised at this conference were not a simple emulation of Third World dependency discourse. Rather, the principal focus of these discussions was Pacific women and their experience of nuclearisation and colonial or alleged neo-colonial subjugation. As such, this type of advocacy grew out of critical and concrete evaluations of Pacific women's lives and how they were being shaped by economic and political forces emanating from outside the region.

In the following section, these trends are discussed in a more situated fashion by examining how YWCA members understood their ability to utilise the political spaces available to them in the independence-era political environment. Emphasis is placed upon the interplaying local and global contingencies that shaped women activists' views of the prevailing political climate and their subsequent negotiations of organisational collectivity, progressive ideas and transnationalism in this period.

---

18 Personal communication with Greg Fry. Fry was an observer at the 1975 conference and witnessed the nature of interaction between delegates. Interestingly, this tension is not mentioned in Griffen's report of the conference proceedings published in 1975, although she does make some mention of disagreement occurring between delegates over the constitution of 'women's issues' in a later piece she wrote discussing the history of women's organising in the Pacific in 1984 (Griffen 1984: 519).

Collectivity

During my interviews with women who had been part of the YWCA during this period, references were frequently made to the group's organisational structures and how these contrasted with those of more established women's organisations. Emphasis was placed upon the protocols that regulated participation within Fiji's civil society more broadly, how these impacted upon women's organisations in general, and how they were alternatively negotiated by YWCA members. In general, the older and more politically conservative women's organisations were characterised in ways which suggested that broader hierarchies of social organisation in Fiji were also replicated within these groups and contributed to the relative authority of individual members. As the earlier discussion has shown, within the mass organisation for indigenous women, the SSVM, questions of social rank were an especially pertinent consideration when determining the appropriate person to assume the leadership of the organisation upon the departure of the long-time expatriate president, Rene Derrick.

According to my interlocutors, these types of relationships were negotiated differently within the YWCA at this time. Unlike other women's organisations, there was an absence of a class consciousness within the YWCA, which allowed Rokotuivuna to rise to a senior position in the organisation despite the fact that she was not a person of high social rank within Fijian society.[19] Moreover, the organisation's members also downplayed the traditional deference to elders that was evident in many other women's groups. Vakatale argued, for example, that 'there were traditional women's groups who felt that young women shouldn't speak out ... they should let the old women speak out first. But here at the YWCA it was different. The older members sat back and got us young women, educated women, to take the leading role' (2002).

The fact that the YWCA embraced a multicultural ethos was also generally viewed as something that set it apart from other women's organisations and challenged the communal identifications so prevalent within the realm of associational life outside the organisation. Discussing the YWCA's ecumenism, Rokotuivuna argued that by 'playing down the traditions of our particular faiths, we felt we were aiming for higher goals' (Rokotuivuna 2002b). These commitments towards inclusion were not only relevant to the ways in which relations between Fijians and Indo-Fijians were negotiated within the YWCA either. For Rokotuivuna, the fact that expatriate YWCA members encouraged local women to voice their opinions on political and social issues and take leading roles within the organisation challenged the hierarchies of ethnicity

---

19   Rokotuivuna had won a scholarship to attend the elite girls' school ACS.

more generally evident in Fijian civil society. She commented, 'remember, this is colonial Fiji! It was the first time for me ever to sit around and talk to a European as an equal' (2002b).

The multicultural ethos had been firmly stated in Stewart's articulation of the organisations' objectives at the time of its foundation in 1962, and was also mandated by World YWCA Council resolutions. My interviews with older members such as Vakatale, Rokotuivuna and Siwatibau, and later YWCA representatives such as Claire Slatter and Sharon Bhagwan Rolls indicated that Lechte and Walker, as YWCA coordinators, played an important role in making these tenets a reality. Their talent for welcoming people from all communities and various age groups into the organisation was recognised as significant and something which set the YWCA apart from the majority of organisations within Fiji's civil society sphere.[20]

These successes contrasted with the agendas promoted by the NCW. Although this entity aimed to act as a national peak body representing many of the older and more established women's organisations in Fiji, it was far less successful in maintaining a multiracial profile. The fact that the SSVM was a member and, at this point, perhaps the most numerically powerful organisation affiliated with the group, meant that the NCW profile in many ways reflected an indigenous approach to women's issues. In general, the organisation was therefore willing to entertain the concept of multiracialism, and indeed women's advancement, only insofar as it did no damage to the broader political, social and cultural agenda promoted by the indigenous establishment, which was committed to the preservation of indigenous paramountcy (Jalal 1997).[21]

Certainly the Fiji YWCA felt no such constraints in this regard. While the organisation's members were conscious of the local political potency of racial questions, key members within the YWCA felt it was also time for this situation to be challenged. By establishing an organisational structure which facilitated participation regardless of racial origin, age or social standing, the YWCA acted in ways that posed an implicit challenge to the protocols which established hierarchical relationships within other women's organisations and which, since early colonial times, had also structured how relationships were forged within civil society more generally.

---

20   The incorporation of young Indian women into the 'Y' was initially helped by the efforts of Denise Hussein, an important figure within the Indo-Fijian organisation, Sri Sewa Sabha, but also one of the first Indian women to become involved in the YWCA administration (Rokotuivuna 2002b; Lechte 2005).

21   Robbie Robertson and William Sutherland (2001) have demonstrated the ways in which the indigenous elite in Fiji maintained control of the politically dominant Alliance Party and were able to use the discourse of multiracialism in a way that suggested a broad commitment to the advancement of all Fiji's peoples but which, in fact, benefited only a narrow indigenous chiefly elite from the country's Eastern provinces—the Tovata confederacy (see also Durutalo 1985; Kelly and Kaplan 2001; Lawson 1991; Firth 1997).

The first regional conference for Pacific women staged in Suva to mark IWY may, on the surface, appear to be a development which suggests an extension of the same type of horizontal collectivity evident within the YWCA to a broader regional arena of women's networking. Yet, efforts to forge pan-regional connections were, in fact, disrupted by disputes amongst the region's gender activists over appropriate frameworks for the interpretation of Pacific women's experience. The means used to resolve these disagreements suggest an emerging hierarchy of knowledge within the regional sphere of women's organising which was shaping how discussions of gender equality took place at this time.

As has been shown, women from the Melanesian regions tended to describe Pacific women's status in ways that regularly made reference to the international political context, and the structural sources of inequality in world politics. This contrasted with the more localised examination of women's subordination offered by delegates from the independent Polynesian states such as Tonga, the Cook Islands and Samoa. During the course of this conference, these women complained that Melanesian women's criticisms of foreign intervention in the Pacific did not reflect their views and that their own divergent opinions on women's status were not given enough recognition (Griffen 1975a, 1984; Rasmussen 1980; Kahn 1980).[22]

Yet, Melanesian delegates to the 1975 Suva conference successfully downplayed these perspectives as lacking a critical edge (Mera Molisa 1991; Rokotuivuna 2002b). The final dominance of the Melanesian women's agenda is evident in the 1975 conference resolutions, which emphasised issues of indigenous sovereignty and Pacific nuclearisation. In this particular context, it seems that an internationalised perspective of women's disadvantage, reflecting trends emerging more generally within the realm of global politics, were considered to have greater 'critical' currency than the viewpoints offered by conference delegates whose approach to gender equality was informed by more localised perspectives.

These types of incidents demonstrate how circumstances within the prevailing political environment shaped the negotiation of collectivity amongst and between women's organisations at the local and regional levels. The protocols that regulated local civil society activity more generally in Fiji clearly impacted significantly upon the operations of organisations such as the NCW and the

---

22   Grace Mera Molisa, a long-time women's activist from Vanuatu (part of Melanesia), argued that such tendencies reflect important cultural differences between the Melanesian and Polynesian women. She claimed that Polynesia's stratified social structures frequently allowed women to rise to positions of leadership due to their hereditary status. For this reason, when women leaders from Polynesia took to the international stage, they frequently denied the impact of gender inequality in their countries (Mera Molisa 1991). Mera Molisa argued that these perspectives denied 'the centrality of gender difference because it is eclipsed by rank' (Jolly 2005a: 149–50). Mera Molisa was scornful of claims made by her Polynesian counterparts that women are not discriminated against within Pacific Island cultures, describing them bluntly as 'a lie' (Jolly 2005a: 150; Mera Molisa 1991).

SSVM. Only within the YWCA was a determined effort made to develop more equitable and inclusive structures of organisational collectivity, in line with a more broadly held conviction that Fiji's independence era would be one of broader political *and* social change. Yet hierarchies were not entirely absent from all the activities undertaken by YWCA members during this period and were certainly evident if we consider the privileging of certain types of approaches to advocacy that featured as part of the networking between Melanesian and Polynesian delegates to the 1975 Suva conference. Once again, broader political contingencies, in this case of an international variety, help explain this situation. Prevailing trends in the global political environment, particularly the rise of critical Third World perspectives of inequality, contributed a certain weight to the structurally inclined perspectives of women's subordination proposed by Melanesian delegates during this period. The corresponding downplaying of Polynesian frameworks for understanding gender equality is indicative of the knowledge hierarchy which structured relations between women's organisations engaged in an emergent Pacific regionalism.

Progressive ideas

In contrast to the many women's organisations in Fiji whose advocacy for women emphasised familial and domestic roles, the YWCA's efforts to progress the women's agenda ventured into far more politicised and often controversial territory. In some instances, the YWCA successfully won government and community support for its stand, most notably in coalition with a range of civil society actors working to promote opposition to French nuclear testing in the Pacific. On other issues, such as legalised abortion or constitutional design, the YWCA position was far more contentious and challenged the central tenets of Christian belief systems and political values such as indigenous paramountcy. These value structures and systems of belief had shaped Fiji's social and political life since early colonial times. Nonetheless, during this independence era, YWCA activists felt themselves to be standing upon a 'new frontier' which could allow these things to be challenged. Rokotuivuna's description of the prevailing political environment at this time indicates how YWCA understood their capacity for political agency. '[A]t Independence there is a marriage of these ideas with the political agenda of the nation. You are in a climate that is like a new frontier. You feel that you are founding a nation and you have a pioneer attitude' (2002a).

Personal recollections of the stand taken by YWCA members during the pre-independence discussions on Fiji's constitution in 1965 frequently highlighted the fact that this was considered an important opportunity to push for political change. The women involved clearly emphasised the fact that they were the first and, at this time, only group to move away from an ethnically or culturally defined appraisal of Fiji's governance structures. They understood these actions to be a progressive departure from the more conventional stance expected of Fijian women on these issues. Rokotuivuna remembers the meeting as:

> one of the defining moments of the YWCA as a group that has a defining ideology that shapes its action. When we met, the *Soqosoqo Vakamarama* stood up and read their statement and it was exactly the same as the Alliance Party had proposed. We walked in and started talking about cross-voting. This was the first annunciation of a *truly* multiracial ideology (2002b).

While the idea that young activists could pioneer change within the local pre-independence-era political environment certainly encouraged these actions, they were also motivated by the idea that Fiji's colonial legacies needed to be challenged. Siwatibau, for example, remembered emphasising the colonially instituted structure of race relations and the need for a new system to be created. She stated:

> We listened to her speak [Eirene White], and then all the others speaking, and I started to get annoyed because no one seemed to be saying anything. I wanted to say we've had enough. So when it was time for us to speak, we said, 'we're ready, we've been a colony for too long.' We said '*we* have to revise *our* system...' (2002).

By their actions, these women challenged orthodox thinking in relation to Fijian paramountcy, prevailing structures of political hierarchy, and also the appropriateness of young Fijian women engaging in debate on such issues. Their contention that Fijians needed to start thinking for themselves and stop following their chiefs was countered with the accusation that they were putting forward an 'Indian' agenda (Siwatibau 2002). As Rokotuivuna notes, 'people were horrified that this group of Fijian women stood up against the Fijian orthodoxy' (2002b).[23]

This stand was not only shaped by dissatisfaction with local political structures, however. International developments also influenced how the YWCA members conducted themselves during this event. Vakatale noted, for example, that the civil rights struggles taking place in the southern US prompted her to consider how more equitable race relations might be developed closer to home. International coverage of these events influenced her to think about the extent to which structures that entrenched discrimination and inequality were taken for granted in Fiji (2002). Similarly, World YWCA condemnation of national political

---

23   The tone of press reports of the proceedings, and the wave of protest letters in the newspapers, reveal the provocative nature of this type of political behaviour (*Fiji Times* 29 April 1965, 4 May 1965).

and social structures promoting inequality was also influential and encouraged Fiji's national association to think about the local impact of discriminatory race relations (World YWCA 1995: 131; Lechte 2005).[24]

Advocacy on the sensitive issue of abortion also occurred in a way that included broader critiques of authority structures in Fiji. In this campaign, prevailing ideas about the location of moral authority in Fiji were challenged and individual citizens were encouraged to think and decide for themselves about questions of morality. The YWCA argued that the Methodist and Catholic Churches' religious teaching tended to erode individual capacity for self-realisation. By emphasising individuals' ability to choose, rather than framing their demands for legalised abortion in ways which simply opposed the church, YWCA members demonstrated a confidence that established structures of authority could be challenged and the time had come, as Siwatibau argued, for Fiji's citizens to 'think for themselves' (2002).[25]

The YWCA drew many of its most active members from the student body of the newly established regional USP, and this also influenced their approach to advocacy on a range of issues. Strands of Marxist political thought were a prominent feature of academic debate on the USP campus in these years (Robertson 1986), and this intellectual environment appears to have encouraged local students to reject the idea that the prevailing structure of race relations and political economy in Fiji was a natural state of affairs. Instead, critical attention was focused upon the legacies of Pacific colonisation and how these might explain the ongoing prevalence of social and economic inequality in Fiji. These ideas proved highly persuasive within the YWCA as well, and organisation members such as Rokotuivuna, Slatter, Siwatibau and Griffen were influential in promoting perspectives on women's subordination which were similarly oriented.

---

24 While the 1963 World Council deliberations in Nyborg Stand, Denmark touched upon this theme, it was examined with greater energy at the World Council meeting held in Melbourne in 1967. At this event, YWCA members were encouraged to recognise the ways in which racial prejudice was manifest in personal social relationships and 'woven into the complex pattern of an entire society'. The council argued that certain groups within society effectively manipulate issues of race in ways that allow them to 'maintain their economic and social position'. National associations were urged to 'give their support to attempts to ensure equal civil and political, social and economic, religious and cultural rights for all racial and ethnic groups' and to assist public authorities to guarantee human rights (World YWCA 1995: 142).

25 This contrasts starkly with how the same issues have been treated in later periods of Fiji's political history. While family planning programs are still carried out by a number of international NGOs operating in Fiji today, the issue of abortion appears to have become something of a taboo subject within the prevailing political environment, and rarely features as an issue of discussion within NGO ranks or national policy-making circles despite the fact that it is still officially illegal. Although procurable privately, as of 2009, abortion remains officially illegal in Fiji. This situation persists alongside a growing public concern and media focus on the subject of teenage pregnancies and many documented instances of abandoned newborn babies (see *Daily Post* 16 April 2002; *Fiji Times* 1 March 2002, 15 April 2002, 6 November 2002).

At the same time, YWCA members viewed advocacy that highlighted the global dimensions of gender disadvantage as also being 'progressive' in an international sense. For example, when recalling the participation of local Fijian women in the first NGO Tribune convened as part of the IWY conference in Mexico City, Rokotuivuna argued that she had gone to Mexico to demonstrate the existence of 'progressive thinking women' in the Pacific region. She argued, 'I think our contribution was to go there and to make the NGO women's movement aware that there is group of women in the South Pacific who are concerned. There is a very strong anti-nuclear group who is also concerned with development issues. It's in an embryo stage but these are progressive thinking women' (2002b).

During our interviews, Rokotuivuna was keen to differentiate the conservative nature of presentations made by Fiji's official conference representatives who, she argued, 'were just making speeches' without 'knowing what was happening', with the more radicalised and internationally informed position articulated by participants to the Tribune (2002b).

Those who articulated structural perspectives of gender disadvantage faced strong opposition from western feminists at Mexico City. Yet, this period of heightened 'Third Worldism' provided an expanded transnational space for civil society actors from developing states to advocate from a similar perspective. Closer to the region, these arguments were lent added legitimacy as Pacific statesmen began to question the prevailing structures of world politics which permitted nuclear testing and continuing colonial rule of Pacific territories. These developments meant that gender activists from the Pacific Islands, particularly those from the Melanesian region, were confident of their ability to promote what they deemed to be 'progressive' perspectives of gender disadvantage at the local, regional and international levels.

Certainly, the YWCA's stand on issues related to racial discrimination or reproductive rights challenged prevailing customary and religious belief systems and stood in stark contrast to the more conventional and narrowly focused approach to 'women issues' undertaken by the other women's groups. Nonetheless, the 'pioneering' attitude of this organisation and its confident challenges issued in a range of areas indicates a broadly held perception within the YWCA that Fiji was being influenced by new political currents and that the country's independence represented a 'new frontier' of progressive political opportunity.

Transnationalism

YWCA members generally described the transnational influences they encountered during this period as both positive and foundational in terms of how they influenced the trajectory of Pacific feminism. Rokotuivuna and Slatter remarked upon the importance of the second wave feminist writings emerging from Australia, Britain and the US during the late 1960s and early 1970s. In particular, they mentioned Germaine Greer's (1970) *Female Eunuch* as a work that was able to speak to women in local contexts. Griffen reiterated this point stating, 'a few of us could grasp, without even coming from that world, that there was a universal element of truth in these writings. We took these ideas seriously and began writing about them, very briefly and simply and crudely in our own student newspaper' (1987: 5).

Local women activists had to struggle against opposition to these ideas within the broader realm of civil society where feminist thought tended to be dismissed as an imported ideology of women's liberation that had no application in the Pacific (Jolly 1996; Douglas 2002). Nonetheless, during this period, feminist works circulating internationally had a broad appeal to those closely associated with the Fiji YWCA.

Certainly, the new institutional willingness to address gender inequality at the UN level during this period,[26] provided Pacific women with important opportunities to represent their region on the international stage, as was demonstrated by their participation at the United Nations IWY conference in Mexico. The issues they debated had important resonances with the contentions shaping world politics more generally during this period. Nonetheless, the starting point for these debates remained the Pacific region and Pacific experience. Many activists were therefore keen to draw global attention to the negative impact of intersecting structural forces in a way which emphasised the regionally specific and cumulative nature of challenges which faced Pacific communities as a whole, and Pacific women in particular.

As Griffen (1987) points out, this was an advocacy framework which feminists from wealthier parts of the world found difficult to accept. The early experiences

---

26 Since the early 1970s, and particularly in the wake of Esther Boserup's groundbreaking work on this subject, the status of women in development (WID) had received increased attention at the level of international policy making. In 1973, an amendment to the US Foreign Assistance Act stipulated that future development aid projects would be required to 'give attention to those programs, projects and activities which tend to integrate women into the national economies of foreign countries, thus improving their status and assisting the total development effort' (Papanek 1975a: 196). In the years that followed, international aid agencies from many Scandinavian countries followed suit, and by the mid-1970s the UN Agencies and the World Bank were also incorporating a WID focus into their policy design for developing regions (World Bank 1975). For an indication of burgeoning academic literature on this subject in later years, see the special issue of *Community Development Journal* edited by Hermione Lovel and Marie-Therese Feuerstein, 1985.

of Pacific women taking part in discussions on the international stage revealed that there was indeed a vast gulf between the feminist perspectives employed by western women and those who approached these questions from a Third World perspective. Western feminists' conceptual approach to women's disadvantage seemed, to Pacific women, to be narrow and unable to accommodate alternative perspectives of disadvantage and subordination. As Griffen states, 'Western feminists did not take into account conditions such as poverty, colonialism or imperialism or racism and white domination in some parts of the world. Western feminists sometimes separated the wider issues of international social and economic relations' (1987: 6).

This scenario left Pacific women with the feeling they were not being heard at the IWY conference. It also made them distrustful of the feminist agenda and its universalist ambitions. 'Sometimes we felt we were on the sidelines,' writes Griffen, 'and were not quite as feminist as Western feminists' (1987: 6).

Of course, local activists did not want to give the impression that a political discourse designed to advance the rights of women was inauthentic to the Pacific context, an imported vein of thought that lacked local legitimacy. There were already many within the region's political classes that were willing to use this line of argument to dismiss women's concerns in blanket fashion (Griffen 1975b).[27] To get around this scenario, many activists chose to avoid calling themselves feminists altogether, given that the term seemed locally unhelpful and was compromised by a western bias in international contexts (Griffen 1987: 6).

Other transnational associations were more positive, however, and appeared to further incline Fiji-based women activists to develop the critical and structurally inclined aspects of their political activity. The affiliation between the Fiji YWCA and the World YWCA seems to have been particularly productive in this regard.

As this chapter has demonstrated, the advocacy positions adopted by the local Fiji YWCA in relation to questions of racial discrimination, reproductive health, peace and disarmament issues, and questions of economic justice, were clearly influenced by the resolutions passed at World Council YWCA meetings held every four years. However, these resolutions were not simply applied

---

27   As Margaret Jolly notes, women in other parts of the Pacific negotiated these tensions in different ways. While calling attention to the ways that patriarchal aspects of local custom 'naturalised' women's secondary status, figures such as Jully Sipolo in the Solomon Islands (Griffen 1987) or Mera Molisa in the newly independent state of Vanuatu 'espoused' feminist values but, in this period, refused the term feminism (Jolly 2005a). Instead, they preferred to articulate their demands for gender equality in ways which called attention to contemporary customary practices which degraded women, and simultaneously ignored the traditional locations of women's customary authority which had in the past been respected. Similarly, Jolly also describes how gender activists in the region have, for many years, rhetorically aligned discourses of women's empowerment with Christian tenets. Such practices clearly indicate how systems of religious belief or cultural protocols shape civil society activity in the Pacific Island region, and, in particular, influence the advocacy of gender activists (Jolly 1996, 2005a; see also Douglas 1998, 2002, 2003).

uncritically at the local level, but developed or adjusted to fit the local context. For example, Fiji YWCA members confronted the issue of racial discrimination in the local context by drawing attention to the ways in which this phenomenon was an unjust legacy of colonial rule in Fiji that must be confronted if Fiji were to be truly independent. And, in their work on issues of economic and social justice, another area in which World YWCA resolutions (adopted in 1971) had urged national associations to take action, Fiji YWCA members had adopted a perspective heavily influenced by dependency-oriented perspectives of economic development that had become a prominent feature of local academic debate.

Of course, it cannot be denied that the Fiji YWCA was affiliated with a transnational organisation whose origins were European and which had, in the past, been heavily influenced by national associations in Britain and the US (Garner 2003: 234). Nevertheless, as the World YWCA evolved throughout the twentieth century and expanded its global structure, the influence of the formerly dominant associations subsided, and the transnational body was well-positioned to articulate objectives which had a relevance to all national associations (Garner 2003: 234). The fact that Pacific women were able to exercise influence within the World YWCA on the question of nuclear testing, reflected in the resolutions passed at the Accra World Council meeting in 1971, eloquently proves this point.

Conclusion

By emphasising the situated experience of YWCA members in Fiji in the 1960s and early 1970s, I have demonstrated how this organisation came to engage in a provocative style of organisational activity that challenged the operations of older and more established women's groups. In its more practically oriented activities, the YWCA clearly adopted a different perspective of 'women and community development' that aimed to meet the needs of women and men together and that challenged the communalist focus of many existing women's groups. Moreover, through its public advocacy work, the YWCA emerged as a provocative voice engaged in debate in highly politicised areas conventionally considered outside the purview of women's organisations.

In a variety of ways, YWCA activity in these years displayed an approach to collectivity, an attitude towards 'progress', and a negotiation of transnationalism which was different to other civil society actors in Fiji, who were more likely to reinscribe rather than challenge the social and political status quo. Yet, contingencies within the prevailing global and local political environment shaped this activity in important ways. Those involved felt that these actions were allowed because Fiji was entering a new era of expansive political possibilities. Within government and amongst Fiji's Church leaders, a more liberal attitude on issues such as nuclear testing or wage protection for low-wage workers seemed to be emerging. Similarly, broader currents shaping regional and global politics were seen to open the way for local civil society actors to question the structural imbalances, political and economic, which were compounding the disadvantage of Third World peoples. Although representatives from the Fiji YWCA faced resistance to aspects of their advocacy from both domestic and international actors, the types of subjects broached by them on the local and international stage indicates a strongly held conviction that this was an era of political promise.

Were these promises realised in the following years? The next chapter continues the story of women's organising in Fiji by examining, once again, the situated experiences of women activists as they pressed their claims for women's advancement on the local, regional and international stages. Many in Fiji anticipated that the continued institutional emphasis placed upon women's issues within the UN would create important opportunities for local women's organisations in Fiji. But ultimately, the concrete gains were few. Some significant developments for women were achieved in this next decade, yet it was also a time when the nature of women's advocacy began to shift in interesting and perhaps unanticipated directions. The next chapter examines how and why these shifts occurred and what they meant for the status of women more generally as the UN Decade for Women continued.

3. Beyond the 'New Frontier'?
Fiji's Decade for Women: 1976–1985

Optimistic about the possibilities for further political change, Fiji's YWCA members envisaged continuing their forthright and often provocative advocacy campaigns for women during the UN-declared Decade for Women. But changing political circumstances, both within Fiji and outside the country, made this difficult. Women activists who had formerly made a strong political stance on issues related to Pacific Island nations' political and economic sovereignty, now found themselves working within a more constrained political environment. As Pacific Island statesmen began to bow to increased international pressure to modify their stance on nuclear testing in the region and Pacific decolonisation, civil society groups saw government support for their activity on these questions begin to wane. This changed political environment caused a number of women's groups to critically assess the utility and appropriateness of provocative political approaches to questions of women's disadvantage.

This did not, however, equate to a terminal loss of momentum within Fiji's women's movement. Other developments, such as the international attention placed upon the 'women in development' agenda, and further conferences held to mark the UN's Decade for Women, provided added political impetus and an international legitimacy to the calls by local activists for Fiji's government to focus more attention and resources on the needs and interests of women. In response, Fiji's political leaders made some rhetorical commitments to the promotion of women's interests, but they rarely followed through with concrete practical initiatives that might boost women's social, political or economic standing.

This meant that Fiji's women's organisations were extremely active during this period as they sought to highlight the disjuncture between state rhetoric and practice. At the local level, they advocated for new approaches to national development which recognised women. They also campaigned heavily for women to gain increased institutional participation within government. Certain activists also began to think about the need for a more concentrated focus upon specific aspects of women's disadvantage.

This thinking gave rise to a new organisation, the Fiji Women's Crisis Centre, formed in the latter part of this Decade for Women to confront violence against women. Through its campaigns designed to raise public awareness of this issue, change social behaviour, and elicit government support for policy reforms that might reduce the incidence of violence against women, the FWCC broke new ground for women's organisations in Fiji. This work introduced a sensitive topic into the public domain and challenged robust cultural protocols which had previously ensured that the subject of violence against women remained firmly located within the private sphere.

Additionally, representatives from Fiji's women's organisations continued to be energetic participants in regional institutional deliberations and at the two UN conferences for women staged in Copenhagen in 1980 and Nairobi in 1985. To begin with, their contributions to global debate on the status of women were marked by a continued focus upon questions of economic and political power distribution across the Pacific region. However, towards the end of the Decade this position tended to be complemented by an increasingly strong focus upon specific phenomena that were also felt to be contributing to women's subordination in a more localised manner. This included a more direct focus upon gender inequalities in the areas of health, education, law and order, and the media. This more concentrated emphasis on particular aspects of women's disadvantage is indicative of an emerging trend evident locally (with the formation of the Fiji Women's Crisis Centre (FWCC)) and internationally. This was a period when women activists became increasingly interested in developing transnational networks to confront specific issues deemed detrimental to women.

While these developments certainly indicate the vibrancy of women's domestic, regional and transnational political engagement, this chapter also shows that not all gender activists in Fiji were content that such activities equated to evidence of women's political agency. Some felt that gender activists' abilities to be heard regionally and internationally were hampered by institutional constraints and a broader international disregard for the Pacific Island region. Others began to question what they felt was an inappropriate expatriate influence within the sphere of women's organising. This contrasted dramatically with the earlier independence era where the contributions made by expatriate women were viewed in a more positive light. As the latter sections of this chapter demonstrate, activists' assessments of collectivity, progressive potential and transnationalism at this time indicate that there was no firm consensus of opinion regarding the appropriate makeup of the women's movement and the goals to which it should aspire.

Local developments

Both the Fiji YWCA and the National Council of Women (NCW) suffered serious internal disputes in the late 1970s which distracted attention away from their advocacy programs. Within the YWCA, internal tensions relating to the organisation's political profile became increasingly apparent and began to spill over into the public arena. Records of the organisation's management committee meetings suggest that the more radical voices prominent within the YWCA in the previous decade were now losing some of their influence. For example, policy submissions devised by the YWCA's Public Affairs Committee (PAC) on matters of economic governance faced strong opposition from YWCA members of a more conservative political persuasion. These members argued that the PAC should remember the YWCA's 'Christian mandate' and interpret its core commitments to 'justice in society' in a less incendiary fashion (Fiji YWCA 19 August 1975, PAC Record Book).

In mid-1976, conflict within the YWCA came to a head when the organisation's board terminated the employment of four executive officers, including Amelia Rokotuivuna, who had continued her outspoken public role. While this decision was partly justified as a money-saving measure in response to the organisation's difficulty in meeting overdraft and mortgage repayments, board-members also argued that the controversial activity of the YWCA had cost the organisation support and needed to be curbed. In particular, they were critical of the 'rudeness' and 'excessively forceful views' articulated by certain executive members of the YWCA which were often deemed to be representative of the YWCA as a whole (Keith-Reid 1976: 16–17). For some, the tone of YWCA advocacy was deemed too aggressive and out of step with local cultural mores which emphasised the importance of 'quiet diplomacy' in political conduct (Robertson and Sutherland 2001: 56). While the sacked executive members were supported by members of the YWCA general staff, who engaged in a series of strike actions, the board remained resolute. This situation badly affected the internal operations of the organisation as well as its public credibility. The YWCA had always sought to use the local media to its advantage. Now it found there was intense media interest in the internal battles for organisational control.[1] A general meeting was held some months later which saw the dissolution of the YWCA board after a no-confidence vote, and a new board elected which immediately reinstated the sacked employees. Nevertheless, this very public split within the YWCA, and clear evidence of serious internal division emerging on questions of public advocacy, was damaging to the organisation. Ultimately, Rokotuivuna chose to temporarily resign from the YWCA in 1977, convinced that she no longer had the capacity to 'pull the conservatives along' (2002b).

With Rokotuivuna's departure, the general tenor of the organisation's political engagement was perhaps less provocative than it had previously been. However, this more muted style of political engagement also reflected broader political

---

1   One notable account of these events was published in the *Pacific Islands Monthly* under the headline of 'Teeth and Talons bared at the Suva YWCA'. In this account, the writer repeatedly uses highly sexist language to describe the struggles for influence taking place within the organisation. In a subsequent edition of the *Pacific Islands Monthly*, letters from YWCA representatives were published protesting at the inappropriate language appearing in the article, its overall disparaging tone, and the damaging picture it presented of the organisation (Keith-Reid 1976; *Pacific Islands Monthly* November 1976).

developments taking place in the politics of the Pacific Islands. As the decade progressed, a more conservative policy focus was also emanating from Fiji's government in many areas and particularly in its foreign policy.

A shift in government policy direction on the question of the Pacific nuclear presence significantly reshaped the local political space available to those women's organisations that had previously taken up the anti-nuclear cause with great energy. Despite the fact that the same governing party and Prime Minister retained power, the Fiji government was under increasing pressure from the US to take a more moderate line on these questions and it began to move away from its earlier international advocacy of a nuclear free Pacific.[2] The previously 'close relationship' that had existed between the Fiji government and the anti-nuclear movement was all but 'lost' by this later stage (Ogashiwa 1991: 50, 52). YWCA members continued to pursue the peace and disarmament cause in the ensuing years, but the changed mood within government equated to a crucial loss of institutional support on this issue.

Like the YWCA, the National Council of Women (NCW) had also experienced internal troubles related to the organisation's political profile, and coordination of member organisations' activities was becoming more difficult. In 1979, the indigenous women's organisation *Soqosoqo Vakamarama* (SSVM) withdrew its support for the NCW on the grounds that younger organisations were becoming too outspoken. This was a substantial blow for the NCW and threatened to damage its standing with the indigenous political elite. However, in her newly appointed role as NCW leader, Esiteri Kamikamica (1982: 42–43) voiced a determination to move beyond these difficulties and refocus organisational efforts upon women.

More generally, local debate about the role that women should play in development was beginning to gather momentum. While this discussion reflected broader themes under examination in development policy-making circles globally (Papanek 1975a), Pacific activists' deliberations in this area tended to begin with a critical examination of the foreign influences at work in the region and how they had diminished the perceived importance of women's economic roles. Such concerns echoed themes that had been prevalent in other aspects of women's advocacy undertaken by the YWCA in the early 1970s.

For example, in 1978 Ruth Lechte authored a study which argued that the influence of European missionaries and colonisers had encouraged Pacific women to internalise the view that they were economically unproductive and

---

2   In 1982, the local government had chosen to ban US nuclear-powered ships from using Fiji's port facilities. This decision was reversed twelve months later, in the wake of strong US pressure and justified by Fiji's Prime Minister on the basis that such actions compromised Fiji's international law obligations as well as the country's strategic, economic and security interests (Ogashiwa 1991: 50).

that the daily tasks they performed in the areas of horticulture or handicraft production required no skill (1978: 161–64; see also Schoeffel and Kikau 1980). Lechte also argued that the position taken by Third World delegates to the UN's Mexico City women's conference in 1975, and their clear articulation of a desire for 'liberation and justice', issued a new challenge to development planners in the current context. When applied to the Pacific situation, Lechte argued that this underscored the need for a new approach to development and economic policy-making which would create greater opportunities for Pacific women's participation (1978: 170).

The establishment of the post of Women's Programme Officer within the Centre for Applied Studies in Development at the University of the South Pacific (USP) in Suva in 1979 increased the possibilities for academic research to be conducted into women's economic productivity. Headed by Claire Slatter, this unit produced studies on the role of women in fisheries, women's access to health infrastructure, and women's uses of traditional medicines and healing practices (Goodwillie and Lechte 1985: 60). Other studies were conducted by local scholars who were closely connected to women's organisations. These focused upon the role played by development aid agencies and found that although increased aid was flowing into the region, consultation with local communities remained limited. A process of 'passive' aid distribution was identified (Siwatibau 1985), whereby development programs were poorly matched to the needs of local communities and became unsustainable as funds were exhausted or foreign expertise was withdrawn (Pulea 1982; Schoeffel 1983; Randell 1983; Siwatibau 1985).[3]

In 1980, women's organisations won the right to take up these questions at the first National Development Summit held in Fiji. While the participation of women's groups at this event was significant in its own right, Rokotuivuna (2002b) also argued that the women's submission was generally well-received. Nevertheless, this did not signal a new era of engagement between government and women's organisations on the women in development (WID) question. Indeed, Rokotuivuna argued that the ability of women to penetrate this meeting was facilitated through personal contacts that YWCA members had made with a member of the national planning office who was friendly to their cause and simply included them on the conference agenda (2002b). While the national development strategy that was formulated during this summit duly reflected the concerns raised by the women present (NCW 1981: 2), concrete policy, which might increase women's economic visibility, was generally not forthcoming.

---

3   Many development initiatives proposed for Pacific Island women were found to be inappropriate to local contexts—for example, encouraging women to use imported products such as flour and rice in food preparation and discouraging the preparation of more nutritious local food staples on the basis that these took longer to cook and consumed more fuel (NCW 1982; Schoeffel 1986).

In 1982, Fiji's NCW incorporated the WID theme into its own programs and held a national workshop on this subject which brought together over two hundred participants from the broad range of organisations affiliated with the council. One of the principal ideas emerging from this three-day event was the need for increased representation of women's interests within government. However the debate was principally focused upon women's bureaucratic representation with the NCW arguing for the establishment of a women's ministry within Fiji's government (NCW 1981: 1).[4] The creation of a women's machinery was felt to be important at this time for, as Dianne Goodwillie notes, Fiji's post-independence government had offered only meagre support for a Women's Office, and this tended to be shunted from ministry to ministry but was most frequently housed within the Ministry of Fijian Affairs. As a result, the office was politically weak and failed to represent the interests of Indo-Fijian women or women in urban settings (Goodwillie and Kaloumaira 2000: 9). Many of the organisations affiliated with the national council of women, argued for the creation of a women's ministry as an independent office or associated directly with the prime-minister's office. The NCW claimed that this location would ensure greater and more consistent attention given by government to the interests of women. Despite intense amounts of lobbying by the NCW on this issue, the government paid little heed to these calls and showed almost no interest in developing a new institutional machinery for women in these years.

Women's Crisis Centre

Towards the end of the Decade for Women, an important new women's organisation was established in Fiji which adopted a more issue-specific approach to advocacy for women than the women's groups that had formed previously. The Women's Crisis Centre (later the FWCC) was founded amid rising community concern over rape and other forms of sexual violence in Fiji. In 1983, a newly formed local research body, the Action Centre for Women in Need (ACWIN), published a significant report entitled *Rape in Fiji* (1983) in which the frequency of crimes of sexual violence, community attitudes towards these acts, and the treatment of rape victims within Fiji's legal system were examined.

This was a bold move in a social and political context where public discussion of such incidents was rare, the stigma attached to these crimes substantial and policing responses to these events generally poor (Adinkrah 1995; Jolly 1996; Ali 1987; McKenzie Aucoin 1990; Lateef 1990; also see Introduction). Up

---

4 It was argued that the machinery should either be designed as a separate and central ministry in its own right, or be attached to the office of the head of government to ensure that it had the requisite political influence. On the question of accessibility, it was argued that it must 'liaise directly with women's organisations and individual women'. It was also stipulated that the women's machinery must be allocated adequate funding and appropriately trained staff (NCW 1981: 5).

until this point, the institutional and civil society responses to gender violence were almost non-existent and the country's political classes and cultural and religious leaders generally showed little willingness to raise this issue in the public domain. ACWIN's 1983 report, therefore, attempted to generate greater public awareness of the prevalence of rape and sexual violence. Additionally, it examined the measures needed to improve state welfare and police responses to rape crimes and considered how judicial processes might be amended to better support rape victims. The report's findings pointed to the urgent need for a government counselling service for rape victims and the establishment of a women's crisis centre (pp. 20, 22).

In 1983, a group of expatriate women in Fiji began to think about how a local women's group could respond to some of the challenges outlined in the ACWIN report. These women saw the importance of developing a multiracial response to the issue of rape in Fiji. To this end, they sought to engage local women as participants within an organisation that would tackle this issue in an ongoing manner (S. Ali 2002). In 1984, the Women's Crisis Centre began operations. At first, the group envisaged using voluntary staff to provide victims of rape with emotional support and information about government support services (Sutherland *et al.* 1986). But Crisis Centre staff soon came to realise that the phenomenon of gender violence was not simply limited to rape and sexual violence. It became evident that the Centre needed to expand its focus to also support the victims of violence in the home, and women and children suffering other types of abuse (Ali 1987).

Therefore, in addition to counselling, the Crisis Centre also established programs of public education and community awareness about violence against women. It distributed posters and pamphlets, undertook media engagements and ran training sessions in schools and with women's groups on the issue of violence against women. It also sought to build links with health professionals, the police and legal practitioners (Ali 1987).

The highly sensitive nature of this work meant that, at the outset, the Crisis Centre faced strong opposition from conservative elements within the broader realm of civil society, including from other women's organisations. These groups often argued that the organisation's discussion of domestic violence threatened the integrity of the family—highly valued within Pacific cultures—and promoted an agenda that was essentially, 'anti-men' (S. Ali 2002; see also Leckie 2002: 169). The Crisis Centre also faced some opposition from government representatives who argued that the use of the word 'crisis' in the centre's title was damaging to Fiji's reputation as a tourist haven and the image of the country as a tropical 'paradise' (Ali 1987: 40). These critiques meant that the Centre faced some pressure to modify its rhetoric and even change its title.

The critiques also made funding difficult, with potential local benefactors often wary of close public association with a group deemed troublesome in national political circles.[5]

Nevertheless, the establishment of the Women's Crisis Centre in 1984 was a significant development, heralding a new trend towards more issue-specific approaches to advocacy and service provision for women. Unlike the NCW or the YWCA, which developed broadly focused engagements with both community and the state on women's issues, the Crisis Centre's approach to the advancement of women was clearly aimed at promoting women's physical security and supporting women who had become victims of violence. Contrasting the Centre's efforts with existing women's groups, Shamima Ali argued:

> Though the Centre might not be contributing to 'development' in the sense of economic growth or being involved in any redistribution of wealth, the Centre is providing a valuable support service for women and the Collective is making decisions and running the Centre on a shoe-string budget. The project is working well in the face of opposition from men and women also (1987: 40)

In later years, the Fiji Women's Crisis Centre would develop an important local and international profile as one of the leading women's organisations in the Pacific Island region.

Regional developments

During this period, regional institutional deliberation on the question of women's advancement began to increase, with a number of significant conferences taking place. Yet, there was a marked variance in the types of access women had to these forums, and the spaces they provided for critical debate on the status of women.

The first of these events took place at the annual South Pacific Commission (SPC) conference held in Port Moresby, Papua New Guinea (PNG), in October 1980.[6]

---

5 In many cases, funding allocations at this time were granted to local organisations from external agencies, but distributed via the state. This meant that local government authorities were able to scrutinise local programs and block funding initiatives where it was felt that the activities of local organisations were inappropriate. From time to time the Fiji government had given small amounts of funding to the Crisis Centre, but it had also used its powers of scrutiny to block access to larger amounts of grant money directed to the organisation from international agencies (Ali 1987: 40).

6 These conferences are held as annual 'general assemblies' of the SPC, a regional intergovernmental institution formed in 1947 and whose membership at this time included the metropolitan countries responsible for the administration of Pacific Island territories as well as independent Pacific Island states. Tensions between delegates from within and outside the region have frequently been apparent and often resulted in efforts made to steer SPC conference deliberations towards areas where all parties have common

The conference agenda required participants to respond to the theme of Women in Development in the Pacific Island region, however, the meeting began as a decidedly male-centred dialogue. Of the two hundred conference delegates, only two were female (Goodwillie and Lechte 1985: 59). It is for this reason perhaps, that the prepared statements read by government representatives gave little or no consideration to the work that women researchers and activists had previously conducted on WID issues, nor to the concerns that they had begun to raise in the public domain.[7]

This state of affairs was not allowed to persist however. During a morning recess in the male-dominated conference deliberations, more than twenty women from a variety of local organisations, including the PNG YWCA, streamed into the conference venue carrying placards and a petition which demanded that the SPC give women greater rights of participation. The placards asked delegates 'Where are the Pacific women?,' or stated 'Only women can understand women.' Another claimed, 'the time will come when you will be sorry that you have left behind half the population—the women—in your clever development programmes' (*Pacific Islands Monthly* December 1980).

The protestors were eventually allowed to address the meeting and called upon the SPC to recognise women's rights to participate in regional intergovernmental deliberations. They also called for the SPC to re-establish the Pacific Women's Resource Centre (PWRC), a short-lived regional organisation for women which was founded in the wake of the 1975 regional women's conference but ultimately disbanded as it struggled to fund its operations (*Pacific Islands Monthly* December 1980; Waqovonovono 1980; Griffen 1984).

This highly visual and confrontational protest was widely reported in the local press across the region. In response, conference delegates agreed that the SPC should hold a special meeting of Pacific women in Tahiti, French Polynesia, the following year, and that this meeting would make recommendations to the 21st South Pacific Conference. Moreover, governments were also requested to 'take action' to ensure effective implementation of the resolutions from the UN's Economic and Social Commission for Asia and the Pacific (ESCAP) sub-regional

---

interests such as the environment, technology and welfare. The aim of this policy has been to override the traditional, cultural and political differences that have often marked relations between the Pacific Island states and the metropolitan powers of the region (Smales 1980).

7   The lack of consultation that characterised the content of the papers presented at this meeting is nowhere more evident than in the presentation made by the delegate from French Polynesia whose paper began with the confident affirmation that women and development issues were 'non-political' (SPC 1980a). In a further section of this paper, the same delegate characterised feminism as innately 'competitive' and argued that this was certainly not something that Pacific Island women were interested in. He claimed, instead, that Pacific Island women were more interested in 'reciprocity, exchange, sharing, cooperation and respect' (SPC 1980a).

Women's Conference that was to be held in Suva only a few days later, and to ensure that they were 'adequately represented by women' at this meeting (SPC 1980b).

The ESCAP regional follow-up meeting duly took place and was attended by government and non-governmental organisation (NGO) representatives from the twelve-member and associate-member states of the Pacific sub-region,[8] and observers from specialised UN agencies, the SPC, a variety of local and internationally based NGOs, and outside states with a strategic interest in the region such as the US and Great Britain (Kahn 1980).[9] The United Nations accorded the meeting a high status, sending both Lucille Mair, Secretary-General of the UN World Conference for Women held in Copenhagen, and the Australian-born Elizabeth Reid, who also represented the UN as Principal Officer of the Secretariat responsible for the UN's mid-Decade conference. Both women had forged close ties with the community of women activists operating in the Pacific during the first half of the UN's Decade for Women, and were understood by Pacific Island women to be sympathetic institutional representatives to the event (Rokotuivuna 2002b).

The principal objective of the conference was to develop a sub-regional Plan of Action that would guide local and regional institutions in the implementation of policy addressing the themes of the final five years of the United Nations Decade for Women. The final document that the delegates produced is noteworthy for the fact that it did not simply provide a Pacific response to issues and problems identified at the international level. Neither did it describe issues of concern in abstract terms. Instead, it offered a regionally specific perspective on the challenges facing Pacific women, identifying issues of concern in concrete language and suggesting pragmatic courses of action as a response to these concerns. For example, the document called for scrutiny of legislation to identify possibilities for gender-based discrimination, the collection of data and research relating to women at the national level, more public awareness campaigns to confront women's health and mental health issues and greater efforts made to combat violence against women, and the impact of alcohol abuse in the community (Danielsson and Danielsson 1981a). In proposals for action at the regional level, delegates called for the re-establishment of a Pacific Women's Resource Centre as an 'autonomous intergovernmental institution' staffed by Pacific women with the aim of facilitating communication on gender issues across the region (Danielsson and Danielsson 1981a: 19).

---

8   Australia, Cook Islands, Fiji, Kiribati, Nauru, New Zealand, PNG, Samoa, Solomon Islands, Tonga, Tuvalu and Vanuatu.

9   The French Ambassador in Suva, reportedly displeased by the ruling that his country's representatives would only have observer status, chose not to send representation (Danielsson and Danielsson 1981b).

In addition to these proposals, the Plan of Action's conceptual framework section was particularly striking for its highly critical interpretation of international regional engagement within the Pacific Island region, and the fact that it was constructed in a way that paid little heed to the sensibilities of those outside observers participating at the meeting. This particular section of the Plan made reference to Pacific Islanders' rights to self-determination, the negative impact of nuclear weapons testing and nuclear waste dumping in the region, inappropriate trajectories of aid and development in the Pacific, and the inability of local communities to exert control over these processes. It also noted the local health, social and cultural costs that followed the regional importation of goods such as potentially harmful contraceptive drugs, manufactured food-stuffs, agricultural methods and alcohol (UNESCAP 1980).

While debate about the wording of this part of the document was at times heated, and saw some delegations, most notably Australia and New Zealand, take reservations upon the whole section, the majority of delegates in the final instance put their weight behind the sentiments expressed (Rasmussen 1980; Danielsson and Danielsson 1981a; Reid 1984). Described by some as a 'poetic' plea for Pacific Islanders' political, cultural and economic self-determination (Goodwillie and Lechte 1985: 59), the sentiments expressed in the document represented the culmination of local and regional advocacy efforts that occurred during the preceding years. It exemplified an activist voice which was regionally focused, conscious of the international, and informed by a redistributive ethos. Here, a strong degree of emphasis was focused upon the subordination of Pacific Island communities in world politics and the global restructuring that was required to ensure that these communities might have greater powers of self-determination.

Within later regional meetings for women, this voice became much harder to detect. These events were convened within a more structured institutional environment, restricted by the agendas of foreign powers in the region, and this slowed the momentum that had previously carried forward critical deliberation upon the status of Pacific Island women. This trend became quickly apparent at the first regional women's meeting convened by the SPC and held in Tahiti in July 1981. At this point, the SPC had finally acceded to the demands made in PNG twelve months earlier and agreed to convene a conference focused solely on the situation of Pacific women. Yet, the conference outcomes were far less significant than many of the attendees had envisioned. Delegates may have hoped that the meeting would provide an opportunity to build upon the Plan of Action developed at the ESCAP forum, but the highly structured environment of the Tahiti event meant that the space for substantive discussion of the issues raised in Suva was not only limited, but actively controlled.

In particular, discussion was thwarted by the actions of the SPC's Director of Programmes. A figure highly sympathetic to the French administration, he frequently acted to inhibit debate and appeared particularly keen to police the issue of French nuclear testing in the region. In this role, he was described in the media as a 'hawk' swooping down from his 'secretarial nest on the conference doves whenever they dared to squeak a little' (Danielsson and Danielsson 1981b: 21).

On a positive note, delegates to the SPC women's seminar agreed to support the reconstitution of the PWRC, and the staging of regional triennial conferences which would bring together government delegations to debate women's issues.[10] Yet, in more general terms, the meeting passed a set of resolutions which had only a faint resemblance to those agreed upon at the previous ESCAP conference in 1981. Many anticipated that the ESCAP resolutions would form the blueprint for a further set of resolutions in Tahiti. They had even had them translated into French. Yet their attempts to distribute this material amongst conference delegates was thwarted by the Director of Programmes. He defended this action on the grounds that objections from 'certain countries' made this impossible (Danielsson and Danielsson 1981b: 20).

While impetus for institutional reform had been building at the regional level, the events of this conference palpably demonstrate the hurdles that remained for women activists working within the SPC. This was an institution committed to working principally with the governments of the region rather than its NGOs and generally disinclined to offend the French government who provided it with substantial funding. The only way that the activist community would be able to influence SPC discussion was through their representation on state delegations. Without this, women activists could attend regional meetings as observers but were unable to actively participate in the meeting's formal deliberations. Hence, they had few opportunities to voice their dissatisfaction over the activities of the region's metropolitan powers.

In line with the recommendations made at this conference, and after a sustained campaign effort on the part of women's organisations in many parts of the Pacific, the SPC finally established a new regional body in 1982, the Pacific Women's Resource Bureau (PWRB), and appointed Hilda Lini as the body's Anglophone representative (Marie-Claire Beccalossie was later appointed to this office as the representative for the Pacific's French speaking territories). Lini already had a strong background as a ni-Vanuatu independence activist and was, therefore, hardly someone who could be relied upon to pursue the type of quietly conservative line that the SPC seemed to expect. And, in the early period of the PWRB's operations, Lini seemed to have some success in widening

---

10   A commitment which the SPC has upheld to this day.

the parameters of debate within subsequent SPC-facilitated conferences on women's issues. On the whole, however, the efforts of the PWRB officeholders to independently define an agenda of women's concerns were hamstrung by the SPC stipulation that this body should deal with member governments only. In the longer term, this meant that the PWRB's operations generally reflected the conservative political course steered by the region's governments rather than the more radical agendas that had been promoted by the region's activist community.

This was made clearly evident during a later women's conference convened by the SPC in Rarotonga in 1985 to formulate regional strategies for the UN's End of Decade Women's conference, upcoming in Nairobi. The report from this conference indicates the increasingly systematic approach taken to women's issues by regionally based women's groups at the end of the Decade for Women (SPC 1985). Rather than the free-ranging debates that were recorded by conference observers at the first Pacific regional conference for women in 1975, the report of this meeting, staged ten years later, indicates a more structured and detailed approach to the issues deemed to be negatively impacting upon women. Delegates participated in workshops on issues related to health, education, employment and women's role in decision-making, with detailed consideration given to the causes of the disadvantage experienced by women in these areas and the types of policy solutions that might address some of these difficulties. In addition, a detailed discussion of issues relating to young women in the region, and the detrimental impacts upon women of alcoholism, drugs and gender violence also took place at this meeting. This was the first time that these subjects had received a special emphasis within a regional forum.

Consideration of the broader international dimensions of women's disadvantage that had been a major feature of discussions taking place in earlier regional conferences of NGO women were not given the same emphasis in this particular forum. Discussions were locally framed and, once again, actively regulated by members of the SPC institutional hierarchy. Nevertheless, there was brief mention made of the Pacific nuclear disarmament issue, something that had not been allowed to occur in Tahiti in 1981. On this question, it was stated that governments should be 'strongly urged to make rapid progress on peace issues such as the Nuclear Free Pacific Zone Treaty' (SPC 1985: 23). The brief references to this issue within the 1985 conference report suggest that the PWRB office bearers were having measured success in creating an institutional environment more tolerant of criticism towards the region's remaining colonial powers.

However, developments in other quarters suggest that the momentum driving this broader structural critique was beginning to wane of its own accord within women's advocacy circles. Some indication of this is evidenced in reports of a final NGO conference for women staged in Sydney in June 1985, in the lead up to the UN's End of Decade Conference for Women. A strictly NGO-only affair, the Sydney meeting brought together two hundred women from across the Pacific Island region, including indigenous activists from Australia and New Zealand, and was organised by the Australian offices of the international women's organisation, Women's International League for Peace and Freedom (WILPF). We might expect that because it took place outside an institutional framework, this forum, with its particular focus on peace, would be a likely venue for the articulation of strongly worded critiques of prevailing international structures and the continued inability of the peoples of the Pacific Islands to gain full rights of self-determination from foreign powers in the region.

While these issues were clearly audible in many of the presentations made by representatives of local organisations, they were not dominant. What is striking about this particular meeting is the extent to which many of the issues raised mirrored the concerns that had been raised by Pacific women at the SPC's Rarotonga meeting a few months earlier. Women's organisations discussed in great detail the break-down of law and order in many parts of the Pacific and the accompanying rise in violence against women. This discussion was also framed as a peace issue, with one speaker from PNG arguing that the high incidence of rape and sexual abuse was a diminution of women's peace and freedom. Other women spoke on issues relating to alcohol abuse, the role and function of women's organisations, funding levels for women's groups and women's access to media (*Pacific Islands Monthly* September 1985).

This shift towards a more issue-specific form of advocacy which emphasised the causes of women's oppression that came from within the region, rather than attributing oppression to the impact of colonialism or global inequality, can be understood in part as a reflection of broader international advocacy trends. During the preparatory meetings for the UN's Nairobi Women's Conference, deliberations upon the shape of the intergovernmental conference document, *Forward Looking Strategies* (FLS), had identified specific areas of concern that contributed to women's disadvantage. These were established as areas that international institutions and local governments should address in their policy-making processes. While this development certainly encouraged activists working in Pacific Island contexts to frame their advocacy in similar ways, the shift towards a more issue-specific deliberation of gender inequality was home grown too, reflecting activists' increasing expertise as gender analysts and their more systematic attention to the local social, political and economic structures that contributed to women's subordination. As a result, this new style of advocacy retained its strong emphasis upon Pacific experience and the struggles to overcome disadvantage waged by women from around the region.

Pacific women on the international stage

Two further UN-convened conferences for women provided a platform for Pacific women to participate on the international stage in these years. The first was held in Copenhagen in 1980 to mark the UN Decade for Women's 'Mid-point'. The second was held in Nairobi in 1985 to close the Decade. Government and NGO delegations from the Pacific attended these conferences, but on each occasion complained that they found it difficult to make their particular regional concerns heard and understood, both within the intergovernmental conferences and the parallel NGO Forums.

Copenhagen 1980

The 1980 World Conference on the United Nations Decade for Women was seen by many at the time to have been a highly politicised and internationally divisive event. Indeed, the signing ceremony for the newly established United Nations Convention For the Elimination of Discrimination Against Women (CEDAW), which saw sixty-four states recognise the instrument, was generally noted as one of the few highpoints. In general, many accounts of this event focussed upon the militancy allegedly demonstrated by Third World delegates on issues of political and economic dependency, and the extent to which this caused divisions that were harmful to the broader conference objectives (Syrkin 1980; Fraser 1987; Tinker and Jaquette 1987; Hill 1980).[11]

On this occasion, Third World political actors appeared determined to make international policy-makers recognise the need for international political and economic negotiations to be guided by a pronounced redistributive ethos. Universal consensus on these issues remained a long way distant, however, as talks gave way to battles over political ideology. Observers of this event argued that official delegations to Copenhagen had a tendency to bloc together into three groups with competing perspectives on the status of women offered by participants from western countries, participants from developing states and those from the Eastern Bloc countries (Fraser 1987; Hill 1980). Intergovernmental debates continued to make reference to contentious international questions such as the establishment of the New International Economic Order (NIEO), the continuing policy of apartheid in South Africa and the status of Palestine in the Middle East (Ashwin 1981). All of this meant that consensus on the final conference document was ultimately unattainable. Opposition to the inclusion

---

11   The intrusion of the Palestinian question into conference debate was interpreted by many as a serious deviation from the official business of the conference and a lost opportunity for a consensus to emerge. When the issue was forced by India, official conference delegates were drawn into lengthy and highly politicised discussions of Middle East politics and the implications of Zionist doctrine (Syrkin 1980; Fraser 1987; Tinker and Jaquette 1987; Hill 1980; Ashwin 1981).

of the term Zionism in the final draft of the Programme for Action meant that twenty-two states abstained from voting while four states (Australia, the United States, Canada and Israel) voted against.[12]

Many interpreted this outcome as a significant defeat for the broader cause of women's advancement, and questioned how such politically divisive issues could be considered legitimate subject matter for an international conference on the status of women. However, as in Mexico City five years earlier, Third World delegates to the Copenhagen conference found structural perspectives of disadvantage to be highly relevant to the experiences of women in their own countries and something that could not be ignored when strategies for improvement were devised. For these participants, arguments for the advancement of women could not be disassociated from broader themes related to the 'common struggle for justice and liberty' (Danielsson 1980: 21).

As they had in Mexico City, Pacific delegates again articulated perspectives of gender disadvantage that supported this idea and blurred the lines between local and international obstacles impeding women's advancement. In so doing, they recalled the idea that the struggles waged by women in the region could not be considered in isolation from the international struggles waged by the peoples of the Pacific to have their economic interests, environment, culture and rights to self-determination better protected (Griffen 1987).

The region as a whole was represented within the Copenhagen parallel NGO Forum by delegates from Fiji, Tonga, Western Samoa, New Hebrides (Vanuatu from 1980), French Polynesia and New Caledonia, as well as indigenous representation from Australia and New Zealand. However, the same misgivings experienced in Mexico City were again apparent amongst the Pacific Island participants at Forum '80 who argued that the organisers had made them 'practically invisible' at this event (Villabos 1980). Lini from the New Hebrides argued that the Forum had been organised in a way that was more accommodating to delegates from 'Europe, Africa, Asia and the Americas'. Lini lamented this as a lost opportunity, for she saw attendance at Copenhagen as a way to draw international attention to the struggle for independence taking place in her country. She argued, 'no one knows about our struggle.... My whole country knows I'm attending this conference and they expect me to publicise our problems and get help' (Lini cited in Villabos 1980).

Out of a sense of frustration, the Pacific Forum participants organised a joint meeting to be held between local NGO representatives and all official delegations to the conference with economic or political stakes in the region. For women from areas of the Pacific still subject to colonial rule, this was considered an

---

12 Conference delegates managed to generate a consensus vote on the National sections of the Programme for Action, which were subject to a far less contentious level of international scrutiny and debate.

especially significant opportunity; one which enabled them to articulate their grievances in an international context and to demonstrate the plight of the 'stateless' who were powerless to resist imposed models of development (Lini cited in Villabos 1980).

Vanessa Griffen's later writing on women's regionalism emphasises the significance of this meeting. Despite the fact that the Forum organisers gave no recognition to the Pacific Island region, Pacific Island women took affairs into their own hands. As such, they appeared far better prepared to challenge their 'imposed silence' than they had been in Mexico City. Working as a 'regional delegation' (Griffen 1987: 520), these women argued that the Copenhagen Program of Action must address themes relevant to Pacific Island women, listing a number of internationally focused issues which should be given top priority by 'all governments and peoples' if disadvantage in the region was to be effectively addressed (Danielsson 1980: 22). These included calls for the creation of a Pacific Nuclear-Free Zone, the banning of nuclear tests, weapons and the dumping of nuclear waste, acceleration of the decolonisation process in those areas of the Pacific still governed as colonial dominions, an end to the continuing exploitation of the Pacific region's natural resources by foreign and multinational corporations, a revaluing of indigenous cultures in the field of local education, an end to large-scale labour migration into Pacific Island countries, and greater efforts to combat racial discrimination (Hill 1980). This agenda was far more challenging, detailed and provocative than the substance of the Pacific Island official government reports to the conference agenda (Slatter 1980).[13] At the same time, the participation of state representatives at this meeting suggests that while not in full agreement with the lines of argument presented, state officials were motivated to give some attention to the provocative perspectives of Pacific women's disadvantage being advanced by the regions' activists.

Pacific delegates anticipated a high level of support from the Australian and New Zealand state representatives attending this meeting, hoping that, as neighbours to the Island region, they would provide leadership within the intergovernmental conference on the issues raised. This leadership was not forthcoming, however, and Pacific women interpreted this as a lack of regional identification. Australian and New Zealand delegations were felt to be displaying a clear determination to protect their own strategic and economic interests in

---

13 Only four Pacific Island states sent delegates to the official conference in Copenhagen—PNG, Western Samoa, Tonga and Fiji. Of these, only Fiji and PNG presented country reports to the conference plenary. Fiji's paper was written in Copenhagen by the delegation's male advisor who came across from New York to assist the three-women delegation. While the paper acknowledged that the government had not committed to a Plan of Action for women, it was also stated that collaborative government and NGO efforts had meant that Fiji had 'come near to meeting all the 14 minimum objectives of Mexico City World Plan of Action recommendations' (cited in Slatter 1980: 15). In a show of regional solidarity with the population of the New Hebrides, the Fiji country paper also expressed a highly critical opinion of foreign interests which were said to be frustrating the independence aspirations of this territory's peoples.

the region and a loyalty towards 'the rich men's clubs of Europe' rather than 'the poor relations of the South Pacific' (Hill 1980). The only point of convergence related to the nuclear presence in the Pacific with Australia and New Zealand co-sponsoring a resolution with the official Pacific Island delegates for a nuclear test ban treaty (Hill 1980: 28; Slatter 1980: 16).

The general lack of receptiveness to the viewpoints proposed by the region's activists reflects the broader conflicts emerging in Copenhagen, particularly when participants from developing countries attempted to explain women's subordination via reference to the international sphere and the uneven distribution of global economic and political power. While Pacific women clearly demonstrated a determination to be heard internationally on these questions, the broader political division evident at Copenhagen tended to overshadow their efforts.

Nairobi 1985

By contrast, the UN World Conference to Review and Appraise the Achievements of the United Nations Decade for Women, staged in Nairobi in 1985, was generally viewed as the 'high-point' of the Decade for Women (Tinker and Jaquette 1987: 419). This was partly due to the enormous number of women involved,[14] but also because deliberations were said to have been driven by consensus-building approaches rather than the adversarial negotiation that had marked the previous two UN Conferences for Women. Many observers argued that this was made possible through the creation of a more cooperative conference environment and a determination to overcome the wide gulf separating Third World and First World women that had been evident in Mexico City and Copenhagen (Berkovitch 1999; O'Barr 1986; Tinker 1986; Hultman 1986; Basu 1986; Çağatay, Grown and Santiago 1986; Galey 1986; Mair 1986). Within both the intergovernmental conference and the parallel NGO Forum, a spirit of compromise was said to have prevailed, prompted by a growing awareness that the factors contributing to women's subordination had become more serious across the decade. Indeed, staging the final women's conference of the Decade in an African location brought home, in stark terms, the disparities between North and South and was undoubtedly influential in increasing the willingness of 'Western women to see issues such as access to clean water as "feminist"' (Hultman 1986).

Within the formal conference proceedings, emphasis upon consensus-style deliberation was encouraged by the Kenyan host-delegation that was eager to avoid a situation whereby Nairobi would be viewed as the 'graveyard of the women's movement' (Galey 1986). Margaret Galey argues that, in this spirit,

---

14 Over 14,000 participants were present at the Nairobi NGO Forum and 2,000 delegates attended the official intergovernmental conference.

Kenyan delegates acted to disrupt the G77 solidarity that had marked the previous intergovernmental conference deliberations and, in coalition with representatives from other African states, diffused tensions over issues related to the status of Palestine that had been a significant sticking point during the previous UN women's conferences (Tinker and Jaquette 1987; Patton 1995). Consensus was also reached on sections of the Nairobi conference document entitled the *Forward Looking Strategies* which paid particular attention to needs of specific groups of women—women victims of violence, women living in drought, urban poor and elderly women, the abused and destitute, and young women—and encouraged a more issue-specific response by states and local women's groups to these challenges.

Within the NGO Forum, this shift towards consensus building was also apparent. Delegates seemed more prepared to concede that feminism needed to accommodate consideration of 'survival issues' if it were to have a global legitimacy (Çağatay, Grown and Santiago 1986: 403). This perspective also required delegates to question how other determinants of social location such as class, ethnicity, religion or culture operate to further compound the already disadvantaged status of women in many locations. Divisions and some conflict were, as on previous occasions, also part of Forum deliberations. Nonetheless, observers generally found that participants showed a determination to 'engage in productive and peaceful dialogue, even on issues that historically divided them by nationality, class or race' (Çağatay, Grown and Santiago 1986: 409; O'Barr 1986: 585).

The experience of Pacific women at Nairobi, on the other hand, reveals some misgivings in this regard. Within both the intergovernmental conference, and the parallel NGO Forum, the region's delegations again experienced significant difficulties in making their presence felt and in drawing international attention to the particular nature of their grievances.

Over sixty Pacific women attended the Nairobi Forum, more than three times the number of regional representatives attending Copenhagen 1980. Nonetheless, delegates generally felt 'overwhelmed' by the sheer scope of the event and the number of women attending (Goodwillie 1985). Fiji's Susanna Evening, representing the Pacific Council of Churches, claimed 'we are drowned in these workshops because we are only a small group. We need to voice ourselves loudly before we are identified' (Chew 1985a). Once again, Pacific delegates were also unhappy that the Forum organisers had failed to provide sufficient space for Pacific women to set up exhibitions and had not included them in Forum workshop schedules (Chew 1985b). This situation was relieved to some degree by the fact that a Fiji-based journalist who regularly wrote on women's issues in the local press, Seona Martin, was also part of the Pacific delegation to

Nairobi, and worked on the *Forum '85* daily newspaper. Martin's efforts ensured that coverage was given to Pacific activities within this conference, and Pacific perspectives of the event in general (Goodwillie 1985).[15]

These reports show that many of Fiji's representatives to the conference continued to identify international factors as contributing to women's subordination in the region. Their advocacy at the Nairobi conference echoed the themes that had been apparent in their presentations to the 1975 and 1980 conferences and again focused upon issues such as the testing of nuclear weapons, calls for decolonisation and greater local control over Pacific Island economic and natural resources. For example, Vanessa Griffen's forum presentation focused upon the negative impact of militarisation in the Pacific and the ways in which the world's major powers had acted to enhance their strategic interests in the region but simultaneously endangered the interests of local communities (Chew 1985e). On another occasion, Fiji YWCA national general secretary, Tupou Vere, spoke of the continuing colonial presence in the region and urged delegates from the states implicated to pressure their governments to withdraw from the Pacific and recognise local communities' rights to self-rule. Arguing that colonial states were imposing their own sense of superiority on Pacific Islanders, she stated '[w]e do not want your white gods' (Chew 1985c). Another highly critical presentation on similar issues was made by Shaista Shameem, also a Fiji YWCA member. Shameem argued that some Pacific Island states may have gained political sovereignty but their ability to retain control over economic resources and production had been compromised by outside influences. In particular, Shameem argued that Fiji's strategic alliances with the US and Australia were compromising the country's independent status (*Fiji Sun* 20 July 1985).[16]

In an effort to promote Pacific concerns within the Forum, delegates from the region again formed a regional committee which aimed to influence Pacific delegations to the official intergovernmental conference. This committee issued a joint statement which drew attention once again to nuclear testing in the Pacific region, the continuing economic dependency of newly independent states, and indigenous populations' rights to self-rule. It read, '[i]t is our responsibility as women of the world to combine to bring this exploitation to an immediate halt' (Martin 1985b).

Like Pacific women participating in the Nairobi Forum, the Pacific region's official delegates to the intergovernmental conference also felt that they were

---

15   The UN also sponsored a local journalist, Connie Chew, to cover the event for Fiji's local press. This ensured that the Nairobi women's conference and Pacific women's participation received far greater coverage in the press than the previous events of the UN Decade for Women.

16   This observation partly reflects local dissatisfaction over the Fiji government's reversal of its previously strong anti-nuclear stance as a result of US pressure.

given little opportunity to present their case.[17] Despite the fact that official Pacific Island state delegations were generally more high-ranking and more numerous than those that had attended previous conferences, there was also some dissatisfaction that delegates were grouped with those from Asia and thus viewed as representing the Asia-Pacific region as a whole. Kuini Bavadra, head of Fiji's official delegation, argued that this common practice within the UN was in need of review, given that Pacific Island countries 'have no similarity' with Asian countries and that their 'tradition and customs are totally different' (cited in Gokal 1985). The fact that significant tensions existed within the Asian group also exacerbated the situation and ensured that the Pacific Island delegates received little support from other state representatives when it came to raising particular issues of concern (Gokal 1985). As in Copenhagen, the region's delegates were also disappointed that Australia and New Zealand seemed reluctant to support a Pacific Island agenda. Once again, they were viewed as displaying loyalties towards delegations from the western states, rather than their local neighbours (Chew 1985f).

Yet, even Fiji's delegates were heartened by the apparent broadening of feminist debate that occurred in Nairobi. While the world may have become 'more aware of disadvantaged women' as Bavadra asserted on her return to Fiji (cited in Gokal 1985), the way had also become clearer for the global articulation of a 'diversity of feminisms, responsive to the different needs and concerns of different women' (Sen and Grown 1987: 13). This development contrasted with the divisions that had been evident during earlier conferences.

The idea that feminist debate had expanded in this period was reiterated by local and international observers of women's organising, and viewed as a progressive development for women in general terms (Tinker 1986; Fraser 1987; Çağatay, Grown and Santiago 1986; Bernstein 1986; Griffen 1987). Important changes were also taking place within the sphere of women's organising domestically—in Fiji and across the region—during this period. Certainly the formation of an important new women's organisation in Fiji and the creation of an agency specifically designed to address women's needs at the regional level provided an energising impetus for women's advocacy in these years. Yet, Pacific gender activists were also encountering influences which made their work difficult. This suggests that the developments described in the previous pages need to be understood in contingent terms. In the following section therefore, I consider how women's political agency was shaped by the contingencies of the prevailing political environment during these years. I focus again on gender activists

---

17   Fiji was represented at this event by Kuini Bavadra, a senior official within the Department of Information, and Ross Ligari, second secretary of the Fiji Mission to the United Nations in New York. This formal delegation was assisted in the various conference committees by local NGO representatives: Esiteri Kamikamica from the NCW; Adi Mei Gauna from the SSVM; and Sabreen Kahn of the Fiji Moslem Youth League.

'situated experience', of the domestic and international political influences that shaped their negotiations of collectivity, their promotion of 'progressive ideas', and their approach to transnational engagement.

Collectivity

The previous chapter demonstrated the important commitments that the YWCA made towards multicultural organisational participation. This was something that contrasted with the communalism and hierarchical structures more generally prevalent within Fiji's civil society, however it was a commitment that also became more difficult to maintain in this later period.

The internal disputes that emerged in the late 1970s within the YWCA are a strong indication of this shifting trend. These disputes often occurred as younger, more outspoken members of the organisation clashed with those who believed they should be accorded greater organisational authority due to their age, or their indigenous rank. For example, some board members of the YWCA who, in their lives outside the organisation, were closely connected with the ruling political elite and, in particular, Fiji's politically dominant Alliance Party, were frequently uncomfortable with the controversial public political profile pursued by other members of the organisation. In 1975, disputes over planned policy submissions to government saw one prominent board member argue that her association with this type of activity conflicted with her political standing outside the organisation (Fiji YWCA 19 August 1975, PAC Record Book).

The later and more serious developments taking place within the YWCA, leading to the strike action in 1976, also reflected internal struggles for influence between younger, more radicalised and outspoken members, and older members who were uncomfortable with the provocative nature of this activity (Keith-Reid 1976). While some acted to protect the early idea of a participatory organisational culture, this position was increasingly challenged by those who could see no reason why the YWCA should challenge social and cultural values more generally respected within Fiji's civil society. Rokotuivuna, in particular, was deeply disappointed that the YWCA leadership had begun to ignore the 'higher goals' it had aimed for in the past (Rokotuivuna 2002b).

The breakdown of relationships within the NCW can also be understood as influenced by these broader socio-cultural protocols and helps explain the SSVM decision to end its affiliation with the NCW in 1979. The SSVM justified this decision in part because it was unable to reconcile its own organisational ethos, which emphasised the importance of respect for seniority and social rank, with that of the younger, more reform-oriented women within the NCW whose conduct challenged these values (Kamikamica 1982). In the short term, this development damaged the NCW's profile. Although the newly appointed NCW coordinator, Kamicamica, vowed to put division behind her, the departure of the SSVM compromised the NCW's ability to speak for Fiji's women in a way that was wholly representative.

Towards the end of this period the creation of the FWCC indicates an emergent shift towards a more issue-oriented approach to women's advocacy; in this case an organisation specifically devoted to combating gendered forms of violence. This was a significant development which reflected trends emerging internationally, and which many viewed as enhancing women's networking opportunities locally and internationally. It was anticipated that developing coalitions around single issues would provide the 'necessary space for a cross-fertilisation of ideas and strategies' and help to minimise the transnational tensions that had been apparent at global conferences in the past (Çağatay, Grown and Santiago 1986: 410). Nevertheless, in Fiji, the personal recollections of those closely connected to the Women's Crisis Centre also demonstrate how these supposed benefits often gave way to a sense of competition and rivalry within the sphere of women's organising more broadly, and made the achievement of a sense of common purpose, even in the domestic setting, a considerable challenge.

The foundation of the Crisis Centre could be read as a development that signalled confidence in the capacity of existing organisations to meet the needs of women in general terms, and an attempt to build upon the earlier groundbreaking work performed by the YWCA. Yet, when outlining the early operations of the Centre, the organisation's coordinator, Shamima Ali, did not articulate this sense of progression, and her references to broader cooperation or collaboration were largely absent. Rather, Ali argued that within the local sphere of women's organising there was some reluctance to concede both political space and funding opportunities to a new organisation. In an environment where funding was tight and WID issues predominant, the task of convincing donors of the relevance of programs on gender violence was described as a challenge. Ali also suggested that the efforts of the Centre were sometimes discredited by other organisations that had pre-existing relations with funding agencies (S. Ali 2002).

Ali claimed that the issue of race was emphasised, in particular, by representatives from other women's groups to discredit the political profile of the Crisis Centre, and to suggest that the early expatriate presence within the organisation compromised its local authenticity. In our discussions, Ali praised the early role of expatriate women within the Crisis Centre and their tendency to 'push' local members to 'take ownership of the issues' (in many ways echoing the sentiments expressed by early YWCA members as they discussed the role of founding expatriate members like Ruth Lechte and Anne Walker). Nevertheless, in this later period, Ali argued that expatriate involvement had harmed the Crisis Centre's profile, with other women's organisations dismissing its importance by arguing 'oh they're an expat organisation' (S. Ali 2002).

Of course, in a political climate where the detractors of the women's movement have frequently accused women's organisations of introducing foreign ideas that are incompatible with Pacific Island cultures, the presence of expatriate women could be viewed as detrimental to the long-term ambition of these organisations to be accepted as locally authentic. Additionally, there continued to be some local resistance towards the 'monolithic' (Çağatay, Grown and Santiago 1986) prominence of western-oriented feminist frameworks which had seemed hostile to local perspectives of gender disadvantage. These tendencies help to explain why local women activists during this period were able to discredit those organisations that continued to incorporate expatriates as members. Yet, such views also tended to overlook the important role that locally admired expatriate figures such as Lechte had played in pioneering critical public debate on gender issues (Moore 2002b; Bhagwan Rolls 2002a).

Ali's suggestion that the racial origins of Crisis Centre members were used to discredit the organisation appears particularly poignant and paradoxical given the earlier efforts that national organisations such as the YWCA or the umbrella group, the NCW, had made to promote ideals of multiculturalism both within society and within their own organisations. The critique of expatriate influence also contrasts sharply with the legitimating role played by expatriates within Fiji's civil society during earlier colonial periods. At this time, women's organisations were practically obligated to appoint expatriate women to positions of leadership if they were to be seen to have any authority by the prevailing colonial elite (Lechte 2005; see also Chapter 2).

Attempts to understand these episodes of ruptured collectivity within and between women's organisations are only possible if recognition is given to the broader socio-cultural influences that shaped civil society behaviour more generally in Fiji at this time. Prevailing hierarchies of age and social status clearly had an impact upon women's groups, influencing the negotiation of organisational relationships and disrupting the idea of horizontal collectivity, so often identified as an ideal feature of women's organisations. Similarly, the legacies of Fiji's colonial history, which have ensured that race remains a powerfully charged local idiom, frequently exploited for local political gain within the realm of institutional politics, clearly also permeated the associational sphere at this time. The ability of some Fiji-based women's organisations to use the issue of race as a means by which to discredit others can therefore also be appreciated as a tactic that reflected Fiji's highly communal political terrain and the contestation that inevitably surrounds questions of racial identification in this setting.[18]

---

18   In her study of gender activist networks in Fiji leading up the Beijing Conference in 1995, Annelise Riles notes in passing that 'generalized conceptions of "race" and "culture" were divisive elements.... In some

Progressive ideas

The increasing international prominence of the WID policy framework in this period expanded the political space available to Fiji's women's organisations as they campaigned for greater government attention to be focused upon 'women and development' issues. While locally focused efforts to improve women's formal representation in Fiji's state bureaucratic structure were generally not successful in these years,[19] activities designed to strengthen the regional network of women's organisations certainly appear to have accrued some significant political dividends, particularly with the establishment of the PWRB within the SPC. The increased focus upon regionalism was, therefore, seen by many activists as a progressive approach to gender advocacy during this period.

When asked about the developing regional consciousness of Pacific Island women at this time, former YWCA member Suliana Siwatibau highlighted the importance of understanding women's regionalism not as a new development, but an aspect of Pacific Island life that was simply enhanced in these years. Siwatibau argued that the SPC's Community Education and Training Centre had, since its foundation in Suva in 1963, played an important role in fostering regional contacts amongst women. Participants who had come together for education or training from across the region still managed to 'keep the network alive' upon their return home, she argued (Siwatibau 2002).

Moreover, in these years, Pacific regionalism was becoming more pronounced at the intergovernmental level. Greg Fry has shown that this was an era when newly independent Pacific Island states, as well as regional neighbours (Australia and New Zealand), were seeking to establish new regional institutions such as the South Pacific Forum (founded in 1971), which aimed to facilitate regional cooperation while also increasing the region's international political influence (Fry 1979, 1994, 1997). Therefore, Pacific women were increasing their level of regional engagement at a time when these same trends were becoming prominent within Pacific Island politics at a more general level.

When asked how regionalism could be empowering for women, many of my interlocutors emphasised how this level of engagement contributed to both organisational learning and political influence. It was argued that the 'regional focus' evident during this period facilitated learning in the shape of 'exchange

---

cases, the racial composition of organizations was explicitly celebrated, while in others, it was vehemently denied.' While Riles also notes how racial stereotypes formed an important part of this discourse, she does not expand upon these observations (Riles 2001: 59).

19 In terms of local institutional outcomes that might be identified as instances of reform-oriented agency, it is clear that positive developments for women at this time were few. The Fiji government was particularly good at making commitments towards women's advancement on the international stage, but generally disinclined to follow these up with concrete policy formulations.

of information and experience' and helped 'shape ... advocacy, and the type of plans to be put in place' (Vere 2002a). Rokotuivuna provided an important example of this when she described the regional ramifications of the PNG government's 1975 decision to establish a women's machinery within the Office of the Prime Minister. Rokotuivuna argued that this development was celebrated by the region's women in general terms, and viewed as strengthening similar demands for the establishment of women's machineries in other Pacific countries (Rokotuivuna 2002b).

Regionalism was also understood to increase the international influence of local women's organisations. Griffen has argued that participation at the 1975 World Conference for Women in Mexico City 'revealed to Pacific women that their individual voices were inadequate if they wished to raise issues; they found that they must present their views as a region' (Griffen 1984: 519). Taufa Vakatale also emphasised this point, stating that, in this period 'Fiji couldn't come and fight its own case. If we wanted to be heard ... we had to organise regionally' (Vakatale 2002). Forming regional coalitions was, therefore, viewed as increasing activists' ability to leverage support for particular causes on the local and international stage.

However, as the previous discussion has demonstrated, fortunes were somewhat mixed in this regard. Certainly, the ability of Pacific NGO representatives to convene a high-level meeting of international delegates to the Copenhagen women's conference in 1980 was significant. Yet the concerns articulated at this meeting were not taken up within the intergovernmental forum. Campaigns waged by Pacific Island women to refocus the policy emphasis of the SPC to accord greater recognition of gender issues resulted in new institutional initiatives such as the triennial intergovernmental women's conferences and the establishment of a new SPC agency for women, the PWRB. However, evidence from the SPC's Tahiti meeting convened in 1981 also demonstrates that Pacific women were not able to make the same types of critical contributions to regional debate that had been a hallmark of their advocacy in the previous decade (Goodwillie 2005).

In later conferences convened by the SPC, debate on questions of gender disadvantage proceeded smoothly when an issue-specific approach was taken. This seemed to allow the thornier questions of structural inequality and international political influence in the region to be avoided altogether. Deliberations on questions of health infrastructure and education, or gender violence were areas where a commonality of experience and concern could be identified without provoking institutional observers. These developments reflected an emerging trend which was locally interpreted by some as taking women's advocacy to a 'new level'. From this perspective, issue-specific forms of advocacy were seen as progressive for the fact that they enabled women's groups to 'move beyond' the questions that had been of particular concern in the past (Vere 2002b).

Within the broader transnational sphere of women's organising, the shift towards issue-specific forms of advocacy was similarly acclaimed as progressive. The fact that the Nairobi *Forward Looking Strategies* focused greater attention upon the disadvantage experienced by women in specific circumstances was viewed as demonstrating how cutting-edge academic research on gender inequalities was beginning to inform gender activism. It was argued that rather than simply documenting instances of women's oppression, this type of work enabled a global understanding of the varied contexts in which women are disadvantaged and the strategies needed to alleviate this disadvantage (Fraser 1987; Tinker 1986: 588).

Arvonne Fraser described these attempts to identify both issues of concern *and* potential solutions as 'hopeful and forward looking'; an acknowledgement of the obstacles impeding women's advancement, but also an attempt to create a sense of progress (Fraser 1987: 168). By its very title, *Forward Looking Strategies* encapsulated this idea of progress for women being made at all levels of policy-making.

This does not mean that women's organisations taking a more issue-specific approach to combating women's disadvantage were strangers to controversy. As Ali's recollections of this period demonstrate, organisations like the Fiji Women's Crisis Centre challenged important socio-cultural protocols which regulated conduct within civil society generally and prevented the issue of gender violence from becoming a topic of public debate. Describing the political environment before the Crisis Centre was established, Ali stated, 'People didn't talk about this issue and rape was not mentioned in the press. You only read about it if it was rape and murder. So reports were quite rare. In terms of open debate—there was none at all…. Rape was seen as a private affair, it was something that was shameful' (S. Ali 2002).

Similarly, Ali also illustrated how cultural and social protocols operated to strengthen patriarchal values in civil society and limit the space available to organisations such as the Crisis Centre. She stated, 'There were cultural restrictions too; the acceptability of treating women like doormats, and the mentality that if these things happen then women deserve it. We were working in a very conservative society … there is the whole patriarchal system in operation here which sanctions the culture of men owning women' (S. Ali 2002).

Ali viewed the activities of ACWIN and, later, the Crisis Centre, as challenging these protocols. Yet, if Ali privately articulated a relatively bald view of the impacts of patriarchy and gender discrimination, she was also careful to point out that in its public advocacy the Crisis Centre had geared its message delivery in ways that reflected cultural values and religious belief systems within the broader community. She stated, 'We have examined culture and religion. We have read the Koran, the Hindu holy books and the Bible. We have learnt all about these religions so we can counter arguments that might do damage to women. This has been an important part of our training' (S. Ali 2002).

These statements suggest that the 'progressive' step towards issue-specific forms of advocacy for women was also shaped in important ways by the contingencies of the local socio-cultural setting. Ali's comments indicate that while the Crisis Centre sought to challenge cultural protocols which reinforced the hidden nature of gender violence, the organisation was also mindful of the need to shape the anti-violence message in ways that were consonant with these influences. This tactic contrasted with the more provocative, head-on approach to structurally inclined advocacy that had been a characteristic feature of YWCA activity in previous years.

Transnationalism

At first glance, the events described in this chapter would appear to support the idea that throughout the UN's Decade for Women, the transnational women's movement developed an enhanced cohesiveness. Many international observers judged the outcomes generated by the Nairobi Conference—both the level of consensus within the forum and the final unanimous intergovernmental vote for the *Forward Looking Strategies*—to be indicative of a broader and more mature level of global feminist debate (Tinker and Jaquette 1987; Berkovitch 1999; Galey 1986; Fraser 1987). Similarly, some Pacific Island gender activists were keen to promote the argument that the international feminist agenda had become wider and more inclusive in this period.

Not long after the end of the Decade for Women, observers such as Griffen, who had previously been highly critical of the efforts to promote a global feminism, made reference to this idea of expansion:

> The idea of feminism has been broadened. A fundamental aspect of it is recognition of the inequalities and exploitative nature of male-female relationships in all societies in the world. That is the universal aspect of women's condition. Women have found that they cannot ignore other issues related to women, such as how their country is organized, who controls the country and the economy, and the dependence of that economy on the world economic system. With a wider perspective, women are able to see feminist struggle as not just changing the little things that affect aspects of women's lives, but as an effort to seek a broader transformation that would improve the position of women—of men and women equally—for a better world (Griffen 1987: 7).

Griffen's views suggest that her earlier mistrust of the universalising aspects of feminism, strongly biased towards the interests of western women, were diminished in this later period. Indeed, she appears greatly encouraged by the idea of an expanding framework for global feminist debate that would be more inclusive and more easily able to accommodate Pacific Islander perspectives of gender disadvantage (Griffen 1987).

Yet, in many parts of the Pacific, a resistance to the term feminism continued. Participants to a 1987 regional conference entitled 'Women, Development and Empowerment', and organised by a number of former Fiji YWCA activists, made this clear. Delegates to this event stated that they felt feminism to be something only relevant to highly educated women. Some argued that it challenged the cultural emphasis Pacific Islanders placed upon the family and the raising of children, or that its ultimate aim was to see women segregated from the rest of society (Griffen 1987). In other contexts, Pacific women also articulated the view that blanket judgements of Pacific Island cultures as anti-women overlooked the many aspects of local culture that celebrated and honoured Pacific women (Kamikamica 1985: 71).[20] This suggests that while increasing numbers of women were motivated to change discriminatory practices against women within Pacific Island contexts, they were, in many cases, as reluctant as they had been in previous years to identify with the term feminism or to articulate their goals in these terms (Griffen 1987).

The emphasis upon issue-defined approaches to gender advocacy which increased in this period provided a way to move on from the more difficult question about the appropriateness of feminism in the Pacific context.[21] At this time, many international observers were celebrating the emergence of smaller and more issue-focused transnational networks, arguing that they contributed a greater international cohesiveness to women's organising by 'providing a necessary space for the cross-fertilisation of ideas and strategies' (Çağatay, Grown and Santiago 1986: 410). The idea here seems to be that while specific phenomena contributed to women's subordination in specific ways in particular settings, it was also possible to talk about issues such as gender violence, women and environmental resource management (Tinker 1986), or women's role in the media, in ways that acknowledged a commonality of experience and avoided hegemonic universalising.

---

20 Colonial interventions also sought to modify these traditions. Colonial and missionary interventions across the Pacific Island region were frequently accompanied by efforts to promote European ideas about women's maternal and domestic duties and the appropriateness of women's work. In many contexts, these efforts helped to undermine the traditional sites of women's authority (Douglas 1999; Jolly and MacIntyre 1989).

21 In an exhortation to move beyond the 'interminable' debate on the Melanesian appropriateness of the term feminism, Jolly has argued that, ultimately, 'the word is not so crucial as the processes and practices of women's collective action to improve their lives' (Jolly 2003: 143).

Broader political factors also help explain this shift towards issue-specific advocacy and a movement away from activity that protested global structural inequality. To begin with, civil-society actors committed to combating global poverty were operating within a far more constrained transnational political space than had been apparent ten years earlier. With the international debt crisis gathering strength and the world economy falling into recession, the rhetoric of Third World leaders also began to change. The political leaders of aid-recipient states were, at this time, more inclined to acquiesce to the stringent structural adjustment conditionalities placed upon them by multilateral monetary institutions such as the International Monetary Fund (IMF) and the World Bank, than to call international attention to the added local hardship such policy-prescriptions were causing (Randall and Theobold 1998).[22] In global political terms, this situation stood in stark contrast to the earlier period of Third Worldism which characterised international politics in the late 1960s and early 1970s and which influenced a range of civil-society actors to also question the structural imbalances that compounded disadvantage in developing countries.

Domestic political developments in Fiji also contributed to this advocacy shift. For example, the previous 'close relationship' that had existed between Fiji's political elite and those civil society actors promoting an anti-nuclear agenda was, in this period, less evident. Fiji's local political elite had begun to develop a foreign policy agenda which more clearly reflected US interests in the Pacific, and this meant a less provocative state line was being articulated on questions of the Pacific's nuclear status and issues of decolonisation. In turn, this created a more constrained political environment for civil-society actors to pursue the kinds of questions that had absorbed their attention in the past.

This is not to say that advocacy examining the structural determinants of women's disadvantage was a thing of the past. Such views were clearly evident in the strongly worded statements made at the Nairobi women's conference by figures such as Vere, who decried the local influence of 'white Gods,' or Shameem, who argued that Pacific Island countries' state sovereignty was being undermined by foreign powers. Yet, the beginnings of a shift to more issue-specific discussions of women's disadvantage was clearly in evidence during this period, and was seen to offer new and potentially less divisive avenues for women's transnational dialogue into the future.

---

22   This approach to development economics was to become 'increasingly hegemonic' during the 1980s and formed the basis of structural adjustment programs, imposed by the IMF and World Bank which required debt-carrying developing states to devalue their currencies, cut spending in areas such as welfare, remove price control mechanisms and establish wage ceilings as part of 'debt rescheduling packages' (Randall and Theobold 1998: 123, 160).

Conclusion

Beyond the 'new frontier', a combination of changing local and global influences was shaping the ways in which Fiji's women's organisations understood their capacity to act. At domestic, regional and international levels, the political space in which advocates might make the case for greater recognition of the gendered impacts of *global* inequality was much reduced. To some degree, these developments can be understood as having encouraged a shift towards a new, issue-driven advocacy focus. Yet the fact that this new advocacy trend was also viewed as a progressive and less contentious transnational approach to promoting the advancement of women was also significant and saw the structural emphases that had been notable features of women's advocacy lose some of their currency.

Efforts to negotiate collectivity within particular women's organisations, and within Fiji's women's movements overall, continued to be shaped by longstanding social and cultural mores regulating social and political life in this context. This was indicated by the tensions which emerged both within the YWCA and the NCW over the behaviour of younger women in these organisations who were accused of acting disrespectfully towards older organisational members or those of a higher social rank. At the same time, race also emerged as an issue of contention within the sphere of women's advocacy as groups used references to ethnicity in ways designed to discredit each other. This inscription of race politics contrasts in stark ways with the organisational ethos promoted by bodies such as the YWCA or NCW in previous years. Earlier efforts to promote a participatory and multicultural ethos appear, in this period, to have given way to a more competitive communalism. Certainly the expatriate women implicated in these developments were disappointed that the politics of race had been used against them (Goodwillie 2005). Yet in this context too, such developments reveal important characteristics about the nature of associational life in Fiji and the relative ease with which the issue of race could be mobilised for political gain.

The next chapter will examine the local, regional and international developments in women's organising taking place from 1986 until the Beijing Conference for Women in 1995. This decade closed in a haze of international euphoria, as women's organisations around the globe celebrated the success of the Beijing conference, the sheer numbers of women represented, and the fact that state delegates once again had showed a strong willingness to unanimously endorse the World Plan of Action. Nonetheless, at the local level in Fiji, this was a period in which local women's organisations had to contend with a series of political developments that threatened the unity of the country as a whole and created a high level of internal tension within many nationally focused women's groups.

Existence was precarious for these groups in this period, as new currents of religious and social conservatism yoked with ethno-nationalism shaped the terrain of local politics and civil society activity.

4. 'Foreign Flowers'? Articulating Rights in the Post-Coup Political Economy: 1985–1995

The period from 1985 to 1995 was one of mixed fortune for Fiji's women's organisations. Overall, it was marked by an episode occurring in 1987 which had a critical political impact on the country and far-reaching social and economic consequences. In that year, the newly elected coalition government, made up of Labour Party and National Federation Party (NFP) representatives, was overthrown in the wake of a military coup. This event marked the culmination of an indigenous nationalist 'insurgency' which had brewed since the country's first Non-Alliance Party government had assumed political office only a few weeks earlier (Kelly and Kaplan 2001: 174). These events had significant ramifications for the political agency of women's organisations as they came to terms with a much-transformed political context and increased levels of need in the local community.

On the one hand, responses to these events were divided, demonstrating that the terrain of women's organising was not immune to the cleavages emerging within the broader local political sphere. On the other hand, these groups were equally confronted with a higher level of practical need in the community, as women of all nationalities struggled to deal with the immediate and serious social and economic impacts that accrued from Fiji's political upheavals. Drawing attention to these circumstances was difficult, however, within a post-coup political climate exhibiting a powerful current of ethno-nationalism. Accordingly, both supporters and detractors of the prevailing military-led regime promptly came to terms with the need to assume a more guarded political profile than had been apparent in previous years.

Women's organisations active at the regional level during this period enjoyed a more enabling political environment. Indeed, the regional presence of Fiji-based women's organisations increased significantly as local groups looked to create regional networks around specific issues such as gender violence, legal literacy and women's electoral representation. These regional initiatives were motivated by local knowledge of the areas in which women faced common challenges and resulted in the formulation of highly distinctive perspectives on gender disadvantage, with each activist network formulating a specific methodology for advocacy.

Regional preparations for the Fourth World Conference on Women, to be staged in Beijing in 1995, were more extensive than in the previous decade and, again, provided an important platform for organisational activity. However, the sectionalised and issue-specific focus of activity predominated, with regional intergovernmental bodies also limiting the extent to which non-government perspectives on these questions could be heard. In the long run, this meant that official documents prepared for Beijing by regional institutions tended to present a relatively moderate picture of gender disadvantage in the Pacific Island context.

Acting in their own right on the international stage, local women's organisations went to Beijing with a determination to be seen and heard, although the underlying issues that had to some extent been unifying factors and emblematic of participation at previous international events seem to be more difficult to detect on this occasion. The tone of advocacy undertaken by women's organisations was, for the most part, of a far more subtle complexion than had been evident at the preceding world conferences. This reflected general trends emerging in gender politics towards the end of the period and the tendency for statesmen and women, together with members of the activist community, to focus more squarely upon the human rights dimensions of gender disadvantage rather than broader redistributive goals.

To make sense of the waxing and waning fortunes of Fiji's women's organisations during this period, the following pages provide a close examination of the intersecting local and global factors that shaped women's advocacy in this decade. This discussion demonstrates how the terrain of women's advocacy was affected by Fiji's 1987 coups and an emergent authoritarian and, at times, chauvinistic political culture. It also discusses the influence of regional and international policy trends which had newly begun to emphasise 'women's rights as human rights'. The latter sections of the chapter focus on the 'situated' experience of women's organising during this period and draw from gender activists' first hand testimonies to examine how these prevailing circumstances shaped organisational abilities to negotiate collectivity, progressive ideas and transnational engagement.

Local developments

In contrast to the latter years of this decade, the period from 1985 to mid-1987 can be considered a generally positive time for women's organising in Fiji. The Fiji Women's Crisis Centre (FWCC) was beginning to increase its credentials as a nationally focused organisation with the establishment of provincial offices within Fiji and a mobile counselling clinic which aimed to extend the centre's reach to outlying areas. It had also begun to develop collaborations with older and more established women's groups such as church groups and women's cultural organisations. In addition, it continued to raise its public profile by publishing newsletters and pamphlet material promoting an anti-violence message. During this period, the FWCC received funding in a fairly ad hoc manner, with partner non-governmental organisations (NGOs) in Australia and New Zealand securing financial assistance for the Centre from state-based funding agencies such as the Australian International Development Assistance Bureau (AIDAB, later AusAID) (S. Ali 2002).

As previously shown, the FWCC was conscious of the need to frame the more political aspects of its activities in ways which did not challenge cultural or religious values in an overly provocative manner. Nonetheless, the political aspects of the FWCC's work threatened to bring it into conflict with some of Fiji's more conservative social elements. To avoid putting the practical focus of the Centre's programs at risk, it was agreed that a new organisation should be created to take a more state-focused and overtly political path (Moore 2002b). Formed with the twin aims of improving the 'inadequate laws' protecting women and enhancing women's political status, the Fiji Women's Rights Movement (FWRM) began operations as a sister organisation to the FWCC in 1986 (FWRM 2000a). Members of the organisation's management collective included a number of women who had been involved in other women's organisations such as Shamima Ali (FWCC), Imrana Jalal (YWCA), Peni Moore (FWCC), Kuini Bavadra (FWCC), and Ema Druavesi, a prominent member of the Fiji Trade Union Council (FTUC).

The principal focus of the FWRM's early activity was the issue of sexual violence against women, with the organisation formulating an anti-rape campaign which was funded through a partnership formed with the Melbourne-based NGO, the International Women's Development Agency (IWDA). While the program aimed to promote awareness of rape, and a more sympathetic response to victims of rape at the grassroots level, this campaign focused principally upon the need for legislative changes to more effectively deal with this phenomenon at the state level (FWRM 2000a). In 1987, the FWRM held the country's first anti-rape march which delivered to Fiji's parliament a petition containing over 5,000 signatures in support of improved state responses to rape victims and stricter sentencing guidelines for those convicted of sexual violence.

The FWRM also aimed to promote women's issues in the lead-up to Fiji's 1987 general election through the surveying and publication of candidates' responses to a number of questions deemed important to women's status. The Fiji Labour Party, in particular, promised a range of far-reaching reforms which included the creation of a government department for women, legislative change to outlaw sex discrimination, the establishment of minimum wages for women employed in the garment industry, and ongoing public funding for the Women's Crisis

Centre. This party was led by Dr Timoci Bavadra, an Indigenous Fijian from the country's western provinces. Bavadra's strong commitments to social justice drew on some of the antithetical traditions within the Fijian hierarchy which were unsettling for the Fijian establishment. Ultimately, he proved to be a strong contender in these elections and, with a coalition of minor parties, Bavadra's Labour Party was able to form government and bring to an end seventeen years of conservative Alliance Party domination in Fiji (Emberson-Bain 1992).[1]

Within a fortnight of victory, the Bavadra-led coalition had begun to act upon some of its electoral promises for women. In particular, Atu Emberson-Bain notes the preliminary work done to establish a Department of Women's Affairs (Emberson-Bain 1992: 148). On 14 May 1987, however, the policy aims of the Labour coalition were abruptly halted when military forces, under the direction of a high-ranking officer, Colonel Sitiveni Rabuka, invaded Fiji's parliament, took members of the government hostage for five days, and installed an interim military regime. This action was defended firstly as an attempt to 'forestall threats to law and order' (*Fiji Sun* 15 May 1987). Later, coup leaders argued that they were acting to uphold the interests of indigenous Fijians. In the weeks preceding the coup, an indigenous nationalist movement entitled the *Taukei*, 'a self-proclaiming insurgency … alleging to speak directly for the … people of the land or owners of the land,' had begun to win strong support for its claims that principles of indigenous paramountcy and Fijian Christian identity were under threat from the newly elected coalition government which included a high proportion of Indo-Fijian members (Kelly and Kaplan 2001: 174).

Following Rabuka's coup, efforts were made to resolve the resulting political impasse with the establishment of a government of national unity which brought together members of the conservative parties and some members of the Labour coalition. These moves did little to mollify the *Taukei* and the military. In September 1987, the armed forces again intervened, overturning this administration and establishing a military government with Rabuka at the helm. Fiji, at this point, was expelled from the Commonwealth. The country's new political leadership declared the country to be a Republican Christian state and oversaw the creation of a new constitution, formulated to protect indigenous paramountcy and the political powers of Fiji's Great Council of Chiefs. This new constitution also put in place a communal electoral system which ensured that indigenous Fijians would retain power should new elections be held (Kelly and Kaplan 2001). These took

---

1   Dr Bavadra's wife, Adi Kuini Vuikaba, was a highly placed public servant who had led Fiji's official country delegation to the UN Conference for Women in Nairobi in 1985. She had also been an active member of the FWCC and the FWRM prior to her husband becoming Labour Party leader. This undoubtedly helps explain the inclusion of women's issues in the Party's platform. When asked about the role she intended to undertake as the wife of the Prime Minister, she stated 'I intend to help champion the rights of women in this country and to help the youth' (*Fiji Times* 15 April 1987; see also *Fiji Sun* 15 April 1987).

place in 1992 and Rabuka, leading the nationalist Soqosoqo ni Vakavulewa ni Taukei (SVT) party,[2] was returned to power with a substantial majority (Sutherland 2000: 205).

Interpreting these events through a lens which highlights how racial cleavages are evident within the political life of the Fiji Islands obscures their class-based motivations and, particularly, how the political and economic ambitions of Fiji's Eastern Chiefs have influenced political developments throughout Fiji's colonial and post-colonial history (Robertson and Sutherland 2001; Sutherland 1992; Durutalo 1985). However, in the day-to-day political life of the nation, it was also easy to exploit the racial dimensions of the 1987 coups, with the result that divisions between Fiji's various ethnic communities intensified in the ensuing years (Davies 2005: 47). Strong support for coup leaders from within the powerful Methodist Church, and Church leaders' increasingly vocal demands that Fiji declare itself a Christian state, made the political environment difficult for civil society actors who were critical of the *Taukei*, the interim government and, in later years, the nationalist agenda of the SVT (Tuwere 1997; Niukula 1997).[3]

Within the sphere of women's organising, tensions developed between those sympathetic to the nationalist cause and those committed to democratic rule in Fiji. Many former members of the YWCA such as Vanessa Griffen, Claire Slatter and Amelia Rokotuivuna were strongly committed to the same principles of equity and social justice articulated by Bavadra. Rokotuivuna, in particular, led protests, public marches and prayer meetings in the days immediately after the coup, and was eventually arrested for these actions alongside women unionists Jackie Koroi and Druavesi (Emberson-Bain 1997; Rokotuivuna 1997; Griffen 2005). Other activist women maintained a strong media profile, with Slatter, Rokotuivuna, Arlene Griffen (also involved with the YWCA) and Peni Moore (FWRM) writing letters to the print media demanding an end to the Fiji military's political role and a return to democracy. Appeals were also made to Fiji's indigenous political elite, and especially the Great Council of Chiefs, to relinquish the idea that political power was their birthright (*Fiji Times* 5 June 1987, 12 June 1987, 22 June 1987; *Fiji Sun* 14 June 1987). In the subsequent months, a national 'Back to Early May' movement was formed to coordinate political activity in support of a return to democracy. Protests, petitions and marches were organised and women of 'all ethnic categories and political persuasions' were prominent campaigners (Emberson-Bain 1992: 159). Those engaged in this type of resistance were also subject to police surveillance and

---

2 J.D. Kelly and M. Kaplan translate this title as the 'Party of the Chiefs' (2001, 175), but also note that the leaders of this organisation dislike its title being translated into English.

3 Divided responses to these events were evident amongst Fiji's powerful Christian leaders, and particularly within the Methodist Church throughout 1987 and 1988. For an account of these differences and the tensions brewing within Fiji's mainline churches during this period, see Niukula (1997).

at times arrested for their anti-government activities (Emberson-Bain 1997: 280–86). On the first anniversary of the coup, a significant protest action was planned but had hardly begun before its organisers, a group which became known as 'Democracy 18' and which included activists Jalal, Emberson-Bain, Druavesi, Rokotuivuna and Moore, were detained by police overnight (Ricketts 1997). After a nine-month trial they were found guilty of unlawful assembly but not convicted (Emberson-Bain 1992: 159).

Other women's groups were equally energetic in their support for the actions of the Fiji military and the *Taukei* movement. In particular, the nationalists drew support from the mass organisation for indigenous women, the Soqosoqo Vakamarama (SSVM), and the National Council of Women (NCW) which followed a moderate political path at this time and appeared keen not to jeopardise its relationship with the state through outspoken or critical advocacy.

Conflicting appraisals of the political situation also threatened unity within single organisations. This scenario was particularly apparent within the Fiji YWCA, a body which, as previous chapters have shown, had formerly voiced strong official commitments to democratic rule and multi-racial electoral representation. By contrast, examinations of the organisation's records for this period demonstrate that some YWCA executive members were quick to dissent from this line, despite the fact that affiliation with the World YWCA required national associations to promote and uphold multicultural values (see Chapter 2).

In particular, the YWCA's general secretary, Adi Finau Tabakaucoro, had been a notable public supporter of the *Taukei* movement, defending the protest actions of Fiji nationalists prior to the coup in letters to the print media (*Fiji Times* 29 April). In the aftermath of these events, she presented the view that democracy was a 'foreign flower' for which Fiji had the 'wrong soil,' a phrase that was to become a catch-cry of the *Taukei* and its sympathisers (*Fiji Times* 28 May 1987). While these comments were made in a personal capacity, YWCA records for the period from May to September 1987 show that Tabakaucoro's association with a publication which ostensibly sought to explain women's responses to the coup but which was written in a tone strongly sympathetic to the indigenous nationalist cause, raised the indignation of a number of YWCA board members, and also the head of the World YWCA's regional office, Salamo Fulivai. The implication that the views expressed within this publication represented those of the organisation as a whole was deemed problematic. While Tabakaucoro acted to reassure the board that any links drawn between the YWCA association and the pro-nationalist publication were purely accidental, the media was not easily convinced on this score and once again showed intense interest in the political divisions emerging within the Fiji YWCA—a situation that was particularly damaging for the YWCA's profile in subsequent years (Fiji YWCA 8 and 10 August 1987, Management Committee Record Books; *Fiji Times* 9 August 1987; Bhagwan Rolls 2002a).

Goodwillie and Kaloumaira noted similar tensions evident within the FWRM membership during this period, arguing that the organisation became 'polarised' along racial lines as its Fijian members struggled to accommodate questions of indigenous political identity with the FWRM's strong commitment towards the promotion of women's rights within a democratic framework. In the short term, these concerns prompted some Fijian members to leave the FWRM. As Goodwillie and Kaloumaira observed, however, this was often only a temporary absence, with some members returning to the organisation in later years (Goodwillie and Kaloumaira 2000: 11).

Quite apart from the political challenges that the coup placed before women's organisations, this was also a period in which local organisations struggled to address, in more practical terms, the urgent and escalating range of economic and social needs borne by women in the post-coup years (see Emberson-Bain 1992; Slatter 1994; Ram 1994; Griffen cited in Dé Ishtar 1994). Emberson-Bain observed that within a post-coup political environment marked by authoritarianism, women's vulnerability was accentuated. Increased levels of violence in Fiji were apparent both in the short term, as a result of waves of race-motivated attacks and, in the longer term, due to a rise in pro-nationalist paramilitary aggression which took the form of vandalism, arson and local abductions (Emberson-Bain 1992: 153; Griffen cited in Dé Ishtar 1994).

A broader culture of political violence and political authoritarianism seemed to compound the risks borne by women in this period. The Crisis Centre observed a six-fold increase in violence and sexual attacks against women by 1989, with the majority of incidents brought to the Centre's attention but not reported to police (Griffen cited in Dé Ishtar 1994). In those cases which were reported to authorities and successfully taken to court in the post-coup context, it was also found that the indigenous practice of *bulubulu* or 'traditional apology' to the victim's family had become increasingly acceptable to Fiji's judiciary as a factor to be taken into account to reduce the severity of sentencing for these crimes (Emberson-Bain 1992: 155).

The unguarded attitudes expressed by the country's self-imposed leaders at this time, seemed to further legitimate the violent treatment of women. Rabuka's widely reported jest that Fijian men use idle hours on Sunday, the 'Christian Sabbath', to kick 'either a football or one's wife around' (*Pacific Islands Monthly* May 1994: 32), evidences the 'proprietorial and contemptuous attitudes towards women' that were commonly held amongst the post-coup political elite (Emberson-Bain 1992: 153–54). Another indication of the regime's extreme gender prejudice was evident when Nationalist sympathiser and parliamentary member Ratu Telemo Ratakele stated that advocates 'who promote legal education and social, economic and political equality for all women, made him feel like raping women' (*Fiji Times* 2 May 1995). Together, these statements demonstrate the depth of chauvinistic thinking amongst the country's political leaders. Beyond their offhand 'normalisation' of gender violence, they also issued sexualised threats against those women who were critical of the systems which upheld patriarchal privilege in their society.

Heightened physical insecurity was not the only thing Fiji's women had to contend with during this period. Intensifying economic pressures were also creating difficulties. Emberson-Bain argued that the predicament of women employed in low-skilled areas such as garment manufacturing,[4] was made even more precarious in this period as the military government developed policy to attract new investment to support a rapidly weakening economy. This included wage deregulation, the creation of tax free zones and restrictions on labour organisation. All of these measures had detrimental economic impacts for low-skilled female workers (Emberson-Bain 1992; Ram 1994). A raft of austerity measures enacted by the government in order to qualify for International Monetary Fund (IMF) and World Bank assistance, only added to this economic pain (Emberson-Bain 1992; see also Slatter 1994; Ram 1994; Singh 1994). These included currency devaluations, the imposition of a value added tax, and a significant reduction in state welfare budgets.[5] During the same period, government military spending doubled.

Within the newly created Ministry of Women, established by the military government in 1987, there appears to have been little willingness to confront or alleviate the types of burdens being placed upon Fiji's women. Creation of this office as part of a broader-based Ministry of Women, Culture and Social Welfare may, on the surface, have appeared as an acquiescence to the long struggle waged by a number of women's groups, and in particular the Fiji NCW, for the creation of women's machinery at the state level. Government detractors, on the other hand, saw this move as a calculated attempt by the military government to portray itself as progressive and forward looking. They were particularly unhappy when the controversial YWCA and pro-*Taukei* figure, Tabakaucoro, was appointed as head of this Ministerial office (Emberson-Bain 1992; Houng Lee 2002).

---

4   Workers within Fiji's garment industry at this time typically had little union representation, and generally relied on employees working long hours for low wages (see Emberson-Bain 1992; Ram 1994).

5   Economic policies enacted by the government in the post-coup years included two currency devaluations that saw the Fiji dollar lose 33 per cent of its value and the introduction, in 1993, of a ten per cent value added tax which meant that those whose wage earnings were previously under the tax-free threshold (65 per cent of all wage earners) were now also contributing to the state's coffers (Ram 1994: 243).

The Ministry of Women generally appeared reluctant to tackle the issue of women's economic disadvantage and, with an operating budget that was largely taken up with salaries and administration costs, was unable to offer much in the way of concrete programs of assistance (Emberson-Bain 1992). In general terms, the government had significantly reduced its commitment to welfare funding and this prompted many women to turn to local women's organisations as alternative sources of welfare support. As such, the practical demands placed upon local women's groups such as the FWCC, the FWRM and trade union servicing sectors with high numbers of women employees were considerable. In response, the Crisis Centre began to run programs assisting families with school fee payments and also coordinated a 'back to school scheme' which recycled school shoes, books and uniforms between families (Griffen cited in Dé Ishtar 1994; Emberson-Bain 1992: 150).

In addition to these relief-oriented activities, organisations such as the FWRM, in close cooperation with the unions, began to lobby the state to provide greater protection for women workers employed in low-wage industries such as garment manufacturing or domestic work. The government made some legislative changes in these areas, for example ensuring the 'far from adequate' minimum starting wage for garment workers at 65 cents per hour (FWRM 2000b). In general terms, however, the establishment of these awards was by no means an assurance that they would be respected by employers or enforced by state representatives (Emberson-Bain 1992: 153).

With the resumption of parliamentary democracy in 1992, albeit within a constitutional framework which concretised principles of indigenous paramountcy, the FWRM began to extend the focus of its activities, lobbying the state to take a greater role in the regulation of discriminatory practices on a variety of fronts. A significant part of this campaign was focused upon government recognition of the United Nations women's convention or CEDAW (Convention for the Elimination of Discrimination Against Women). The FWRM acted as a secretariat for the local CEDAW committee which was comprised of a number of other Suva-based women's organisations. After a series of meetings between government representatives and the committee, and a two-day convention in April 1995, Fiji acceded to CEDAW in August of the same year, only a few days prior to its participation at the UN Fourth World Conference for Women held in Beijing. While this move was generally welcomed by the local community of women activists, and reported by the local media as 'an indication of Fiji's firm commitment to equality of rights and respect of human dignity' (*Daily Post* 14 August 1995), it was also felt that the timing of this event was designed to provide the Fiji government with increased political credibility at the international level (Bhagwan Rolls 2002a; Vere 2002a). Of particular concern for organisations such as the Crisis Centre and the FWRM, however, were the reservations noted by Fiji on articles 5(a) and 9 of the convention; articles which oblige states to eliminate customary practices that are prejudicial towards women and also require men and women to be granted equal citizenship rights (FWCC 1995). Such reservations reflected post-coup sensitivity to questions about the discriminatory aspects of custom, citizenship and land-rights entitlements. The nationalist government's accession to CEDAW with these reservations was clearly a political strategy which aimed to appease gender activists while also quelling *Taukei* fears that this step would lead to cultural sabotage or the subversion of indigenous paramountcy.

In 1993, Peni Moore, a Fiji citizen of European origin, who had been formerly employed as a coordinator of the FWRM, formed a new women's organisation in Suva. This move was motivated in part by Moore's dissatisfaction with the state-focused legalistic advocacy strategies being employed by the FWRM, which she felt were failing to make an impact for the substantial numbers of women in need at the grassroots level. Moore's decision also came about in response to the increasing opposition she felt from some members within the FWRM who argued that having a white woman at the helm of the organisation was becoming a political liability (Moore 2002b). Convinced that she was well-positioned to make a valid contribution towards the advancement of Fiji's women, but disappointed that her ethnicity was becoming a point of contention, Moore decided to leave the FWRM in March 1993. In November of the same year, she registered Women's Action for Change (WAC) as a charitable organisation. In forming this new organisation, Moore was particularly interested in investigating how community theatre might be used as a tool of education to 'empower and assist women' (WAC 1999).

The primary aim of WAC's activities during this period was to develop 'alternative media' such as drama, song, dance or story-telling as vehicles for advocacy in political contexts where there were often strong levels of resistance to advocacy messages which were felt to challenge traditional or cultural values (WAC 1999). The strategies employed by WAC aimed to soften the delivery of these messages by building upon local religious, cultural and social reference points while also creating a more empathetic response amongst grassroots communities towards those who suffer forms of discrimination. In later years, WAC became adept in a variety of community theatre techniques, but remained committed to the idea of developing alternative advocacy methodologies that might have a strong impact at the grassroots level.

The emergence of WAC demonstrated a new direction in women's organising in Fiji, encouraged by the political events taking place at the beginning of this decade. The advocacy methodology developed by this group was an attempt to develop a more creative and covert style of operation within a relatively restrictive political climate. This shift is understandable given the prevailing political conditions which shaped organisations' understandings of what was 'permissible' in these years. For example, women's organisations were clearly well aware of the significant level of material disadvantage being borne by women in Fiji. Yet, they also demonstrated a general reluctance to be overly critical of the state. The punitive nature in which political power was being exercised was coupled with a potent and chauvinistic indigenous nationalism. In this environment, advocacy to advance the status of women was easily dismissed as a seditious attempt to sabotage Fiji's national interests. This severely constrained the political space available to women's organisations.

For example, campaigns to alleviate the economic predicament for women that were articulated in legalistic form and focused upon wage regulation, achieved a limited success. Such strategies were clearly more acceptable to government authorities and less likely to meet with hostility than strike action or public protest activity, as the Fiji Nursing Association had found to its detriment when it chose to challenge the government through a prolonged strike action in 1990 (Leckie 1992). Certainly the post-coup regime's decision to create a state-based machinery for women seemed hopeful, yet the general abrogation of institutional responsibility for the disadvantaged status of women in the post-coup political climate was also disappointing (see Slatter 1994; Singh 1994). Ultimately, this meant that women's organisations were forced to work creatively and from their own limited resources to provide practical assistance where they could. And within WAC, alienation from the state was more pronounced as Moore began to develop advocacy strategies which aimed to bypass the state completely and promote the rights of women in ways that might encourage grassroots social change. This conviction would see WAC's activity branch out in a number of different directions in later years.

Regional developments

Establishing new networks

While developments occurring within Fiji's national political realm made it difficult for women's organisations to legitimate their agendas locally, a developing focus upon regional engagement within organisations such as the FWCC and the FWRM helped raise the profile of these groups beyond Fiji's borders. In particular, these groups worked to build upon the regional contacts established between women's groups in earlier periods by organising a series of regional conferences and workshops to focus upon single issues which were felt to be contributing to gender inequality in ways that were common across the region.

The first of these events occurred in 1992, when the FWCC staged a regional meeting on violence against women. In part, this initiative was a response to requests from women activists throughout the region for literature and training materials on gender violence (S. Ali 2002). Through these requests, the FWCC became aware of an area in which it could potentially expand its operations.[6] The 1992 meeting provided an important opportunity for the FWCC to develop a region-wide network of activists who were focused upon gender violence issues, and to also gain some idea of how they might develop a broader regional advocacy and training program to confront this issue (S. Ali 2002).

In the same year, a regional meeting staged by the Development Alternatives with Women for a New Era (DAWN) network in Suva, brought together a number of activists and academics to examine the trajectory of political and economic development in the region. Participants included Emberson-Bain, Vanessa Griffen, and Claire Slatter from Fiji. Together, these women delivered a critically informed appraisal of aid practices, development projects and governance in the region. They also argued for more accountability in Pacific Island politics, greater grassroots participation in decision-making and the creation of alternative models of development that extended the focus from economic growth to economic and environmental sustainability (see Emberson-Bain 1994). Many of the presentations at this conference were highly critical of the aid and development agencies engaged in the Pacific Islands, and also drew attention to compliant behaviour of local governments in accepting restrictive and harmful development aid conditionalities (Slatter 1994; Singh 1994). Yet, such provocative readings of the region's political economy appear not to have had a significant influence upon the activity of other women's organisations engaged at the regional level in later years.

The legalistic focus of regional activities undertaken by the FWRM in this period provides further evidence of a predominating issue-specific approach to gender advocacy. In 1994, the FWRM conducted a regional seminar on Women and the Law in the Pacific, in association with the International Commission of Jurists. This conference brought together forty women lawyers and activists to examine how the law could be used as a tool for women's empowerment. The FWRM's legal literacy programs conducted in Fiji were discussed as possible models that could be applied in other Pacific Island contexts. In the same year, the FWRM, together with the Fiji NCW, staged a roundtable for women politicians and activists from across the region to discuss the issues that prevented women's participation in electoral politics and how they might be circumvented. A

---

6 The Centre's newly found international benefactors also encouraged this regional concentration. In 1990, the Crisis Centre's regional partner, Community Aid Abroad, negotiated a four-year grant for the Centre from AIDAB (FWCC 1998a). While this money provided the Centre with its first core-funding, it was allocated through AIDAB's regional funding window and required the Crisis Centre to develop a regional focus in its work, in addition to its Fiji-based operations.

Women In Politics (WIP) project was established in the wake of this meeting which, in later years, would become an important focus for the Pacific Office of the United Nations Development Fund for Women (UNIFEM). In 1995, the FWRM also hosted a regional forum on Women, Law and Development which focused on the subject of legal literacy and the regional promotion of CEDAW. Here, FWRM representatives discussed their campaign experiences on CEDAW and advised women's organisations from across the region on how to promote this international instrument in their own countries.

The strong emphasis upon state-based reform in the areas of political representation and law reflected the primary focus of the FWRM's activity at the local level. Nonetheless, the tone of deliberations taking place at these events suggests a far more positive assessment of women's ability to have their concerns recognised at the state level, both within local parliaments and the law, than the more critical appraisals of this terrain that had been evident in the DAWN-sponsored regional meeting. Such differences illustrate the distinct nature of the methodologies employed by each of these networks as they identified various aspects of gender disadvantage, and the limited extent to which cross-cutting perspectives were identified or a cross-fertilisation of ideas took place. The issues raised by the DAWN network reflected concerns that were a strong focus of women's advocacy in former years and tended to place the question of local disadvantage in an international perspective. By contrast, organisations such as the FWCC or the FWRM appear not to have given prolonged consideration to these questions or how they might also be relevant to their own more specific work aiming to promote the institutional visibility of women in law or politics.

Regional preparations for Beijing 1995

In addition to the growing number of regional events coordinated by women's organisations from Fiji, the South Pacific Commission (SPC) continued to play an important role in the coordination of triennial regional conferences for women during these years. In the lead up to the UN's Fourth World Conference on Women, to be held in Beijing in 1995, a greater sense of energy became apparent in these deliberations as government and non-government representatives worked towards the production of a Pacific Platform for Action (PPA) for women's advancement. It was hoped that the creation of a Pacific document would increase the profile of Pacific Island women and their capacity to inform global debate in Beijing (Fairbairn-Dunlop 2005). This was a need identified by the region's government and non-government regional representatives who lamented the poor visibility of Pacific delegations at the previous UN Women's conferences (see Chapters 1 and 2; Fairbairn-Dunlop 2000: 64).

In early 1994, the Pacific Women's Resource Bureau (PWRB) encouraged member states of the SPC to conduct local research on the status of women; research which addressed areas of concern identified in the Nairobi Forward Looking Strategies (FLS) but which also noted the types of challenges that might be unique to the Pacific context. These reports were then sent to the PWRB and reviewed by a regional development specialist, Peggy Fairbairn-Dunlop, in order to prepare a Draft Plan of Action. Two key meetings were held in May 1994 to oversee this process. The Sixth Regional Conference of Pacific Women staged by the SPC in Noumea (2–4 May), brought together over 200 government delegates and NGO observers from the region. At this meeting, government representatives worked on the draft document and formulated a regional declaration which became the preamble to the Pacific Plan of Action (SPC 1994a). At the follow-up SPC-convened ministerial level meeting, held a few days later, the PPA was delivered to, and accepted by, the region's state representatives (SPC 1994b).

Fairbairn-Dunlop argued that the collaborative effort that went into this document reflected women's growing regional sophistication and their ability to 'look beyond their own immediate concerns' and accept 'different viewpoints' (Fairbairn-Dunlop 2000: 65). With the PPA in hand, and these new skills in place, it was anticipated that regional representatives would be well-placed to make themselves heard at the final pre-Beijing consultation for the Asia Pacific region, staged by the United Nations Economic and Social Council for Asia Pacific (ESCAP) in Jakarta in 1994. While Fairbairn-Dunlop acknowledged that not all the concerns raised in the PPA were recognised in the final Jakarta Declaration, on the whole, she judged the exercise to have been successful. She was also confident that the document would provide an important list of considerations to be recognised in future 'Pacific development interventions' (Fairbairn-Dunlop 2000: 66).[7]

Nonetheless, comparisons made between this document and the regional NGO Programme of Action, formulated during consultations staged by the ESCAP in Manila (November 1993) and Suva (February 1994) in preparation for Beijing, give a particularly powerful indication of the extent to which the broader political agendas of governing regimes in the Pacific Islands region also informed the perspective of women's subordination evident in the official SPC version of the PPA (UNESCAP 1994). This fact, although not acknowledged by Fairbairn-Dunlop, is perhaps not surprising given the SPC mandate which bound its women's office, the PWRB, to work principally with Pacific Island governments

---

7   Further refinements to this Pacific Plan of Action were made in the final twelve months before the Beijing conference, during four sub-regional intergovernmental caucuses which were convened by the SPC to further consider the Plan's provisions and recommendations. Three of these meetings were organised according to geographic location, with sub-regional caucuses formed in the Melanesian, Micronesian and Polynesian regions of the Pacific Islands. The fourth sub-regional caucus brought together representatives from the French Pacific—New Caledonia, French Polynesia, Wallis and Futuna.

rather than the region's women advocates (see Chapter 2). The need to appease Pacific state representatives' sensibilities seems to have had a profound influence on the final shape of the PPA.

The distance between government and non-government perspectives on women's disadvantage was perhaps nowhere more evident than in the Regional and Global Framework section of the official PPA which suggested that the introduction of 'democratic forms of government' has placed 'serious strains on the traditional ways' of Pacific Islands communities (SPC 1995). While this was a position that corresponded to the perspective on democracy being endorsed by the incumbent nationalist political elite in Fiji during this period, fears about the appropriateness of democracy in Pacific Island contexts were nowhere to be found in the NGO Plan of Action.

Similar contrasts were also evident in the corresponding sections relating to women's economic status. In the formal PPA, this discussion took place under the heading of women's economic empowerment. Here, a highly entrepreneurial view of women's wage-earning potential was promoted. The report noted the increase of women in formal employment due to the creation of industrial zones and commercial industries in the region. The increasing numbers of women successfully involved in micro-enterprises were also celebrated for the fact that they allowed local women to combine household and familial responsibilities with income-earning activities. The PPA did concede some failings in this area, noting that women's rate of formal labour participation was lower than that of males, and that across the region, women were under-represented in senior business or management positions (SPC 1995: 12–13).

Yet, these issues were addressed from a far more critical perspective in the NGO Programme of Action. In this report, the section entitled 'Economic Empowerment', focused upon the issue of wage equality between men and women. It also discussed the lack of recognition given to the work of Pacific Island women in the domestic sphere and also in areas such as agricultural production where women's contributions continued to be overlooked by economic and development policy-makers. In an additional 'Labour' section which focused more centrally upon the rights of working women, attention was drawn to the challenges facing women who undertook the dual roles of domestic duties and paid employment. Reference was made more clearly to the negative aspects of women's factory work within industrial zones and particularly garment manufacturing and fish-processing, with attention drawn to worker exploitation and sexual harassment, the lack of adequate child-care and maternity leave for working mothers, and the need for more 'responsible fathering' in order that women's wage earning and reproductive roles might be more easily balanced (UNESCAP 1994: 11, 17–18). As we have seen, these were concerns that had been pursued by women's organisations in Fiji, and local feminist academics with close connections to the women's movement (Emberson-Bain 1992; Emberson-Bain and Slatter 1995). They had not met with a sympathetic response from Fiji's government when raised in the domestic public domain however. It is not surprising, therefore, that a more labour-oriented perspective of women's economic status was not present in the official PPA.

While there were some significant differences in the perspectives of women's status evident in each document, the same sectionalised and issue-specific approach to gender disadvantage that had been evident in other aspects of women's regional organising was also obvious here. This issue-specific focus diverted attention away from the identification of cross-cutting issues of a structural nature which contributed to women's disadvantage in a more general sense. As such, the more internationalised perspectives of women's economic disadvantage that called attention to the activity of international monetary institutions or the impact of international aid conditionalities were absent. This suggests, once again, that while regional networks were strengthened in these years, regional dialogue on questions of gender inequality tended to be more cloistered. Action on issues such as global economic equality or post-colonial political empowerment, were clearly a far less common advocacy focus for Pacific women than they had been in the past.

International developments

During the early 1990s, the United Nations sponsored a series of international conferences focusing upon specific areas of international policy-making. These included the World Summit for Children (1990), the Earth Summit (1992) and the World Conference on Population and Development (Cairo 1994). While women's organisations were generally well represented at all these events, their participation at the World Conference on Human Rights in Vienna 1993 is generally celebrated in feminist academic literature as being of particular significance. Their use of this occasion to successfully promote the issue of violence against women as a violation of women's human rights, a campaign spearheaded by US-based activist Charlotte Bunch and her Center for Women's Global Leadership (CWGL) at Rutgers University, is argued to have been instrumental in gaining broad legitimacy for women's rights to be recognised as human rights (Joachim 1999, 2003; Keck and Sikkink 1998). This campaign sought to widen what feminists had often viewed as the 'gender myopia' evident in human rights law which failed to recognise 'oppressive practices against women as human rights violations' (O'Hare 1999: 364).[8] In Vienna, networks

---

8   In so doing, the traditional western privileging of civil and political rights over social and economic rights was challenged. In defence of the claim that the human rights framework needed to be broadened, Bunch argued that 'much of the abuse against women is part of a larger socio-economic web that entraps women,

of women activists successfully campaigned for violence against women to be recognised as a human rights concern and an issue that states should be internationally obligated to combat (Keck and Sikkink 1998; Joachim 1999: 2003). Further international activity on this issue saw the UN General Assembly adopt a draft declaration on the Elimination of Violence Against Women in December 1993, which again recognised these principles. This session also saw the nomination of a special rapporteur appointed to investigate violence against women and its causes.

Keck and Sikkink argue that these developments 'increased the synergy of diverse national and international efforts on violence against women' (1998: 187). Bunch's activities, both as the head of the CWGL, and as an international advocate for women, had a substantial impact upon the local work of the FWCC. In the same year that these developments occurred internationally, the Crisis Centre staged its first public march protesting against violence against women, and used this occasion to reproduce the 'women's rights as human rights' message that had been endorsed in Vienna (S. Ali 2002). In later years, FWCC coordinator Shamima Ali undertook training with the CWGL in public advocacy around issues related to gender violence. In particular her training centred on ways to promote the 16 Days of Activism against Gender Violence (S. Ali 2002). Commencing on 25 November (International Day Against Violence Against Women) and concluding on 10 December (International Human Rights Day), this event, established by the CWGL and staged by women's organisations around the world since 1991, draws attention to the links between violence against women and human rights. In Fiji, the early Crisis Centre '16 Days' campaigns included radio programs, street theatre and public discussions on the issue of violence against women (Keck and Sikkink 1998: 185). Ali described the advocacy methods she had learnt at the CWGL, and particularly the Centre's focus upon human rights, as highly influential and 'important for what we do here' (S. Ali 2002).

The UN's Fourth World Conference on Women in Beijing 1995 provided further international endorsement of human rights perspectives on gender disadvantage. The fact that the final intergovernmental conference document, the Global Platform for Action (GPA), 'subsumes feminist goals under an umbrella of human rights' and applied this perspective to a wide variety of issues apart from violence against women, such as health, sexuality and reproductive rights, was viewed as an indicator both of the success of this new strategy, and of the political agency of the women's organisations that had worked transnationally to promote this perspective of gender disadvantage (Pietilä and Vickers 1996;

---

making them vulnerable to abuses which cannot be delineated as exclusively political or solely caused by states' (Bunch 1990: 488). Bunch's challenge to international policy makers to give recognition to women's rights as human rights struck a chord with many women's groups across the globe (Joachim 1999).

Keck and Sikkink 1998; West 1999; Joachim 1999, 2003; Jaquette 2003). These deliberations did not take place without serious resistance from some delegations who felt the focus on human rights challenged religious values and promoted an 'excessive individualism' (West 1999: 189).[9] Yet the fact that consensus was achieved on the GPA was generally hailed as a momentous achievement for women. As the intergovernmental meeting was brought to a close, UN Conference Secretary General Gertrude Mongella was moved to claim that the delegates present had 'significantly expanded the horizons of previous conferences' (Pietilä and Vickers 1996: vii).

Even so, the GPA's incorporation of a human rights framework generally tended to 'obscure' the connections between 'human rights abuses' and 'current economic structures', particularly in relation to the issue of violence against women (Guest 1997: 112; Bishop 1997: 11).[10] Indeed, while the GPA noted the fact that women around the world were enduring the negative consequences of structural adjustment policies and deregulated markets, imposed as a conditionality of multilateral lending institutions, it also described structural adjustment programs as 'beneficial in the long term' and noted the importance of 'trade liberalisation' and 'open, dynamic markets' (UN Commission on the Status of Women 1995: para. 18, para. 16). This faith in the power of markets to lift women out of poverty linked empowerment with cash income but simultaneously overlooked the exploitative nature of women's employment in many developing countries (Bulbeck 1998: 176–79).[11] As one observer put it, the problem of women living in poverty was conceptualised within the GPA as 'liberal capitalism's bête noir … nothing that a bit of targeted credit, business training and entrepreneurialship won't cure' (Guest 1997: 112).

Reports from the NGO Forum at Beijing, on the other hand, indicated that issues related to poverty and women's economic deprivation were at the forefront of discussion for delegates from both North and South. Bulbeck (1998: 171) notes that of the 3,000 workshops convened during this event, 500 confronted aspects of poverty and their effects upon women. The critique of economic globalisation became something of a 'mantra' within the forum (Guest 1997: 110), emerging as 'the single most critical issue' overall (Agarwal 1996: 28). However, as Pacific Island women noted, the sheer number and diversity of presentations made at

---

9 As West (1999: 189) notes, representatives from the Vatican, countries with a majority Catholic population, states headed by Muslim fundamentalist governments, and conservative Christian lobbies within the US, all objected to the language used in many sections of the Platform for Action and in the preparatory conferences leading up to the 1995 Beijing conference.

10 This situation stems, in part, from the fact that sections of the platform devoted to economic issues and poverty elimination were agreed upon in the New York preparatory conference. This left little bracketed language in this area of the document to be considered in Beijing (Bishop 1997).

11 This was particularly so in the Southeast Asian region where economic development in countries such as Taiwan, Korea, Hong Kong and Singapore was celebrated as the 'Asian miracle' but overlooked the fact that this miracle relied upon the low-wage labour of women (Bulbeck 1998: 176–79).

the Forum, which attracted over 50,000 participants, made it difficult to come to terms with the ways in which perspectives on disadvantage raised in one session might have implications for women in other areas (FWRM 1995).

For some Pacific women attending the Beijing Forum, the economic aspects of gender disadvantage were an over-arching consideration. This was particularly true for the DAWN Pacific network members. However, this question was by no means the primary focus of Pacific women's activity at the 1995 conference which represented a diverse array of interests.

Over two hundred Pacific women participated at the Beijing Forum with over twenty participants present from Fiji alone (Rokotuivuna 2002a). Having learnt from previous international conferences, these women were keen to make their presence felt. Indeed, this was one of the key aims of the Beneath Paradise project, which involved a number of regional women activists and whose sub-theme was 'See Us, Hear Us, Beijing'.

This project, funded by the IWDA, had brought together fifteen groups across the Pacific, including the FWCC, and aimed to document and 'faithfully' represent the 'first hand statements, stories and declarations of Pacific Women' (Beneath Paradise 1994). The project focused upon themes such as traditional and subsistence lifestyles, cultural events and practices, violence against women, education, political participation and health (Beneath Paradise 1994). In preparation for Beijing, the IWDA had funded the publication of a book edited by Emberson-Bain which brought together a number of the papers presented to the Pacific regional meeting of DAWN in 1992, and which was available from the Beneath Paradise booth at the Forum. Other perspectives on the status of women in the region were presented in a more immediate and interactive form. These included dance and theatre presentations, discussion on the work done by women's organisations, participation in networking events and seminars, and meetings coordinated with regional aid partners and state representatives (Beneath Paradise 1995).[12]

Pacific women's enthusiastic participation at Beijing was disrupted by the French government's untimely announcement of its decision to resume its nuclear testing program at Muroroa Atoll in French Polynesia. This development

---

12   While IWDA provided support, training and funding for the project, the focus was upon building the capacity of local organisations to work on their own documentation projects in a way which would allow 'grassroots women' and organisations working with women to 'speak for themselves to an international audience' (Beneath Paradise 1994). Annelise Riles' discussion of this project suggests that the 'Australian design consultants' brought in to provide training for local participants to this project compromised its authenticity (2001: 131, 207). While she claims this to have been a point of contention amongst local project members, my discussions with the Fiji-based women who took part in this project revealed no such misgivings. The collaboration between the IWDA and local organisations was said to have been highly beneficial, and in Fiji, formed the basis of an ongoing relationship between the FWCC and the IWDA that was much valued (S. Ali 2002; Costello-Olsen 2002).

was met with 'anger and sadness' by Pacific participants in Beijing (Beneath Paradise 1995). As it had in the past, this issue once again focused attention upon the twin issues of the Pacific nuclear presence and decolonisation in the region. And, working as a regional group, Pacific Island women used what means they could to draw attention to the nuclear testing issue—a task aided by the presence of members of another IWDA-funded project, *Omomo Melen*, which specifically focused upon bringing international attention to questions of Pacific decolonisation through participation at Beijing.

This project was headed by Susanna Ounei, a prominent Kanak activist from New Caledonia and member of the Pacific Concerns Resource Centre.[13] It brought together representatives from East Timor, New Caledonia, West Papua, Tahiti and the indigenous communities of Australia and New Zealand. In 1995, Ounei represented the *Omomo Melen* Project at the final global preparatory conference for the Beijing conference which took place in the UN New York Headquarters. Here, she successfully argued that consideration of the plight of women in colonised territories should be included in the draft GPA (Riles 2001: 177). The regional preparations undertaken by the *Omomo Melen* network ensured that this group of Pacific women was well-prepared to lead regional activity on the nuclear testing issue in Beijing and employed a clearly defined conceptual framework which focused upon colonialism and indigenous rights to self-determination. Ounei spoke at a Forum plenary session entitled 'Obstacles to Peace and Human Security' and also participated in a global tribunal staged by the Asian Women's Human Rights Council (Beneath Paradise 1995).[14]

On the other hand, domestic political developments in Fiji meant that the country's official delegation to Beijing articulated a soft line on nuclear testing issues within the intergovernmental conference, despite the fact that the newly appointed Minister for Women, former YWCA President Taufa Vakatale, had been involved in anti-nuclear protests after the French announced their plans to resume testing.[15] Vakatale had, in fact, been relieved of her ministerial post for these actions. This was hardly surprising. Official relations between France and Fiji had become much closer in these years, particularly after a bilateral aid arrangement which saw the French government inject over FJ$10 million

---

13 This is a regional organisation that had grown out of the earlier Nuclear Free and Independent Pacific Movement.

14 Riles' account of the impact of the *Omomo Melen* Project focuses on the difficulties encountered by Pacific Island women during their participation in Beijing and discusses only one, apparently poorly attended press conference in which project participants attempted to draw attention to their particular cause. Riles' account does not mention the fact that Ounei represented *Omomo Melen* at these more significant Forum events and the attention accorded her presentations as the nuclear testing issue took on greater urgency (see Riles 2001: 177–78).

15 While some local women activists such as Rokotuivuna had been disappointed with Vakatale's political involvement with the post-coup regime, they welcomed her support on this particular issue, and recognised the courage of a political stance which contravened official government policy on this question (Rokotuivuna 2002b).

into Fiji's national coffers (Emberson-Bain 1997). This aid was seen to provide a vital boost to a stagnating post-coup economy. It also ensured Fiji's relatively compliant official response to Jacques Chirac's renewed nuclear ambitions in the Pacific.[16] For these reasons Fiji's government representatives in Beijing delivered a conservatively focused country paper to the intergovernmental conference which avoided any mention of the regional nuclear testing issue, even though this would become a pointed advocacy focus for Pacific delegates to the NGO Forum in the final days of the meeting.[17]

Such developments are indicative, once again, of the shifts which had occurred within the domestic political setting, both in the areas of foreign policy and Fiji's economic development. Official silence on the nuclear testing issue clearly contrasts with the Fiji government's earlier pursuit of this issue in the immediate post-independence context. The government's punitive response to Vakatale's involvement in anti-nuclear protests was also a clear demonstration of a shift in attitude amongst the dominant political class. At the same time, the framework employed to discuss women's economic status was clearly more geared towards an entrepreneurial perspective of economic empowerment. Thus, the questions of wage equality or wage justice that had been prominent features of local academic research into women's employment at this time were not apparent in government statements.

As we have seen, within the domestic post-coup political climate, these questions were not a political priority for the local political elite which was looking to promote Fiji's economic credentials internationally in ways that emphasised a liberal approach to wage and industry regulation. This meant that all civil society actors, including women's groups aiming to take up these types of issues at the local, regional or international level during this period, were operating within a far more constrained political environment than had been evident in the past.

At the domestic level, the rise of ethno-nationalism and political authoritarianism, together with the absence of constitutional democracy for over five years, inclined some women's groups to alter their advocacy strategies towards a more cautious style of public engagement or to experiment with new advocacy methodologies. Similarly, within an international political environment shaped by an unswerving faith in neoliberal approaches to development, gender

---

16 French President François Mitterrand had announced a moratorium on nuclear testing in the Pacific region in April 1992.

17 On the other hand, in response to Australian calls that Beijing be made a conference of commitments, the Fiji paper stated that the government would increase support for the financing of women's small enterprise ventures, aim to increase the participation of women on the boards of business and in local councils to 50 per cent, aim to increase the representation of women in all levels of government also by 50 per cent, take measures to eliminate violence against women, sexual harassment and child abuse, and eliminate gender discrimination in law (Beneath Paradise 1995).

activists were clearly less inclined to frame their advocacy in terms which emphasised how global political or economic structures were contributing to local disempowerment and disadvantage. Certainly, some discussion of these questions was apparent within networks such as the DAWN Pacific or *Omomo Melen*, yet this did not have the same far-reaching impact that was apparent in the past.

In the following section, I turn my attention more explicitly to the factors which shaped women activists' negotiations of collectivity, progressive ideas and transnationalism during this period. I do this by again emphasising the 'situated experience' of the women in question and their own appraisals of the political contingencies that shaped their advocacy in these years.

Collectivity

Developments taking place within the terrain of women's organising in the period 1985–1995 would, on the surface, appear to indicate that local and regional networks were flourishing. The creation of two new nationally focused women's groups, the FWRM and WAC, and the establishment of a number of regional networks which were focused upon specific issues of gender disadvantage seem to support this idea. As we have seen, however, communal politics were also amplified in this period within Fiji. This dramatically constrained the political space available to those civil society actors who aimed to resist government authoritarianism and ethno-nationalist intolerance. And these conditions had important implications for the ways in which collectivity was negotiated by women's organisations.

For example, in the immediate post-coup context, the YWCA and the FWRM had both issued strongly worded statements in support of a return to democracy. In the longer term, however, these actions contributed to internal divisions and, in some cases, loss of membership, as indigenous members struggled to reconcile loyalties to their communities with the political stance adopted by the organisation. The difficulties experienced by the FWRM in this respect were generally played out in private, and eventually saw Fijian members who had left the organisation voluntarily return in later years (Goodwillie and Kaloumaira 2000). The post-coup tensions within the YWCA were a much more public affair, however, and ultimately did long-term damage to the organisation. While the fortunes of the YWCA had been declining for several years, the organisation struggled to recover from its coup-related divisions (Lechte 2005; Goodwillie 2005; Slatter 2002). Ultimately, membership waned as the YWCA began to look more politically conservative, and young women's interest in the work of newer women's organisations such as the FWCC and the FWRM began to expand (Rokotuivuna 2002b; Vakatale 2002).

Moore's recollections of her experiences as the FWRM coordinator are also telling and suggest that questions around ethnicity were not always resolved amicably within the newer women's organisations. Moore's decision to depart from the FWRM was motivated, in part, by the fact that she felt continually subjected to the questioning of her ethnicity (Moore 2002b).[18] In the longer term, Moore found the situation at the FWRM untenable and began to explore the possibility of establishing a new women's group with a more creative style of advocacy which might in some ways diffuse the focus upon race that had been problematic for her at the FWRM.

However, Moore's recollections suggest that it was not only communal politics which created tensions within the sphere of women's organising on the domestic stage. Her descriptions of the early years of WAC operations suggest that the competitive environment between women's organisations that was described in the previous chapter had not abated and, if anything, had become more pronounced as groups became aware of the need to secure local and international institutional recognition for their work. Moore argued that pre-existing women's organisations demonstrated a degree of wariness towards her new organisation, with some expressing concerns that WAC would duplicate other organisations' work. A more collaborative environment did evolve in later periods, with the FWCC employing WAC to assist in its anti-violence campaigns. Nonetheless, the overall lack of enthusiasm which greeted the appearance of a new organisation, also working on women's issues, continued to make the early years of WAC's operations difficult, despite the fact that this group was developing a strong grassroots base of support for its operations (Moore 2002b).

This guarded response to the formulation of new women's organisations is perhaps more understandable if we consider the limited civil society space available to women's organisations struggling for recognition in the post-coup political environment. As we have seen, Fiji's government was generally unresponsive, and sometimes openly hostile, to the demands made by women's groups. In the short-term, it was only willing to make concessions to the indigenous women's group SSVM, or the politically moderate NCW. In later years, it is clear that the FWRM and the FWCC did establish more cordial relationships with the government, particularly with Vakatale at the head of the women's ministry. Yet, within a political climate where all political issues were interpreted through an ethno-nationalist lens, any territory gained by local women's groups was hard-won, guarded defensively and not willingly conceded to newcomers.

---

18   Moore acknowledged the limitations she faced in this role as a white woman and made reference to the strong level of resentment she faced from indigenous political leaders such as Tabakaucoro, when she called for an examination of the uses of *bulubulu* (traditional apology) in rape trials. This was clearly a difficult topic to raise within a political culture where any questioning of indigenous tradition could easily be framed as an attack upon indigenous cultural identity and an attempt to dissolve traditional values (Moore 2002b). On the other hand, Moore argued that 'being white' gave her advantages as a women's activist in the post-coup era. She felt this allowed her to take a provocative stand in the public domain in ways that might not always have been possible for women from other ethnic backgrounds (Moore 2002b).

At the same time, funding issues were also a concern for all local women's organisations and contributed to an increased level of competitiveness between groups (Lechte 2005). During this period, development agencies encouraged the participation of civil society actors in development programs. In particular, bilateral and multilateral development agencies began to boost funding for women's groups as a result of increasing awareness that institutional development initiatives for women were, in fact, not meeting their stated goals effectively (see Chapter 2). Moreover, at this time, development agencies with connections to Fiji found engaging with civil society groups preferable to funding agencies of an authoritarian regime with undisguised ethno-nationalist sympathies. Nonetheless, the communal aspect of associational life in Fiji also influenced how donors working with women's organisations negotiated these relationships, for they were careful to avoid accusations of partisanship. For these reasons, donors generally directed their support to issue-focused organisations rather than faith-based or cultural bodies whose affiliations to Fiji's various ethnic communities were more clearly identifiable.[19]

A wariness of civil society communalism in Fiji meant that organisations such as the FWCC and the FWRM were the principal beneficiaries of external institutional assistance (in these years, usually brokered through partner NGOs located in donor countries). But overall, the pool of externally managed funds that might support such groups was limited. The fact that new organisations such as WAC were now also asking to be considered as deserving recipients of overseas assistance only helped to intensify the competitive aspect of inter-organisational relationships in these years.

Progressive ideas

In keeping with a trend that was emerging towards the end of the Decade for Women, a more issue-specific approach to women's advocacy continued to be evident within the sphere of women's organising in Fiji. This approach was viewed as progressive because it allowed women's groups to develop expertise and advocacy methodologies that were particular to their areas of concern. For example, FWRM was principally engaged in state-focused advocacy programs designed to promote the rights of women through the law or through increased parliamentary representation. By contrast, WAC was engaged in advocacy which was disengaged from the state, and aimed to encourage social change at the grassroots level through programs of community theatre. And the DAWN Pacific network, which focused upon the regional impact of neoliberal economic development strategies, presented another, more research-focused, advocacy model.

---

19   The negative aspects of this situation are considered in greater detail in Chapter 5.

On the one hand, this trend towards issue-specific organisations and differing advocacy methodologies had important benefits. It allowed organisations to gain specialist knowledge and professionalise their operations. It also allowed them to create their own particular organisational identity, something that was necessary to avoid the accusation from potential funders of women's groups duplicating each others' work (see previous section). This increased specialisation also appealed to the media[20] and donor agencies who increasingly sought out engagement with individuals or groups who might claim 'on the ground' expertise.

On the other hand, the issue-specific focus also encouraged a cloistered style of dialogue on women's issues which worked against local organisations and regional networks identifying cross-cutting issues that compounded women's subordination. This was an important development which contrasted with the way women's organisations had functioned in earlier decades.

This shift towards an issue-specific emphasis is certainly evident in the activities undertaken by women's organisations operating at the domestic level in Fiji. It is also starkly apparent in the text of the PPA and the corresponding regional NGO Programme of Action, formulated prior to the participation of Pacific women at the 1995 UN World Conference for Women in Beijing. Those who described the PPA, in particular, as a 'manifesto' for Pacific women (Fairbairn-Dunlop 2000), clearly saw this document as representing a significant institutional outcome and a clear testimony to the long struggle women had waged for regional recognition since the days of the protest outside the SPC meeting in Port Moresby in 1980. Yet, such celebration tended to ignore the extent to which this document was predominantly focused upon government perspectives of gender disadvantage and, hence, provided a relatively moderate analysis of the factors contributing to women's subordination across the region. This is not surprising, given the role that the SPC and the PWRB had played in its production; these regional entities were primarily committed to working with Pacific Island governments rather than the region's NGOs.

Nonetheless, the failure to incorporate an analysis of the cross-cutting factors contributing to gender disadvantage in the Pacific becomes more clearly apparent when we consider the remarkably offhand manner in which the issue of women's poverty is treated within both the PPA *and* the NGO regional documents prepared for Beijing. For women's organisations operating in Fiji, and particularly the FWRM and the FWCC, increasing economic disadvantage

---

20   This idea of specialisation is particularly relevant to the media profiles that women's organisations have established in Fiji. The FWCC is routinely cited in media reports of gender violence and sexual abuse. The FWRM is generally the first women's organisation called upon by journalists to comment on broader political developments in the Fiji Islands. By contrast, the WAC's media profile tends to be generated through feature articles which examine its community-theatre programs or projects designed to assist a particular disadvantaged group.

in the post-coup years was a concern which intensified, particularly in the wake of the military government's retreat from involvement in the welfare sector. Local women's groups were under increasing pressure to fill this gap and provide assistance from their own limited resources. The fact that no discussion of poverty or economic hardship borne by women appears in the pages of the NGO Programme of Action, therefore, seems at odds with the practical experience of women's organisations in Fiji in the post-coup years.[21] It also runs counter to the observations made by participants in the DAWN seminar staged in Suva in 1992, where the economic marginalisation of women was described as an increasingly prominent phenomenon across the region (see Emberson-Bain 1994).

As I have shown, women's organisations in Fiji were operating in a highly restrictive political climate in the post-coup years and drawing regional or international attention to the incidence of poverty was not a strategy welcomed by the prevailing political elite. Indeed conduct of this type tended to be viewed as an attempt to sabotage Fiji's international reputation and damage its future potential for economic growth (Slatter November 2001).

The apparent inattention of gender activists to the local and regional incidence of poverty in the ESCAP documents can also be explained by the pervasive nature of the free-market economic ethos both regionally and internationally. Slatter's examinations of Fiji's political economy at this time described the considerable influence of the IMF and World Bank and the extent to which these institutions had successfully encouraged the Fiji government to adopt structural adjustment policies as a means by which to increase Fiji's global economic competitiveness (Slatter 1994). Slatter argued that many Pacific Island governments had succumbed to similar pressures from the Bretton Woods institutions but were generally keen to present these policies to domestic constituents as of 'their own inspiration' (Slatter 1994: 17). Premjeet Singh suggests that such strategies helped to circumscribe the political outlook of local civil society actors and discouraged critical political activity on questions of economic disadvantage (Singh 1994: 57–58).

Domestic, regional and international political contingencies, therefore, meant that women's organisations were disinclined to engage in sustained campaigns on questions of women's material disadvantage. Although the perspectives of regional development outlined during the 1992 DAWN regional conference appear as a noteworthy exception to the rule, in general it can be said that

---

21   In the official PPA, the issue of poverty is raised, although this discussion takes place in a highly abstract form, justified by the fact that poverty 'was not presented as a critical area of concern for the region' (SPC 1995: 26). While it is acknowledged that poverty does exist, and is of particular concern within women-headed households, the chief emphasis is placed upon the incorporation of women into the wage-earning market as a mechanism of poverty alleviation. Ultimately the Platform argues that '[p]ublic policies and private initiatives that address women's skills and potential by providing the necessary resources and opportunities will lead to equitable economic growth' (SPC 1995: 27).

women's organisations tended not to engage in advocacy that criticised the prevailing economic orthodoxies which promoted entrepreneurial models of economic empowerment rather than welfare as the key to alleviating women's economic disadvantage.

If structurally inclined perspectives of gender disadvantage were no longer viewed as progressive, human rights advocacy frameworks were gaining in ascendancy and increasingly seen as providing women's groups with a progressive and politically empowering agenda. This is clearly evident at the international level, where institutional recognition of the human rights dimensions of women's subordination increased dramatically during these years. At the same time, groups such as the FWCC viewed these strategies as particularly important in the local context.

In a local and international political environment which was clearly not conducive to women's groups engaging in a structurally inclined critique of women's subordination, the shift towards human rights can be considered a 'neat fit'. This type of advocacy tended, in practice, to encourage a more localised examination of state capacity to protect women's human rights rather than scrutiny of more contentious internationalised themes such as the gendered impacts of global inequality.[22] It is therefore not surprising that the human rights advocacy focus employed by the FWCC was clearly supported by aid agencies attached to governments with strong interests in the region, such as AIDAB (Australian International Development Assistance Bureau, later AusAID) which, in the 1990s, provided core funding to the FWCC for a four-year period through an NGO partner scheme coordinated by Freedom From Hunger (FWCC 1998b).

The FWCC's good fortune in this regard contrasts significantly with that of *Omomo Melen*, a gender advocacy network whose emphasis upon Pacific colonisation and nuclearisation more closely resembled the style of advocacy employed by women's organisations in previous decades. It was anticipated that in the post-Beijing context, the *Omomo Melen* project would continue to support women activists living in Pacific territories still subject to colonial rule. The project ultimately proved to be short-lived, however, failing to secure continuing financial support as potential donors worried about the political implications of being seen to meddle in the affairs of another country through their support of local independence activists (Riles 2001: 175–76). The Third Worldism of the 1960s and 1970s may have increased the political weight of issues such as indigenous populations' rights to political self-determination, and broadened the local and transnational space in which they could be pursued by civil society actors, but the international political currency of such questions had waned significantly in this later period.

---

22 This view is similar to the critique of human rights advocacy advanced by legal anthropologist Sally Engle Merry (2003a, 2003b).

Transnationalism

In this period, the concept of women's human rights became 'transnationalised' (Merry 2006a: 48) and increasingly important to the terrain of women's advocacy (Ackerly 2001; Joachim 1999, 2003). This occurred largely as a result of sustained and successful NGO-advocacy campaigns which called upon international policy-makers to recognise aspects of women's subordination as violations of women's human rights. These efforts accrued important institutional dividends at the Vienna Human Rights conference in 1993, and the UN World Conference for Women in Beijing in 1995.

This type of advocatory strategy was said to be about much more than a universalist position that reinforced the global cultural hegemony of the west. Increasing numbers of feminist scholars argued that women's rights advocacy could be articulated or 'translated' (Merry 2006a) in ways that accommodated specific reference to locally specific factors—cultural, political or religious. For these reasons, women's human rights advocacy was said to have an important transnational resonance which directly contradicted the allegation that feminists' use of a 'human rights framework' necessarily denigrated the local and the traditional as backward or retrograde (Jolly 1997, 2003, 2005a; Ackerly 2001; Wing 2002; Douglas 2003; see also Chapters 1 and 2).

The human rights advocacy undertaken by women's groups in Fiji during this period had both global and local resonances. Since its formation in 1983, the FWCC had become adept at articulating its opposition to gender violence in ways that accommodated prevailing religious and cultural sensibilities (see Chapter 4). In the post-coup context, these skills were of even greater political significance. Therefore, while the FWCC clearly embraced the internationally endorsed human rights approach to violence against women, it also saw the value of framing this discussion in ways that did not antagonise a political elite highly protective of indigenous cultural values and clearly suspicious of such 'universalised' frameworks. The Crisis Centre's strategies to promote women's human rights were therefore often articulated in a way that emphasised local religious and cultural reference points. Its advocates did this by aligning human rights perspectives of gender subordination with arguments about respect for women and gender reciprocity framed in theological terms. Similarly they also described how customary values encouraged a complementarity of gender roles and did not necessarily sanction discriminatory relations between the sexes, or the blanket acceptance of patriarchal authority (FWCC 1998a; S. Ali 2002).

Yet, when asked more explicitly about this idea of articulation or culturally appropriate advocacy methodologies, I frequently found that my interlocutors had views of these processes which were difficult to reconcile. Figures such as

S. Ali, Rokotuivuna and Gina Houng Lee, former director of the FWRM, all acknowledged that the promotion of 'universal values' was particularly difficult within a political climate shaped by ethno-nationalist sentiment, increasingly audible demands that Fiji declare itself a Christian state, and a wave of political rhetoric which described democracy as a foreign flower (Houng Lee 2002; Rokotuivuna 2002a; S. Ali 2002). A more flexible articulation of human rights claims was therefore recognised to be a critical campaigning strategy for gender advocates at this time. Yet, in the same breath, these figures would often counter this position by also stating their steadfast commitment to universal models. Often, I seemed to be hearing two codes of feminist discourse at the same time; one that was internal to the organisation and its sympathisers and that appeared highly critical of the patriarchal values evident in local religious, political and social life, and one for a broader level of political consumption which was far more moderately framed.

For example, when asked about the need to negotiate religious and cultural sensitivities, Ali argued that contextually appropriate frameworks were 'definitely' crucial to the FWCC's work, but later argued that these were employed 'much against my will' (S. Ali 2002). On the same subject, Rokotuivuna also appeared to have something of a dual position. On the one hand, she argued that cultural sensitivities could be dealt with 'fairly easily' and did not require a sensitive type of negotiation. Then, some minutes later, she also conceded that in certain contexts concessions were important. Describing her dealings with government she argued, 'You don't want to create a situation whereby you're talking to government but they're not there, they're not listening. When I'm talking to government it's within the paradigm that they establish' (Rokotuivuna 2002a).

Similarly, Houng Lee (2002) argued that she personally favoured a 'universal model' for the promotion of human rights, but later also acknowledged that women's groups had to think carefully about how they 'deliver the message'. And another FWRM member voiced similar sentiments. She argued adamantly that human rights were universal, that there was no need for advocacy to be modified and that there were 'no Pacific rules'. Yet only a few minutes later, when discussing a new public campaign she also advised her colleagues to engage someone to find passages from the Bible that supported women's rights, and to locate a sympathetic Methodist church minister who might appear alongside a FWRM staff member for a scheduled television panel interview.

Houng Lee's (2002) stated fear that women's groups could become 'boxed in' if they conceded too much ground to more parochial actors was instructive on this point and perhaps helps explain this tendency towards contending positions on the place of local culture within advocacy, and points to the importance of understanding these processes of articulation in a contingent fashion. It is certainly clear that cultural articulation was strategically important for women's groups operating within a public sphere where communalist values predominated. Nonetheless, activists also voiced strong concern that the normative content of the human rights message could potentially be compromised through these practices. For example, such strategies presented clear contrasts to the ways that earlier YWCA activists had confronted the issue of customary or religious influence. Independence-era gender advocates' activities on issues such as political representation or reproductive rights regularly challenged those aspects of tradition or religion which they argued effaced individual will and capacity for choice (see Chapter 2). While activists in this later, post-coup period, were operating in a much altered political context, there also appears to have been a fear amongst some members of the local gender activist community that conciliatory efforts to 'culture' the human rights message were too indulgent of ethno-nationalist particularism and compromised the values of equality and justice which lay at the heart of the human rights message.[23]

Conclusion

The threat of being 'boxed in' by culture, religion and broader political division hung over Fiji's women advocates in the years between 1985 and 1995. At the local level, Fiji experienced an intensification of communalist politics as a result of the 1987 coup, and the rise to power of an authoritarian, ethno-nationalist regime. The hardened ethnic divisions that were evident within the local realm of associational life were also manifest amongst women's organisations. Divided responses to the political upheavals of 1987 compromised the unity of some groups, and tensions surrounding individual members' ethnicity also became problematic. At the same time, competition for resources and political influence undermined relationships between women's groups.

While many women's organisations struggled for political recognition in a domestic setting where all political questions were now scrutinised through an ethno-nationalist lens, the regional and international realms of political engagement appeared to provide more enabling avenues of political engagement. Yet, in these contexts too, the contingencies of the prevailing political environment shaped the political agency of Fiji-based groups. Regional network building certainly flourished at this time, but tended towards a more issue-specific style of advocacy. While this increased organisations' specialist

---

23　Sally Engle Merry describes this scenario as 'the paradox of making human rights in the vernacular' (2006a: 49). She contends that the human rights translators must walk a 'fine line' between 'replication' and 'hybridisation'. On the one hand, they must ensure that human rights ideas are presented in ways that do not alienate local communities. On the other hand, they are required to develop culturally appropriate 'translations' that do not skew or undermine the human rights message, making it unrecognisable to the 'global community' (2006a: 49).

knowledge in particular areas, it was not an approach that encouraged groups to engage in more structurally focused critiques of the factors contributing to women's subordination.

Certainly, many activists and scholars were inspired by the international ascendancy of the human rights gender advocacy frameworks that occurred at this time and that were seen to augment the transnational political agency of women's organising. However, such strategies tended to 'localise' the focus of advocacy in a more 'state-centric' direction, diverting attention away from the broader issues of global economic and political inequality that had been such powerful concerns of Third World gender advocates in the past. In addition, as my discussion of the costs of 'culturing' the human rights debate has shown, the political contingencies that shape the associated processes also need to be clearly understood. While activists from this period clearly acknowledged the importance of framing advocacy in ways that were considered appropriate to the local socio-cultural context, in the post-coup setting, they were also worried that they were conceding so much territory to the more parochial actors on Fiji's political landscape that the normative content of the human rights message was potentially being undermined in the process.

The following chapter will consider the period from 1995 to 2006, and demonstrate once again the need for a contextual appreciation of women's political agency. Political reforms introduced at the beginning of this period were greeted with great optimism within the local terrain of women's organising and it was widely anticipated that less communally oriented civil society actors would enjoy a more enabling and tolerant political environment. This hopeful political outlook was ultimately short-lived, however. Developments occurring in later years forced organisations to reassess their capacity to act within a domestic political environment where race and the protection of indigenous paramountcy were again predominant themes and efforts to contain political instability resulted in new waves of political authoritarianism.

5. 'A Gentler Political Engagement': 1995–2002

In November 2002, Fiji's Prime Minister, Laisenia Qarase, addressed a meeting convened by the Fiji Women's Crisis Centre (FWCC) as part of its annual 16 Days of Activism Against Violence Against Women. He voiced his support for the FWCC's anti-violence message and declared the government's shared commitment on this issue to be a clear demonstration of NGO-state 'partnership in action' (*Fiji Times* 22 November 2002). Ironically, in the next breath, the Prime Minister took a more critical line, admonishing the Centre for its uncompromising public profile. '[S]ometimes you might more effectively serve your cause with what I would describe as a little quiet diplomacy,' Qarase argued (*Fiji Times,* 22 November 2002). These oddly matched sentiments seemed hardly befitting of the occasion and certainly detracted from the central message of the FWCC's '16 Days' campaign. When understood from a contextual perspective, however, these sentiments were hardly incongruous. By 2002, Fiji's political climate engendered tense relationships between civil society and the state. This meant that for many women's organisations, a path of 'gentle' engagement was considered the most politically expedient (Jalal cited *fem'Link* 2002a).

While the scenario described above might appear to suggest that not a great deal had changed in Fiji since the early 1990s, in fact the immediate post-Beijing era was anticipated with a sense of optimism by many gender activists. During this period the beginnings of a softening policy agenda from the formerly hardline nationalist government was discernible as the government initiated a process of constitutional review and also formulated a Plan of Action to see commitments made in Beijing reflected in local policy. The change of government that brought Fiji's Labour Party to power at the head of a multiparty coalition in 1999 was viewed as further evidence that Fiji was entering a new and more liberal phase. While tensions between the state and civil society were not entirely absent, the ground for productive and sometimes unorthodox collaborations between women's organisations and government agencies was more fertile in this period than in the early 1990s, and inclined many women's organisations to increase their faith in the state.

Local and international political developments in 2000 disrupted this optimistic mood. In May 2000, a civilian-led coup again saw Fiji's parliamentary processes overturned, the elected government ejected from power, and the installation of an interim, nationalist-led regime which aimed to abrogate the country's new constitution. Amongst local gender activists the mood swung from optimism to despondency as their relations with the state again became more fraught. Many women's organisations joined with a range of broader civil society actors who rallied in support of the 1997 constitutional reform process and advocated for return to democracy, thereby avoiding some of the organisational rifts that had occurred in the wake of the 1987 coup. Yet, they also faced considerable difficulty in making issues of specific concern to women resonate within a political environment where ethno-nationalism was again politically dominant.

On the international stage, the initial post-Beijing euphoria evident within the transnational realm of women's organising appeared, by 2000, to have also dissipated significantly. A highly reactionary, transnational religious lobby, disgruntled by the policy developments advancing women's rights in previous years, had gained international influence at this time (Steans and Ahmadi 2005; Chappell 2006; Reilly 2009). This network of state and non-state actors demonstrated a steady determination to stall the momentum of international consensus on women's human rights which had been gathering in Beijing. Dubbed the 'unholy alliance' by some feminist observers (Chappell 2006), this grouping had some success in reducing the transnational space available to women's groups looking to expand UN debate on women's human rights into new areas.

International norms of 'good governance' which, at this time, constituted 'the language of negotiations' for international development institutions (Larmour 1998: 1), encouraged close institutional engagement with civil society actors in these years.[1] The idea was that such practices would help make domestic and international structures of global governance more participatory and accountable.[2] Yet, in the Pacific, organisations who were willing to partner external agencies' development initiatives were also under some pressure to 'dovetail' their agendas with the broader tenets of the 'good governance' agenda (Slatter 2002). As we shall see, these developments were understood by local activists to have both positive and negative implications for the political agency of individual recipient organisations and the sphere of women's organising in general.

The following pages will examine the contingencies of women's political agency in Fiji in this period by describing how broader domestic and international

---

1 Within international aid agencies and development banks, 'good governance became the "language of negotiations" in policy-making during this period and highlighted the importance of transparent and democratic public institutions, an independent judiciary and liberal market economies' (Larmour 1998: 1).

2 Two key liberal assumptions about civil society informed this view. The first emphasised civil society as a site of procedural reform. Here the focus was upon institutional procedures and the capacity of civil society organisations to place an 'important democratic check' on the state to encourage greater accountability within the institutions of governance (Elliot 2003; Howell and Pearce 2001: 39–41; Anheier, Glasius and Kaldor 2001: 15). The second related to the 'normative' idea of civil society and the capacity of organisations within this sphere to act as 'schools of virtue', able to promote a democratic culture amongst the local citizenry (Elliot 2003: 18; Kenny 2003). More critical accounts of civil society tend to be sceptical of this liberal and idealised view and problematise the notion of civil society as discrete from the state or the market (Chandoke 2001, 2003; Khilnani 2001; Keane 2003).

political trends and developments shaped women's organisational activity on the local, regional and international stage. In the later part of the chapter, greater emphasis is placed upon the situated experiences of activists themselves. Here, once again, consideration is given to their subjective appraisals of the prevailing political environment and how this influenced organisations' efforts to promote collectivity, progressive ideas and transnational connection.

Local developments

A climate of reform?

Women's organisations observed with some satisfaction the mood for reform which was building in Fiji in the mid-1990s. While a number of political developments occurring in these years suggested that the formerly hardline nationalist agenda promoted by the Soqosoqo ni Vakavulewa ni Taukei (SVT) government was beginning to alter, the most significant of these was Prime Minister Sitiveni Rabuka's decision in 1994 to commission an independent process of constitutional review (FCRC 1997a, 1997b; Norton 2000: 91).

This development offered an important opportunity for women's organisations to draw attention to those aspects of constitutional law that discriminated against women.[3] Both Fiji's 1970 and 1990 constitutions included citizenship clauses that were discriminatory, granting full citizenship rights only to children born outside the country whose fathers were Fiji citizens, and granting the right to apply for Fiji citizenship only to foreign wives of citizen males of Fiji. Indigenous nationalists regularly defended these laws, citing the Indo-Fijian community's tendency to arrange marriages with Indian men from the subcontinent as the chief concern. The Fiji Women's Rights Movement (FWRM) opposed this view, arguing that existing citizenship provisions were unacceptably discriminatory and also contributed to a local brain drain by encouraging those professional and educated local women married to foreigners to live outside Fiji (Goodwillie and Kaloumaira 2000).

Building upon the success that the FWRM had achieved in coordinating action on CEDAW in the lead-up to the Beijing Conference in 1995, this organisation again sought to lead a coalition of women's groups to take up this issue at the various Constitutional Review Commission hearings held around the country.[4]

3 The work done by women's groups on this issue has been ignored in academic descriptions of the CRC which focus more on how questions of ethnicity and political representation were present in these deliberations (see Norton 2000; Kelly and Kaplan 2001; Lal 2002, 2003).
4 The commission was comprised of Professor Brij Lal, an eminent Indo-Fijian Pacific historian, Tomasi Vakatora, an indigenous parliamentarian and former Speaker of the Fijian parliament and Sir Paul Reeves, a former Governor-General of New Zealand.

The idea was to build upon the impetus for reform that was generated through the constitutional review process. This coalition eventually incorporated sixteen women's organisations, and could boast well-established networks around the country and support from all of Fiji's ethnic groups (Goodwillie and Kaloumaira 2000).[5] One of the members of the constitutional commission was later to comment that wherever the CRC convened its hearings, it was confronted with women wanting to make submissions on the citizenship issue (Lal 2005). This was surely testimony to the important network building on this issue that was encouraged by the FWRM and its partners.

When the CRC's final recommendations were presented to Fiji's President, Ratu Sir Kamisese Mara, on 6 September 1996, it was clear that the work of the Women's Citizenship Rights Coalition had been influential. The discriminatory aspects of citizenship law were now removed from the constitution and in addition, the constitution's Bill of Rights also stipulated that discrimination on the basis of sex and gender was to be outlawed. This made Fiji's reservations on Articles 5a and 9 of the CEDAW convention now unconstitutional and these were duly removed.

Despite some 'tinkering' with the commission's recommendations, particularly in the contentious area of electoral representation for Fiji's ethnic communities (Kelly and Kaplan 2001: 179),[6] the general academic and civil society view was that the 1997 constitution provided 'greater equity in rights between indigenous Fijians and other groups' and reduced 'racialism in politics' (Lal, cited in Kelly and Kaplan 2001: 179; Citizens' Constitutional Forum (CCF) 2005). This view was not shared by more parochial local actors who were aggrieved at many of the provisions within the constitution's Bill of Rights. Almost as soon as the constitution came into effect in 1998, it faced challenges from indigenous nationalist interests who argued that it was incomprehensible to the grassroots, and established principles that ran contrary to indigenous interests and concepts of identity. They also claimed that the constitutional review process had been a hurried affair with inadequate consultation (Lal 2002; CCF 2005). For local women activists, however, acceptance of the 1997 constitution was viewed as a victory and an important demonstration of what could be achieved with a collective effort (Sharma, cited in Goodwillie and Kaloumaira 2000).

---

5   These included the FWRM, FWCC, WAC, NCW, PPSEAWA, YWCA, the Fiji Women Lawyers Association, the women's wing of the National Federation Party and the Fiji Labour Party, and a number of Indo-Fijian organisations—the Fiji Girmit Council for Women, TISI Mathar Sangam, and Stri Sewa Sabha.

6   The final version of the 1997 Constitution gave explicit recognition to indigenous rights and allocated two-thirds of Fiji's parliamentary seats as communal seats with local electorates defined by ethnicity (Fijian, Indo-Fijian and Others) and one-third of the seats declared common role or cross-voting seats, for which voters of all races could cast a ballot (Kelly and Kaplan 2001: 179). The decision to have the positions of President and Vice-President appointed by the Great Council of Chiefs was seen to adequately protect the principle of indigenous paramountcy.

The government's decision to establish a ten-year national Plan of Action for Women reflecting commitments made during the 1995 World Conference in Beijing, was also broadly welcomed by women's groups as a signal that institutional gains for women were being made in this period. The Women's Plan of Action was formally launched by the Prime Minister on 9 October 1998 and five priority policy areas were to be tackled to improve women's status: gender mainstreaming in government planning and policy; women's status in the law; micro-enterprise development; gender balance in decision making; and political representation and domestic violence (Fiji Ministry of Women and Culture 1998).

The plan's discussion in each of these areas was remarkably frank. It cited statistics from a 1997 UN Development Programme (UNDP) report which stated that 25 per cent of Fiji's population was living in poverty, with many more at risk of 'becoming impoverished' (UNDP with Government of Fiji 1997) and speculated upon the impact of this scenario for local women. The plan also touched on some highly sensitive areas, for example discussing the availability of family planning services and the negative impacts of the continued criminalisation of abortion (Fiji Ministry of Women and Culture 1998). The fact that the report's forthright discussion on subjects such as reproductive health was acceptable to the government, clearly indicates the extent to which aspects of the prevailing political environment had transformed in the late 1990s. By raising these provocative questions in the public domain, the government certainly appeared to clear the way for civil society actors to take this debate further, even in the face of local religious sensitivities. By contrast there had been no deliberation on the issue of women's reproductive rights in the previous decade.

But this more liberal attitude was not evident in all areas of the report. The fact that micro-financing initiatives were viewed uncritically in the plan, described as providing important mechanisms by which to tackle economic disadvantage and integrate women into the market economy, indicates other areas in which space for public debate was constrained. The perceived success of Grameen Bank micro-financing schemes for women in Bangladesh had seen this model widely endorsed by 'most of the mainstream development agencies' and replicated in many parts of the developing world (Rankin 2002; Bergeron 2003). Fiji was no exception. By the end of the 1990s, micro-financing schemes were held to be important national development strategies for women. Fitting neatly with the broader good governance paradigm which championed market-led economic growth as an efficient means of wealth distribution over other more literal forms of social provisioning (Schild 2002), these development models placed an important emphasis upon the positive benefits that would accrue if women's entrepreneurial capacity and market participation were encouraged.[7] The Fijian incarnation of micro-finance discourse clearly reflected broader tenets

---

7   For more critical perspectives on micro finance projects for women see Rankin (2002), Schild (2002), and Goetz (1997).

of neoliberal thought that had achieved a hegemonic status in global politics and seemed increasingly difficult for civil society actors around the globe to challenge.

In 1999, new elections were held in Fiji which resulted in a shock defeat for Rabuka's SVT Party. The Fiji Labour Party won an outright majority and gave Fiji its first Indo-Fijian and former unionist Prime Minister, Mahendra Chaudhry. While the constitution's power-sharing mechanisms stipulated that every party with a level of parliamentary representation that exceeded 10 per cent be included in the cabinet, the SVT steadfastly refused to join the newly established 'Peoples Coalition' government.

Fijian nationalists may have reeled from the electoral results, but women's organisations celebrated the fact that the new parliament included eight women. Five took up cabinet positions as ministers or assistant ministers within the new government. The most prominent of these was Adi Kuini Speed, widow of the former Labour Party leader, Dr Timoci Bavadra deposed from government in 1987. Speed was appointed to the senior position of Deputy Prime Minister and Minister of Foreign Affairs (FWRM 1999). Lavinia Padarath, former Secretary of the Fiji Nurses Association, was appointed Minister for Women, Culture and Social Welfare.

In the months that followed, Fiji's women's organisations enjoyed a productive working relationship with the state. This allowed the FWRM to make significant headway in its objective to reform Fiji's colonially inherited family law statutes, a campaign which had begun two years earlier. In 1997, Imrana Jalal had been named as Family Law Reform Commissioner and, in conjunction with the FWRM and the Fiji Law Reform Commission (FLRC), had initiated a two-year series of public consultations on family law which was funded by the UK's Department for International Development (DFID) (FWRM 2000a). The redrafted Family Law Bill, which was presented to the 'Peoples Coalition' government in 1999, established a separate division of the Courts to hear family disputes and established an 'irreconcilable differences' rather than 'fault-based' regime for divorce rulings. The 'Peoples Coalition' government demonstrated confidence in the processes of consultation that had preceded the bill's drafting and, by mid-2000, the bill had been read twice before Fiji's parliament (Jalal 2002).

FWCC advocacy was also framed by similar legalistic objectives in this period as the organisation mounted a strong campaign for law reform in the area of sexual offences law. In 1996, for example, the Centre made a submission to the FLRC on new domestic violence legislation and as a result, the commission began a review of the country's rape laws and a two-year process of public consultations. The commission's final recommendations argued that rape in marriage be given clearer legal status, and that sexual offences be reclassified and mandatory sentences increased. It also argued that the evidentiary burden placed upon victims of rape be reduced and recommended that *bulubulu* no longer be recognised within the courts for cases of sexual abuse and rape (Vasakula 2002).

In these years, Women's Action for Change (WAC) radically expanded the scope of its operations and also developed some unorthodox collaborations with government agencies and the private enterprise sector. The WAC umbrella provided support to a newly formed Sexual Minorities Project (WAC/SM) which aimed to advocate for, and provide support networks to, Fiji's gay and transgender communities.[8] WAC also established a childcare facility for women employed in garment factories in the Kalabo Tax Free Zone on the outskirts of Suva. This centre was partly funded by factory owners and was one of the first in Fiji created to meet the needs of low-income workers (Pande 2002; WAC 2000).

Additionally, the WAC Theater continued to concentrate upon community-development work, creating plays on issues such as teenage pregnancy and incest, environmental protection, domestic violence, drug and alcohol abuse, and mental health, and performing them in schools, tertiary educations, and at more public venues across Fiji's main islands. The WAC Theater also began to develop 'playback' theatre techniques which Peni Moore described as a 'theater about feelings'. These sessions required audiences to describe their own emotional responses to the issues presented in the plays and then to describe when they might have experienced similar situations in their own lives.[9] Moore argued that in combination with community theatre, playback sessions proved a highly successful advocacy methodology. While these activities required audience members to think and act, rather than simply watch and listen, Moore also argued that playback theatre allowed WAC to stay in touch with local communities' concerns (Moore 2002b).

In 1999, WAC was invited to work inside Fiji's prisons as part of state rehabilitation education programs.[10] The organisation formulated a series of drama and music workshops which aimed to improve prisoners' communications skills, increase their self-esteem and provide them with non-violent means of dealing with problems.[11] WAC also sought to introduce a gendered dimension into this program

---

8   At this time, the WAC/SM negotiated funding through partner NGOs in the US and Europe, receiving grants from the New York-based Astraea Lesbian Foundation for Justice, the Umverteilen Foundation in Berlin and Mama Cash, a Dutch organisation supporting the work of innovative women around the world.

9   During these sessions, audience members were invited to describe their emotional responses to the material being presented and then to describe scenarios where they might have encountered similar situations in their own lives. The cast members then 'playback' this story before the whole audience, aiming to increase understanding amongst all audience members of the storyteller's experiences (Moore 2002b).

10   At this time, WAC was performing a play titled *Homecoming* which illustrated the difficulties ex-prisoners face when trying to combat prejudice and stigma in the community. Their efforts were brought to the attention of Fiji's Justice Department.

11   WAC worked with young offenders at Suva's Nasinu Prison, a pre-release unit at Naboro Prison, Natabua Prison in Fiji's Western Division and Korovou Women's Prison, visiting each of these sites on a weekly basis.

by focusing upon the ways in which prisoners related to women (Moore 2003: 128). The programs incorporated activities such as games and exercises, music and song writing, acting improvisation and playback theatre sessions. Moore argued that the utilisation of playback theatre in the prisons was particularly beneficial both in increasing inmates' understandings of the ramifications of their actions and in improving self-confidence. She stated, 'within an hour and a half we could get men going from looking at the ground to smiling ... they could look you in the face, they could laugh, they could talk' (Moore 2002b). Prison authorities also noted marked improvement in the attitudes of prisoners taking part in the WAC programs, with inmates demonstrating increased capacities for self-expression and concentration (Moore 2003: 134) and increased abilities to cope with feelings of 'anger depression and loneliness' (*Sunday Times* 20 February 2000).

The WAC's work in local schools, and particularly the close association developing between this organisation and the Prisons Department, demonstrated the government's lateral attitude towards NGOs during this period, for the methodologies employed by WAC within these institutions certainly had an unorthodox quality. Amongst women's organisations more broadly, there was a general confidence in the government's willingness to create gender-sensitive public policy and to enact legislation reflecting internationally endorsed conventions on human rights and gender equality. State support for women's organisations involved in law reform activities, prisoner rehabilitation programs, and the promotion of human rights were indicative of the more tolerant political environment which prevailed during this period.

Civil insurrection

This climate of increased political tolerance was abruptly altered in May 2000, ironically on the eve of the third and final reading of the Family Law Bill in Fiji's Parliament. On 19 May, a group of insurgents invaded Suva's parliamentary complex, taking government members hostage and demanding that the country's leadership be returned to the Fijian community. Allegedly, this group was supported, 'behind the scenes', by influential members of the indigenous political establishment who had continually sought to undermine the legitimacy of the incumbent government. The public face of this action, however, was George Speight, a local business identity who, although of part-European ethnic origin, described his attempts to bring down the government as both a defence of the *Taukei*, and a long overdue reassertion of the Kubuna confederacy's entitlement to political power (Fraenkel 2000; Fry 2000).[12] Within

---

12 Drawing on substantial support from clan members in the Tailevu provinces, Speight claimed to be representing the Kubuna Confederacy and challenging the political position of the Tovata Confederacy of Eastern chiefs which had maintained political dominance of Fiji since the colonial period (Fraenkel 2000; Fry 2000).

only a few hours, hundreds of nationalist sympathisers who had been protesting in Suva earlier that morning, flooded the grounds of the parliamentary complex and provided the initially small group of insurgents with a 'human shield' that effectively protected them from police or military intervention to restore order (Robertson and Sutherland 2001; Tarte 2001).

During the following days of tense political negotiations between the rebels, Fiji's armed forces, President Ratu Mara and the Great Council of Chiefs, waves of violence swept Suva and many outlying regions of the Fiji Islands.[13] On 29 May, the head of Fiji's military services, Commodore Voreqe Bainimarama, attempted to reassert some semblance of stability in the country. He convinced the incumbent president, Ratu Mara to step down, formally abrogated the 1997 constitution, on the basis that it provided 'no framework for resolving the crisis' (cited in Robertson and Sutherland 2001: 24), and declared martial law. However, the rebels remained in parliament and the violence continued. In part, this violence was a spontaneous and opportunistic reaction to the events unfolding in Suva. In part, it was a coordinated and sustained campaign by the insurgents to weaken state authority (Robertson and Sutherland 2001: xv–17). Much of the violence was racially targeted and included the alleged rape of Indo-Fijian women, and the occupation of Indian-held leasehold farms and Indian businesses.[14] As the political standoff continued, however, the nature of this violence became more brazen, with a number of public infrastructure sites targeted. The coup conspirators seemed eager to demonstrate to their adversaries their capacity to wreak coordinated havoc (Robertson and Sutherland 2001: 23).[15]

The majority of women's groups responded to the hostage crisis and the prevailing environment of lawlessness with extreme disappointment. However, given the tense political environment, they were also careful to voice their opposition to the rebels' actions in ways that did not make them targets of nationalist aggression. YWCA members attracted early press attention by condemning Speight's actions and calling upon women to demonstrate their resistance to his message of 'indigenous rights' by wearing black (*Fiji Times* 21 May 2000). As in 1987, other organisations voiced their opposition to these developments by writing letters to Fiji's daily newspapers. In one letter, the FWCC described the actions of the nationalist rebels as a 'severe blow to the efforts of all those who have worked tirelessly towards the goal of peace and multicultural prosperity in our country' (*Fiji Times* 22 May 2000).

---

13   For a detailed account of these developments, see Tarte (2001), and Robertson and Sutherland (2001).

14   In isolated settlements in the regions of Tailevu, Naitasiri and Muaniweni, on Vanua Levu, the violence was so serious that Indo-Fijian refugees began heading westward towards camps in the Lautauka region where they sought protection from 'marauding gangs of Fijians' (Robertson and Sutherland 2001: 28).

15   Around the country, police stations came under siege, as did telecommunications infrastructure, Suva's main source of electricity (the Monasavu Hydro-electricity plant), army bases, tourist resorts, a tuna cannery in Levuka, the Fiji Water bottling plant at Rakiraki and regional airstrips.

While nationalist sympathisers were once again calling for Fiji to declare itself a Christian state, the Church also provided women's organisations with an important platform for demonstrations against the coup leader's actions. Within days, Suva's Holy Trinity Anglican Cathedral became the venue of a daily peace vigil which was coordinated by the Fiji National Council of Women, and which brought together women from all of Fiji's faith communities. Dressed in black, they mourned the 'threat of violence' that hung over the nation, and expressed the hope that a 'peaceful resolution' might be negotiated (*Fiji Times* 22 May 2000, 28 May 2000). Women attending this vigil also drafted a series of letters to President Ratu Mara and the Great Council of Chiefs calling for a return to constitutional government in Fiji.

After fifty-six days, the political standoff was brought to a resolution which saw the incumbent government dismissed, the chief coup perpetrators charged and placed in custody, and an interim government installed, headed by a Lauan businessman, Laisenia Qarase.[16] While requests from the Women's Peace Vigil for equal representation of women and men in the new administration were initially ignored, increased lobbying saw the interim cabinet include a woman as interim Minister of Women, and four women also assume the positions of assistant ministers (FWCC 2000). Gender activists supporting a return to democracy were particularly disappointed to see the interim administration appoint Adi Finau Tabakaucoro as Assistant Minister for Women. Tabakaucoro's public statements expressing sympathy for the motivations behind the coup-plotters actions indicated that her political allegiances to the *Taukei* remained as solid in 2000 as they had been in 1987 (FWCC 2000; *Fiji Times* 25 May 2000, 27 May 2000).

If women's organisations needed further proof of the interim regime's ethno-nationalist sympathies, this was clearly provided by its hasty formulation of an indigenous affirmative action policy presented to the nation in mid-July. Entitled 'The Blueprint for the Protection of Fijian and Rotuman Rights', this policy outlined plans to establish a new constitution by 2001 that would enshrine Fijian rights to political and economic self-determination and correct the perceived lack of opportunities faced by Fijians in areas such as private enterprise or education.[17] The new administration may have declared its opposition to the coup plotters' methods, but the release of this policy clearly demonstrated a strong resonance with many of Speight's stated aims (Tarte 2001). Defending their right to rule on the basis of indigenous paramountcy, members of this regime regularly repeated the refrain first heard in 1987, that democracy was a 'foreign flower' which contributed to local instability because

---

16 Qarase had close allegiances to the Tovata-based political establishment in Fiji, which, thanks to the military's intervention, was again in a position of political power.

17 Many of the 'affirmative action' provisions within this Blueprint later appeared in the SDL government's Social Justice Bill, which came into effect in February 2002, after general elections in August 2001, won by Qarase's Soqosoqo Duavata ni Lewenivanua (SDL) Party.

of its 'conflict with custom' (Qarase, cited in *Pacific Beat*, Radio Australia, 19 May 2001). Qarase also claimed his rise to the position of interim Prime Minister was part of 'God's plan' (cited in Field 2002). By invoking values associated with the *vanua* (indigenous custom) and *lotu* (Church)—powerful and intersecting sites of authority for Fiji's indigenous communities—the interim political leaders attempted to undermine potential challenges from pro-democracy civil society groups and legitimate their ethno-nationalist agenda.

The new government seemed keen to ignore the depths of economic hardship confronting all of Fiji's ethnic groups in the wake of the 2000 coup. This was particularly so for many local women, once again placed in a situation of extreme vulnerability as the social and economic impacts of the May 2000 political upheavals began to take effect. At the height of the nationalist violence, reports began to emerge of women allegedly raped and sexually abused in the Tailevu and Muaniweni areas where outbreaks of interracial violence had been most serious. There were also allegations that within the parliamentary complex, women were also subject to various kinds of violence and sexual abuse (Robertson and Sutherland 2001; Jalal 2002). The FWCC responded to these reports by sending teams out to the provincial areas to document these incidences of violence and to draw national attention to the 'human rights violations' that had been suffered by women at the hands of the rebels (FWCC 2001b).

Negotiating the post-coup environment

In the longer term, both the FWCC and Save the Children Fiji (SCF) noted increases in the prevalence and severity of domestic violence as families sought to deal with the psychological and financial pressures that had increased as a result of the 2000 coup. Fiji's daily newspapers regularly featured reports of wage-earners with responsibilities to extended families describing the impact of their retrenchment from employment in industries such as garment making and hospitality. These sectors suffered a serious downturn as the international sanctions applied to Fiji began to take effect (*Fiji Times* 5 June 2000, 13 June, 2000).[18] In research undertaken by SCF in the twelve months following the coup, it was argued that income loss occurring in this period equated to far more than a mere reduction in 'purchasing power'. Increasing economic pressures were said to have intensified a range of 'social problems' such as domestic violence, child abuse, suicide and drug and alcohol abuse, as people of all ages reported feeling 'fearful, frustrated, angry and powerless' (Carling and Peacock-Taylor 2001: 9).

---

18   In line with calls for international support from the Fiji Trade Union Congress (FTUC), Australian and New Zealand unions placed an international ban on freight handling to and from Fiji. The rapid impact of these sanctions meant that within less than a month over 2000 jobs had been lost within local garment manufacturing and tourism—industries which were largely dependent upon women's labour. (*Fiji Times* 10 June 2000, 9 June 2000).

While the FWCC documented the gendered fallout from the coup, and provided support for local communities where they could (FWCC 2000, 2001a), they also felt the impact of the changed political environment in a more direct fashion. As part of its '16 Days' campaign in 2000, the FWCC planned to hold a peace rally and anticipated the attendance of a large group of supporters. Although public marches of this type had been a regular feature of FWCC activities since the early 1990s, they were viewed in a more sinister fashion in the post-coup political climate. This march was cancelled at the last minute when government officials revoked their original authorisation of the planned march—a move reminiscent of the heavy-handed responses to the pro-democracy demonstrations that occurred in the wake of the 1987 military coups.

The FWRM engaged in a strenuous campaign for a return to constitutional democracy, arguing that this was a necessary precondition if women's rights were to be realised. The interim regime's decision to stall further political debate on the Family Law Bill dealt a serious blow to the long-term ambitions of the FWRM and particularly Jalal, who had been closely involved with this reform process. Although pro-democracy campaigning had proved costly to the organisation in 1987 (with some members finding it hard to reconcile their loyalty to indigenous political leaders with the group's broader commitment to democracy), the FWRM once again pursued the line that 'democracy is a precondition for the attainment of women's rights'. With this, they pursued a public course of action which pushed 'aggressively … for the return to constitutional rule' (FWRM 2001b: 15).

This stand included the controversial step of contributing legal support to a High Court case defending the 1997 constitution. This case had been launched in the name of a displaced Indo-Fijian farmer (Chandrika Prasad) and was supported by a multi-ethnic, pro-democracy civil society group, the Citizens' Constitutional Forum (CCF). Although it was later referred to the Court of Appeal, this action was ultimately successful and saw the interim administration's attempts to formulate a new constitution halted (Lal 2003; Yabaki 2004). This did not build increased support for the FWRM however. Some figures who had previously championed the organisation withdrew their support as members of Fiji's post-coup political leadership publically condemned the FWRM stand as 'inappropriate for a women's organization' (Houng Lee 2002). The FWRM continued to pursue its pro-democracy campaigns undeterred.

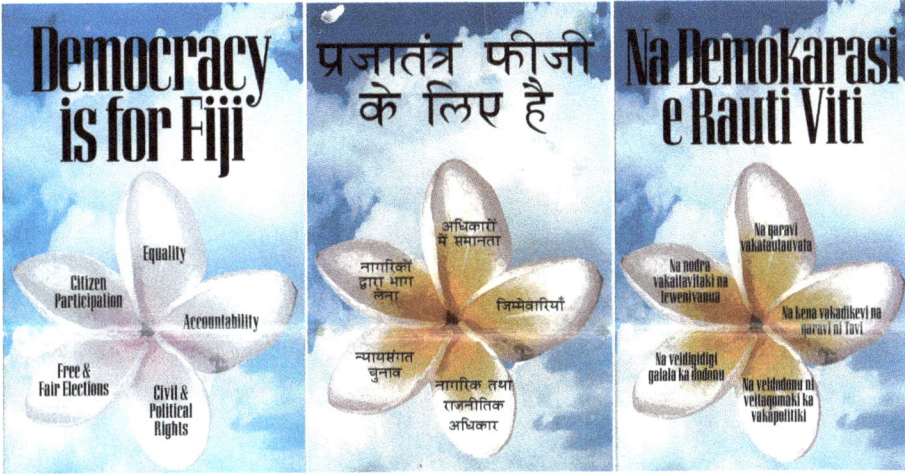

Figure 5.1. Democracy is For Fiji: FWRM's 'frangipani' poster.

Source: Fiji Women's Rights Movement, Suva, 2001.

This situation contrasts with the post-coup scenario in 1987. In this later period, a range of civil society groups had evolved a strong pro-democracy position. The CCF had, since 1996, been running programs to educate Fiji's citizens on their constitutional rights, and had been strong supporters of the reform process. In addition, the Ecumenical Centre for Research Education and Advocacy (ECREA, formerly the research wing of the Fiji Council of Churches) also promoted a strong multicultural political agenda and a determined commitment to social justice and political and economic equity for all Fiji's citizens. While the communal aspects of associational life in Fiji were still highly apparent in this period, the presence of these new groups meant that those women's organisations embracing a pro-democracy position were able to find support from other organisations adopting a similar political stand. From here they could engage in range of much stronger pro-democracy initiatives than had been evident or indeed permitted in the post-1987 context.

In later months, the FWRM became involved in the creation of a community paralegal program which targeted civil society representatives. The long-term goal of this project was to establish a team of people who would be able to spread a message of support for democratic ideals, constitutional values and a human rights culture in Fiji (FWRM 2001b). Additionally, the FWRM sought to counter nationalist opposition to democratic models of power-sharing through a 'Democracy is for Fiji' campaign. The posters and pamphlets used in this campaign were translated into English, Hindi and Fijian and featured the symbol of the frangipani, a blossom native to Fiji, to counter the nationalist refrain describing democracy as a 'foreign flower'.

In contrast to the FWRM, WAC's fortunes were more precarious in this period. The organisation's programs were under significant pressure as a result of the hardening of nationalist sentiment, and the general shift towards a more conservative style of politics that followed in the wake of the 2000 coup. Previously, the successful WAC initiatives in the area of prisoner rehabilitation or low-cost child care had relied upon the collaboration of government agencies or industry partners, yet these collaborations proved far easier to negotiate in the pre-coup period of liberal political reform and relative economic stability, than in the post-2000 context.

WAC's prisoner rehabilitation project was the first to feel the impact of the post-coup regime's altered approach to civil society collaboration. Almost immediately, the interim administration demonstrated some mistrust of the unconventional approach to prisoner rehabilitation undertaken by WAC and repeatedly signalled its intention to end WAC's drama programs within the prisons. When a WAC cast member was caught entering the prison in possession of a small quantity of marijuana in early 2001, this provided the new ministerial authorities with the pretext they needed and the program was concluded (Moore 2002b).

WAC responded by redesigning this program to focus more squarely on the needs of ex-prisoners in the community. Conscious that, upon release, ex-prisoners faced poor employment prospects, social stigmatisation and peer pressure to resume criminal behaviour, WAC felt that programs which aimed to increase ex-prisoners' income-earning opportunities as well as their self esteem would still be useful on the 'outside' and could contribute to ex-prisoner rehabilitation (WAC 2001).

WAC's childcare centre at Kalabo also faced serious difficulties in the wake of the coup. Funding withdrawals from local garment manufacturers who were facing their own economic pressures along with heightened racial tensions amongst the centre's staff, and declining enrolments due to job losses in the area, all took their toll on the centre and positive sentiment within the project began to evaporate. Continued efforts were made to keep the centre running on a small budget and with a reduced number of staff. In August 2001 it was finally forced to close (WAC 2001; Pande 2002).

Despite these setbacks, WAC's theatre advocacy, particularly its use of playback theatre, were viewed by other civil society actors as having an important potential for peacebuilding efforts. In the post-coup climate, the interim administration had created a program around community reconciliation and had gone as far as establishing a Ministry for Reconciliation with the declared aim of restoring 'peaceful coexistence' amongst Fiji's ethnic communities (Ministry of Reconciliation, cited in the *Daily Post* 2 April 2002). Pro-democracy groups such as the CCF and ECREA had been highly critical of these efforts, however, arguing that the rhetorical and ceremonial focus upon reconciliation was not matched by concrete evidence showing that the government was committed to move beyond the 'politics of race' (Yabaki, cited in the *Daily Post* 3 April 2002; ECREA, *Fiji Times* 13 November 2002, 16 November 2002; Rao 2002).

In contrast, the advocacy methodologies employed by WAC were recognised by other civil society groups as providing a more empathetic starting point for peacebuilding efforts. The Fiji and New Zealand offices of Save the Children provided important financial backing for a theatre-based project established by WAC which targeted children in regions where coup-related violence had been most serious. Save the Children Fiji and WAC felt it appropriate to target children from the ages of twelve to sixteen. WAC's program aimed to encourage this demographic group to think critically about how questions of ethnic difference were manifest and politicised within their communities (Carling and Peacock Taylor 2001: 27; SCF 2001).[19] Later assessment of the program found that it had contributed to the beginnings of closer inter-ethnic relations in the community and helped rebuild a measure of social stability (I. Ali 2002; SCF 2001).

The Women's Peace Vigil, coordinated by Fiji National Council of Women secretary Sharon Bhagwan Rolls, continued to act as another platform for women's post-coup peacebuilding efforts. This vigil met on a monthly basis in Suva through 2000 and 2001, and from there, various other campaigns calling for the restoration of Fiji's democracy were formed.[20] This ecumenical vigil also encouraged some to think about alternative platforms for gender activism. Bhagwan Rolls was concerned that media representations presented a perspective of Fiji's coup which focused neither on the efforts made by women to encourage peaceful resolution of this crisis, nor the heavy burdens borne by women as a result of the civil and political instability (Bhagwan Rolls 2002a, 2000). In September 2000, Bhagwan Rolls therefore established an organisation called fem'Link which aimed to give greater prominence to the voices of women within the mainstream media and correct its tendency towards 'unconscious and unrecognized' gender bias (Bhagwan Rolls 2000). Through this initiative, Bhagwan Rolls sought to profile the contributions made by grassroots women towards social and political change and peacebuilding (Bhagwan Rolls 2002a). With small pockets of funding provided by external partners such as the International Women's Development Agency, and the bilateral development agencies, DFID and Canada Fund, fem'Link produced a series of videos documenting women's experiences in the post-2000 coup context. These were entitled *Mothers in Dialogue* (2000), *Fem'talk Not Just Sweetalk* (2001) and *Keeping Watch* (2002b).

---

19   The fear that Fiji had entered a 'coup cycle', in which repeated instances of political and civil unrest could become more likely in the future, was felt keenly by organisations such as the SCF who argued that many of the perpetrators of violence during the 2000 coup would have been in their teenage years during the 1987 military coups and thus potentially understood the events taking place at that time as a legitimation of discriminatory and lawless behaviour.

20   These included the Fiji Blue Day Democracy Campaign which was supported by business, labour unions and a variety of NGOs and the Women's Action for Democracy and Peace or WAD'aP (Bhagwan Rolls 2000: 63).

Figures 5.2 and 5.3. WAC performing *Bats and Birds* in a rural school. This play aimed to show school children how different communities can live together cooperatively.

Source: Photographs by Nicole George.

Resumption of parliamentary democracy: August 2001

While women's organisations were generally pleased to see the resumption of constitutional democracy with national elections held in August 2001, the victory of the newly formed indigenous nationalist party Soqosoqo Duavata ni Lawenivanua (SDL), headed by the former interim Prime Minister Qarase, meant that the parameters for critical political debate on gender equality remained narrow. As contestation between the government and Chaudhry raged over Labour Party entitlement to Cabinet representation, the SDL nominated Asenaca Caucau to the post of Minister for Women. A staunch *Taukei* supporter, and daughter of a prominent pro-nationalist Minister within the Methodist Church, Caucau's appointment once again ensured that Fiji's women were represented in government by a figure whose understandings of gender equality were strongly influenced by her ethno-nationalist sympathies. This was made clearly apparent in August 2002 when, during the course of debate, Caucau likened Fiji's Indian population to 'noxious weeds' with the capacity to 'choke the land' (*Pacific Islands Report/PINA Nius Online*, 4 August 2002).

While the SDL government was clearly doing its best to encourage a return to communal politics, the government's hostile reaction to the CCF activity in these years warned all civil society actors that the parameters of government tolerance were limited. This was starkly demonstrated immediately prior to the 2001 elections when the interim government deregistered the CCF as a charitable organisation. The CCF's involvement in the Prasad case, and its stated intention to take the Fiji President to court for his refusal to call elections, had been major irritations for the nationalist interim regime, with the Prime Minister branding the organisation 'constitutional zealots' (*Pacific Magazine* December 2001). Yet, the deregistration of the CCF did not quiet this organisation's criticism of the interim government (CCF 2001). Neither did it dissuade donors from continuing their support for the organisation with bodies such as AusAID continuing to provide the CCF with funding, albeit in a less public manner (AusAID representative April 2002; Yabaki May 2002).

After the elections, the government's retaliatory posture towards civil society groups continued. In 2002, for example, the government began to use the media to raise doubts about the 'mandate of the CCF' and the interests that the organisation claimed to represent. The Minister for Information, Josefa Vosanibola, argued that the CCF was 'dependent on foreign donor assistance' and, as such, derived 'its mandate to speak on national issues in Fiji from … foreign donors' (*Fiji Times* 4 April 2002).

In addition, public protest marches continued to be banned and public meetings on government policy were subject to surveillance. For example, in November 2002 a CCF-coordinated event staged in collaboration with the FTUC to protest a planned 25 per cent budget increase in Fiji's value added tax (VAT) was the subject of intense state interest, with regular police patrols passing the FTUC premises where the meeting was held (author's observation).

In this political environment, women's organisations adopted a more cautious style of political engagement (Jalal, cited in *fem'Link* 2002a; Vere 2002a). This was clearly evident in the FWCC's 2002 '16 Days' campaign which focused upon the links between development and domestic violence. In the opening address for this campaign, delivered by Savenaca Narube, Governor of Fiji's Reserve Bank, it was argued that violence against women should be understood as a development issue because of the national economic consequences of this phenomenon. Narube described the days lost in employment, welfare liabilities, and law enforcement and health care costs incurred by the state as a result of violence against women. He calculated that this phenomenon cost the Fijian economy roughly FJ$300 million per annum or 7 per cent of the country's GDP (*Daily Post* 26 November 2002).

Choosing Narube to open this somewhat unusually focused campaign was certainly a move designed to win support from the conservative political elite.[21] However, this strategy also meant that all questions relating to the gendered impacts of economic disadvantage were left aside. This was ironic given that the campaign followed immediately after the SDL government announced its decision to increase Fiji's VAT; a development widely opposed by a range of other groups including the Fiji Council of Social Services, the FWRM, and the CCF who argued that it could only contribute to further economic hardship (*Fiji Times* 9 November 2002, 18 November 2002). This cautious path can be explained, in part, by the fact that FWCC operations and training programs frequently involved the participation of state authorities and their advocacy and community-support programs had also begun to receive substantial levels of financial support from government departments.[22] On the other hand, FWCC trustees were also keen not to see the practical focus of the organisation's activity jeopardised by more politically oriented engagement (Yabaki 2002). And, as the opening paragraphs of this chapter show, even when adopting this more cautious advocacy route, the FWCC was still subject to censure from the SVT leadership for the tone of its message and its failure to adhere to indigenous cultural protocols which emphasised 'quiet diplomacy'.

---

21   Debate of this kind has more frequently examined how processes of development or financial pressures of underdevelopment increase the potential for women to be exposed to violence (see Carrillo 1992; Bradley 1997). In this FWCC-sponsored debate, however, the Fijian economy was placed at the centre of the argument rather than a consideration of the ways in which economic variables might increase the likelihood that Fiji's women would be exposed to violence in their daily lives.

22   On 14 November 2002, the FWCC received a FJ$38,000 grant from the Ministry of Women to assist its upcoming '16 Days' program.

While the FWRM had made a provocative pro-democracy stand during the interim government period, with the return of parliamentary democracy this organisation also began to moderate its advocacy in relation to some issues. This was particularly evident in its decision to use the issue of women's economic status as a platform upon which to relaunch political debate on the Family Law Bill. In the post-coup political environment, liberal agendas of reform were more easily cast as threatening to indigenous paramountcy or in contravention of Christian principles. This meant that increased political attention was given to the Methodist Church's claims that the Family Law Bill's regime for divorce would encourage family breakdown. Similarly, the Soqosoqo Vakamarama's concerns about the Bill's recognition of putative fathers' rights to child custody and maintenance support were also received with greater weight by the political elite (Colowai 2002).

Aiming to circumvent these reservations, the FWRM restructured its defence of the Bill in 2002 to dovetail with broader economic agendas. The FWRM argued that the proposed Bill would have a 'major and positive impact on alleviating poverty in the poorest sectors of the community' (Regional Rights Resource Team (RRRT) 2002b). In particular, the organisation claimed that the Bill's maintenance regime offered more just and efficient mechanisms for divorced and separated couples and particularly women attempting to provide for and educate their children on a single wage.[23]

While the SDL government re-tabled the Bill in April 2002, pressure from its backbench members again stalled movement of the legislation through parliament. Despite the fact that the FLRC had been engaged in a two-year period of national consultations on family law reform in 1997, the SDL government launched a further round of public hearings on the proposed Bill in 2002. While the FWRM was bitterly disappointed with this decision, it continued to lobby in support of the Bill in a conciliatory fashion. Like the FWCC, the FWRM was clearly aware of the narrow limits of government tolerance with regard to critical advocacy in this period, and the organisational implications if these limits were transgressed. Clearly, 'gentle engagement' and the foregrounding of economic benefit were perceived to be the most expedient ways of framing solutions to gender disadvantage at this time (Jalal, cited in *fem'Link* 2002a).

---

23   Fiji's current system gives little support to women to pursue their husbands for maintenance payments, with only 15 per cent of 'poor women' successfully accessing regular income of this type. Unlike the existing regime, the new Family Law Bill does not require women to appear before the courts. Instead they are required to put their case before a Maintenance Officer empowered by the courts to collect payment from fathers. The FWRM argues that the Bill also ensures that the unemployed or those living in rural areas do not escape their maintenance obligations by instituting a system of payment in kind rather than the cash-only payments that are a feature of the current system (Colowai 2002).

Regional activity

During the period from 1995 to 2002, regional activity on gender issues continued in much the same manner as it had in the previous decade, with priorities placed on issues such as gender violence, women in politics and legal literacy. During this period, the South Pacific Commission (SPC) hosted two more triennial regional conferences for women in 1997 and 2001 which were coordinated by the Pacific Women's Resource Bureau (PWRB). Deliberations at these events were generally framed by the provisions of the Pacific Platform for Action (PPA), which the PWRB continued to promote as a flagship achievement of the agency (SPC 1997: 33).

However, within advocacy circles there seems to have been a flagging enthusiasm for the provisions of the PPA and indeed the PWRB in these years. As the Fiji example indicates, the Beijing Plan of Action and CEDAW were generally the key international instruments cited in deliberations on gender issues by both representatives of women's organisations and government agencies during this period, and the PPA was not generally prioritised as a policy guide or a local lobbying tool in the post-Beijing context.[24] This suggests the emergence of a disconnect between domestic, regional and international policy-frameworks being utilised to address questions of gender inequity across the Pacific Islands region.

Moreover, the issue-specific focus of the PPA, and its identification of thirteen areas of critical concern for women's advancement, limited the extent to which emerging issues in Pacific politics could be considered from a gendered perspective. Regional moves towards trade liberalisation and restructuring were gathering pace in these years and threatened to have important implications for the domestic political economies of Pacific Island states and the economic status of Pacific women.[25] These questions did not feature as areas of contention at the SPC regional women's conferences however.

---

24   This also made difficulties for government representatives and gender advocates who had trouble articulating local priorities in ways that matched the regional gender policy priorities of the PWRB. This disconnect between national and regional policy frameworks created substantial difficulties for Pacific Island governments when drafting country reports on the implementation of the PPA for the triennial conferences (SPC 2001: 12).

25   In response to Australian pressure, Pacific Island states had begun to consider a range of trade liberalisation measures for the region. The Pacific Islands Forum Secretariat had drawn up two key agreements which aimed to ease trade restrictions in the region and ultimately facilitate the creation of a Pacific Islands free trade region. Formally endorsed and signed by Pacific Islands Heads of State attending the Forum Meeting in August 2001, the Pacific Island Countries Trade Agreement (PICTA) and the Pacific Island Countries Agreement on Closer Economic Relations (PACER) both came into effect by 2002 (Scollay 2001). In addition to these agreements, Pacific Island states that were originally signatories to the Lome Trade agreements through their participation in the African Caribbean Pacific-European Union Accord (ACP-EU) were, in the late 1990s, also in the process of new trade negotiations which became formalised under the Cotonou Agreement of 2001. While countries such as Fiji had enjoyed privileged access to European markets for their sugar exports, the Cotonou Agreement proposed the phasing out of these systems of preferential trade by 2008 in accordance with World Trade Organization regimes (Firth 2000). Argumentation defending these reforms emphasised the need to create competitive and sustainable local industry in the Pacific that would no longer rely on external support (ACP-EU).

In part, this reflects the fact that political classes across the region adopted a relatively uncritical response to trade liberalisation at this time. The view put forward by Fiji's Permanent Secretary for Foreign Affairs and Trade, Ratu Isoa Gavidi, that Fiji's accession to the World Trade Organization was necessary to ensure local economies were not left behind as globalisation processes intensified (Gavidi, cited in the *Fiji Times* 31 October 2001), was widely replicated by bureaucrats and political leaders across the Pacific (Slatter 2006).

On the other hand, the PPA policy framework also limited the extent to which non-state actors within the SPC institutional environment might raise such questions. The PPA approached questions of women's economic empowerment in ways that were consistent with the neoliberal ethos of market liberalisation and state streamlining, emphasising women's entrepreneurial capacities and market participation. By contrast, regional NGOs, such as the Pacific Concerns Resource Centre and a range of local academics, were offering far more critical perspectives on the long-term impacts of these policies for local industry and employment levels (Firth 2000; PCRC 2002). The distance between these two perspectives indicates that within the SPC regional forum there was little room for critical appraisal of the regional political economy.

After nearly twenty years of operations, the PWRB seemed not to have achieved the ambitions envisaged for it when Pacific women began lobbying for institutional representation at the regional level in the 1980s. The broader SPC institutional mandate which had made deliberation on region-specific issues, such as nuclear testing or colonisation in the Pacific, difficult in the 1980s, continued to function in the same way two decades later. This mitigated against the emergence of critical debate on regional economic policy issues of concern to local women.

The establishment of the United Nations Development Fund for Women (UNIFEM) Pacific, in 1997, offered Pacific women a new institutional platform from which to address issues of gender equality. Given that the United Nations Economic and Social Commission for Asia and the Pacific (UNESCAP) had provided a more enabling institutional environment for regional deliberation of gender concerns in past years, the creation of this new Pacific agency affiliated with the UN appeared to provide the scope for more critical, gender-sensitive, regional policy analysis than had been possible within the SPC. Ultimately, however, this UN-funded agency did not act as a counter-weight to the many political figures in the region that were uncritical advocates of trade liberalisation. In a UNIFEM pamphlet entitled 'Women, Men, Globalization and Trade Liberalization', women were urged to become involved in local decision-making processes so that they could have a greater impact upon policy outcomes which might mediate some of the negative impacts of globalisation in the region. The ratification of CEDAW was seen as important in this regard, and said to provide women with improved access to decision-making and a 'framework for equity'. Women were also urged to join local women's organisations so that they might become better informed on issues of trade and economic development and more politically active (UNIFEM Pacific 2000). A strong emphasis was placed upon the need for women to assume a level of personal responsibility in becoming politically active on these questions. At the same time, the intensified climate of neoliberal economic reform in the region seems to have been viewed as an inevitability, rather than a force to be resisted.

Certainly, the creation of a regional UNIFEM office saw stronger support offered to women's organisations at both the local and regional levels than had been provided by the PWRB. Collaborative efforts between UNIFEM and local women's organisations were able to take place in a more ad hoc manner, and were not structured by the restrictive mandate that made PWRB-NGO relationships more difficult. This also meant that UNIFEM provided important financial support for the activities of regional issue-specific NGO networks established by Fiji-based organisations such as the Pacific Women Against Violence Against Women network, coordinated by the FWCC. Through this network, established in the previous decade, the FWCC continued to provide training to gender advocates from most Melanesian states and also established contacts with women's groups in New Caledonia, the Federated States of Micronesia and Samoa. The Crisis Centre also focused greater attention on the situation of Pacific women living in conflict zones, emphasising the predicament of women in Solomon Islands and Bougainville. In December 2000, the FWCC attempted to coordinate simultaneous rallies in Solomon Islands, Bougainville and Fiji to reflect upon the vulnerability of women in conflict situations. While the interim government in Fiji thwarted plans for the Suva march, rallies took place in the other two locations.

The FWCC also staged two regional meetings on Violence Against Women in August 1996 and February 2001. The 1996 meeting was used to conduct a review of regional strategies to combat violence and to locate areas in which additional training might be useful to local women's organisations. The 2001 meeting again drew attention to women in conflict and the negative consequences suffered by women when a widespread breakdown in social services occurs (FWCC 1996, 2001a).

A new Fiji-based regional organisation established in 1995, the RRRT, sought to expand upon the FWRM's previous regional work in the area of legal literacy promotion. Under the leadership of Jalal, former coordinator of the FWRM, the RRRT was principally concerned with the promotion of women's human rights. However, in later years, the organisation expanded its focus to provide more general education on human rights issues in the region. One of the key aims of the organisation was to inform people of their ability to make demands upon the state when their rights had been violated. To this end, the RRRT aimed to promote local awareness of international conventions and how they might be used to promote greater equality for marginalised groups. While RRRT was committed to the promotion of CEDAW therefore, it also focused upon other international instruments such as the Universal Declaration of Human Rights, the Convention on the Rights of the Child and the Convention on the Elimination of Racial Discrimination (Masura 2002). Improving local communities' knowledge of the content of their nations' constitutions, and the protections these documents offered local citizens, was another of the organisation's aims. All members of the RRRT staff were trained in law, human rights, civic awareness and government-civil society relations.

While the scope of the RRRT's operations was broad in geographic terms, its activities were constrained by the funding relationships it negotiated with its chief benefactors; initially the UK Department of International Development, and later the UNDP. The RRRT was conceptualised as a project, rather than an NGO, and this influenced how it formulated its programs of rights awareness training. Rather than acting in an autonomous fashion, it was required to respond to requests for intervention from NGOs across the region. In this way, benefactors hoped to avoid a situation whereby they were seen to compromise the domestic sovereignty of Pacific Island states. In Fiji, for example, the RRRT regularly worked with organisations such as the Fiji Council of Social Services, the CCF, Soqosoqo Vakamarama (SSVM), the FWCC and the FWRM. Ostensibly, these organisations identified issues of need in the community, and then approached the RRRT for assistance in developing targeted human rights awareness programs. In practice, the order of these processes was more blurred (Masura 2002). Nonetheless, through these interventions, the RRRT aimed to train and support a network of Legal Rights Training Officers that were based in local NGOs and, once provided with the skills, to undertake public awareness programs, provide individual advice and participate in policy dialogue with government agencies (UNDP-RRRT).

International developments

New funding relationships

During this period, neighbouring states with an interest in the Pacific Island region placed an increasing emphasis upon developing collaborative relationships with civil society and non-government groups as part of efforts to promote good governance. The Australian government, the region's largest bilateral aid-provider (von Strokirch 2003), incorporated these principles into its development policy programs with the Australian Minister for Foreign Affairs arguing, in 1997, that foreign aid must support NGOs that aim to increase local participation in governance (cited in Larmour 1998: 1). By 2000, AusAID's policy on good governance emphasised the importance of a 'strong and pluralistic civil society' supporting the values of 'freedom of expression and association' (AusAID 2000). And in line with this focus, AusAID's Pacific Regional Strategy, released in 2002, stated a commitment to strengthening local civil society capacity and an increased role for local organisations in community and humanitarian programs (AusAID 2002).

The coup in Fiji, continuing civil war in Bougainville, and violent civil unrest brewing in Solomon Islands in these years, were all seen to justify this shifting emphasis in aid delivery to the Pacific. The increased purchase of the 'arc of instability thesis' amongst Canberra-based policy makers in 2000 encouraged the view that conflict in the region was endemic, and economic development, stagnant. Deficiencies in local political processes and poor governance were identified as contributing to the problem (Reilly 2000; Henderson 2003; von Strokirch 2003; Hughes 2003).[26]

Such concerns shaped aid distribution decisions made for Fiji. International donors were reluctant to support a post-coup government that did little to hide its ethno-nationalist and class-based allegiances (Robertson and Sutherland 2001; Kelly and Kaplan 2001) and they were far more comfortable developing aid partnerships with non-state actors. Within this environment, civil society groups that were able to 'dovetail' their advocacy aims with broader agendas related to good governance were certainly able to attract the support of external aid-providers engaged in the region (personal communication, AusAID official, Suva, March 2002; Personal communication EU official, Suva, March 2002). As we have seen, the CCF's pro-democracy activities were viewed favourably by external donor agencies such as AusAID during this period, despite the organisation's difficulties with local political authorities. In addition, some women's groups also benefited from this shift in emphasis and, at this time, received substantial amounts of core funding directly from aid agencies. In 1999, AusAID made a substantial increase in funding to the FWCC through its Pacific Regional Program, granting FJ$2.2 million to fund the organisation's core expenses over five years (FWCC 1999a). Similarly, increased donor interest in supporting civil society organisations also translated into funding commitments for the FWRM from development agencies such as the Canada Fund and the DFID. International engagements of this type clearly created important opportunities for some women's organisations in Fiji during this period. However, as I

---

26 Criticisms of the 'doomsday' imagery used to frame analysis of the Pacific Island region have been made by Fry (1997, 2000), Fraenkel (2004) and Chappell (2005).

will later demonstrate, aid agencies' prioritisation of particular political and economic ideals also began to influence how recipient organisations articulated their political goals.

Beijing + 5

The participation of Fiji's women on the international stage was dominated by two key events in the period from 1995 to 2002. The first was the Beijing+5 United Nations Generally Assembly Special Session (UNGASS) convened to review the global implementation of the Beijing Platform for Action. The second was the presentation of Fiji's country report to the United Nations CEDAW Committee in 2002.

Preparations for the Beijing+5 UNGASS began under the Chaudhry government in 1999, with the production of a national report on the implementation of the Beijing Platform for Action (BPA) (Fiji Ministry of Women and Culture 1999b). Compiled during a period when women's organisations were enjoying a high level of support from the state, this report noted with some satisfaction the 'positive movements forward' in government-NGO relations in the latter half of the 1990s, described as a 'definite improvement upon the last decade'. The report described the influence that women's organisations had been able to generate within government to promote 'the integration of gender concerns' in the areas of law reform, domestic violence, rape and sexual harassment. At the same time, the report also included a frank account of the types of obstacles impeding women's equal and active participation in development. It stated that women contributed disproportionately to the ranks of employees within low-skilled and unregulated industries such as garment production or domestic and household work, but were poorly represented in professional fields and in senior management positions. It also described the situation of low-skilled single women attempting to support families as particularly concerning (Fiji Ministry of Women and Culture 1999b).

In the final instance, this report was never taken to New York. The events of May 2000 were still unresolved by the time of Beijing+5 UNGASS, which convened in early June 2000, and therefore no official delegation from Fiji attended this meeting. Nonetheless, the content of the national report drafted for this event gives some indication of the extent to which critical appraisal of government policy was possible both from within the national administration, and outside it, immediately prior to the 2000 coup. This situation altered dramatically in the post-coup political environment.

The events of May 2000 made it difficult for NGO delegations from Fiji to attend the Beijing+5 UNGASS, with many preferring to stay in the country rather than face the possibility of being stranded overseas should the crisis worsen.

Three women from the FWRM—Gina Houng Lee, Raijeli Nicole and FWRM board member Dianne Goodwillie—were in attendance. These participants used the opportunity to draw international attention to the negative impacts of the coup upon women, and the efforts being undertaken by local women towards reconciliation and peacebuilding.

However, these efforts were greatly overshadowed by broader political debates taking place on this occasion. The UNGASS may have been envisaged as an opportunity to 'breathe fresh life and stimulate further momentum' in government and civil society efforts towards the implementation of the BPA, yet much of the debate during the preparatory stages had a retrograde quality that continued during the formal Beijing+5 session (Steans and Ahmadi 2005: 239). In particular, there was a determined push made by a coalition of conservative faith-based NGOs, the Vatican and Islamic states such as Pakistan, Iran, Algeria, Morocco and Syria, to have references to women's reproductive rights and women's sexual orientation excluded from the BPA Outcome Document which was to be voted upon at the conclusion of the session (IWTC electronic communication, 29 March 2000; Slatter 2001; Chappell 2006).

These tensions ensured that the final version of the BPA Outcome Document accepted by the UNGASS did not include references to the terms 'sexual rights' and 'sexual orientation'. While this was a cause for disappointment, many observers noted that a good number of government representatives at the Beijing+5 Special Session demonstrated a general unwillingness to make commitments towards further action on the BPA, and a reluctance 'even to restate' the commitments they had made at Beijing 'five years before' (Slatter 2001; Chappell 2006). For these reasons, Amnesty International suggested that the UN Special Session might be more accurately described as 'Beijing Minus Five' rather than 'Plus Five' (Amnesty International 2000b).

Gender activists from Fiji were generally disappointed with the nature of debate taking place at this meeting and the apparent lack of willingness on the part of many official delegates to consider what needed to be done to take the BPA 'to the next stage' (Houng Lee, cited in FWRM 2000b). However, their principal aim in New York was to draw international attention to the domestic political crisis in Fiji. While the FWRM delegates were keenly aware of the limitations they faced in this regard, particularly given the fierce international debate amongst hundreds of participants, they made a particular effort to frame their concerns in ways that resonated with broader conference themes. In particular, they drew links between the issue of democratic rule in Fiji and the realisation of women's human rights, arguing that democracy was the 'foundation' upon which these rights would be established and protected and that restoration of constitutional governance was a central contention amongst Fiji's gender activists (FWRM 2000b).

UN CEDAW Committee Hearing 2002

When representatives from Fiji next appeared before the UN, this time to present the initial country report to the CEDAW committee in New York in 2002, parliamentary democracy had been re-established. As we have seen, however, with a pro-nationalist regime in power, the terms of political debate on gender equality were greatly constrained. As such, Fiji's NGO 'shadow' delegation appearing before the CEDAW committee used this event to again draw international attention to the domestic political situation and the local obstacles which jeopardised efforts to improve women's status.

The preparation of Fiji's first CEDAW country report had been a thorn in the side of the Rabuka-SVT government since the late 1990s, and the report taken to New York in 2002 was in fact the third in a series of drafts; the previous two had met with SVT officials' disapproval. This situation was turned around with the change of government in Fiji in 1999. The Minister for Women, Lavinia Padarath, became aware of the previous government's inaction on the CEDAW reporting process and began a round of government-NGO consultations in 1999 which resulted in the production of the final report sent to the UN CEDAW committee prior to Fiji's scheduled appearance in mid-2000. The events of May 2000 once again interrupted this process, however, and it was another eighteen months before Fiji appeared before the commission.

When this hearing finally took place, representatives of the SDL government's Ministry for Women were required to speak to the country report originally submitted by the Chaudhry government in 2000 and to verbally update the Committee on recent political developments. While the government's representative, Assistant Minister for Women, Losana Salabula, was frank about the civilian coup and the overthrow of Fiji's elected government in 2000, these events were also described in a way that suggested that the interim regime had consistently been focused upon the restoration of Fiji's constitutional democracy and left aside any discussion of the ongoing hostilities between the SDL and Labour over Cabinet representation or the difficult environment existing between the government and sections of Fiji's civil society (RRRT 2002a). The Assistant Minister's presentation was also laced with references to the SDL government's Social Justice Act (formerly the interim government's *Blue Print for the Protection of Indigenous Fijian and Rotuman Rights*) which, it was asserted, would 'promise positive benefits for women' (Fiji Mission to the UN 2002).

Fiji's NGO shadow report told a different story.[27] This report began by acknowledging the work done by Fiji's government in various areas to improve

---

27 Although this shadow report was prepared at short notice by the FWRM in collaboration with the FWCC, ECREA, WAC, the Fiji Nursing Association, fem'Link, the Fiji Women's Catholic League and Stri Sewa Sabha, the general impression it created of the post-coup political climate from 2000 onwards contrasted in important areas with the official line taken by Fiji's government representatives (FWRM *et al.* 2002).

the status of women, and also stated that the official country report presented by the government to the committee was accurate up until May 2000. However, describing the institutional environment since 2000, the authors were more critical, arguing that the nationalist ambitions now predominated within Fiji's government and that this was detrimental to women. The NGO report, therefore, provided CEDAW committee members with a more up to date account of political developments since 2000. It also offered a more critical perspective of the government's *Blueprint* legislation, arguing that no gender perspective was evident in this legislation, and that it ignored the economic predicament of underprivileged Indo-Fijian citizens. The report called attention to the economic costs of the coup and, particularly, the resulting disadvantage suffered by women as a result of job loss and industry decline. It also described the hostile and retaliatory nature of government dealings with women's organisations, arguing that this 'severely obstructed further work towards gender equality' (FWRM *et al*. 2002). Personal statements made to the Committee by RRRT and FWRM board member Jalal, FWRM coordinator Virisila Buadromo and Wati Seeto-Dubain, also of the RRRT, reiterated many of these themes (RRRT 2002a) and ensured that committee members received with some scepticism the Fiji government's claim that CEDAW was a 'living reality in Fiji' (UN CEDAW 2002).

Despite many of the criticisms made of the Fiji government in this report, CEDAW committee members stated that they had never read a shadow report that was 'so complimentary' of government efforts to advance the status of women (FWRM 2002). In part, these comments attest to the fact that the NGO concerns were raised in a non-confrontational tone, reflecting a decision made by the lead author-organisation, the FWRM, to avoid 'bashing the government in an aggressive manner' or embarrassing them on the international stage (RRRT 2002a). It was suggested that critical analysis of government policy could be framed in subtle tones and yet still be persuasive in front of the CEDAW committee. This tactic also ensured that the reports' collaborators would not be subject to a hostile reaction from government once the reporting process was complete.

UN CEDAW committee members used the information provided during the NGO hearing to scrutinise the government report on an article by article basis. Committee members made over two hundred requests to the government delegation for further information and elaboration (RRRT 2002a; FWRM 2002). These queries focused upon the relationship between CEDAW provisions and domestic law, the mainstreaming of gender perspectives within the government's social justice legislation, the uses of *bulubulu* in Fiji's courts, the functioning of Fiji's newly established Human Rights Commission and the prospects of legal reform in the areas of family law and domestic violence law.

The government delegation was required to formulate answers to these questions before taking part in a 'constructive dialogue' session before the CEDAW committee six days later. It was able to respond to only half of the queries, however, and held over many questions until Fiji's next appearance before the committee. In a final press release issued by the UN CEDAW committee at the conclusion of the dialogue, Fiji was congratulated as being a 'pace-setter in the region,' but also criticised over the status of Fiji's family law, described as 'medieval,' and the uses of traditional reconciliation practices within the court system, particularly in relation to the prosecution of domestic violence cases. While government representatives argued that this was a 'vital custom,' used to cement indigenous kinship ties, the committee urged the government delegation to pay increased attention to the 'negative aspects of the … practice of *bulubulu*' (UN CEDAW 2002; see also Merry 2006b).

Fiji's NGO representatives were generally proud of the fact that they were the first representatives of the Pacific Island region to make an appearance before the UN committee. They also claimed that important dividends had accrued in the wake of their participation which vindicated their decision not to adopt a more aggressive tone in their criticisms of government policy. Participation in the CEDAW reporting process had put the Family Law Bill back on the government's agenda, it was argued. In the wake of the New York hearing, Jalal was reappointed to the position of Family Law Commissioner by the Attorney General, and requested to prepare parliamentarians for the Bill's first post-coup reading in April 2002 (RRRT 2002a).[28]

Yet, there were differences of opinion amongst women activists as to the broader utility of the CEDAW process, particularly given the costs of complying with CEDAW reporting requirements (Moore 2002a) and the strongly legalistic basis of the deliberations (RRRT 2002a; Chung 2002). These differences of opinion indicate the contending ways that political agency was understood by gender activists in this period. Some felt that prevailing local and global political conditions required a dovetailing of agendas in order that policy gains for women could be effectively negotiated. Others were more despondent about the formal realm of institutional politics and tended to adopt strategies of disengagement. However, these courses of action were shaped by activists' appraisals of the prevailing political environment and their own judgments of their capacity for political agency in these years. The following section examines the 'situated' experience of gender activists and asks how subjective understandings of the prevailing political environment influenced activists' negotiations of collectivity, progressive ideas and transnationalism.

---

28   Aside from a number of informal reports which were circulated around the Pacific Islands region by the RRRT and the FWRM in 2002 describing the NGO delegations experiences before the CEDAW committee (RRRT 2002a; FWRM 2002), the RRRT also published a more formal technical manual on the CEDAW reporting process drawing on the lessons learned by Fiji-based NGO delegates (RRRT 2003).

Collectivity

Funding opportunities for women's organisations increased significantly in this period as institutional donor agencies focused greater attention upon increasing civil society participation in local development initiatives. Yet the increased availability of funding also encouraged an intensification of competition amongst local women's groups. Australian aid officials fully recognised this consequence of the Pacific civil society funding assistance regime, but this was not viewed as a fault. Indeed, the intensification of competitive relations between organisations was described by AusAID's Pacific regional policy coordinator in September 2002 as 'the price of doing business with the Australian government' (March 2002).

From the perspective of AusAID officials, treating the civil society funding environment as a competitive 'market place' may have been seen as encouraging transparency and efficiency. Yet in practice, these conditions were generally only advantageous to the small number of women's groups who had the organisational infrastructure and expertise that enabled their market participation. In Fiji, this meant that bodies such as the FWRM and the FWCC were routinely rewarded. By this date, both these organisations had developed sophisticated aid proposal writing techniques which allowed them to formulate projects that were consistent with donor priorities but which were also framed in ways that recognised local needs. These organisations also had the administrative infrastructure that allowed them to comply with donor agencies' increasingly stringent and complex reporting and accountability requirements.

By contrast, this system tended to penalise other groups whose limited resources were stretched when producing detailed funding proposals. WAC's eclectic and unconventional approach to gender advocacy meant that it was not recognised as a destination for core funding in the good-governance aid environment. The organisation led a perpetual 'hand to mouth' existence (Moore 2002b). In 2002, fem'Link faced similar pressures. Locating the next source of funding was an overriding priority for the two-person organisation, which at this stage did not have a solid track-record of media production achievements (Bhagwan Rolls 2002a). Faith-based women's organisations such as the Fiji Catholic Women's League, or the Fiji Muslim Women's League, were also under-recognised in this funding environment. Donor agencies' preference for working with secular rather than faith-based women's organisations in Fiji dated back to 1987, and was explained by a fear that association with this type of organisation would be viewed as partisanship. Yet, this practice also meant that donor agencies generally underestimated the substantial district networks of these faith-based women's organisations, and the importance of the community advocacy and welfare assistance projects they had developed for their constituents (Buksh 2002a; Evening 2002).[29]

The impact of increased competition over funding encouraged a 'turfiness' between women's groups, one local observer argued, with issue areas jealously guarded so that domestic and regional influence could be maintained (Chung 2002). Certainly tensions between women's organisations over funding were exacerbated as opportunities for engagement with donor agencies appeared to increase, but the same high profile secular women's groups were routinely rewarded.[30] Others commented that this tendency corrupted the spirit of voluntarism that had previously been critical to women's organising, observing that 'true activists were now an endangered species' (Slatter 2002).

These funding arrangements tended to encourage relationships between organisations to take on a hierarchical quality, with well-funded organisations generally viewed as more successful and influential than other groups. Certainly, well-funded groups were proud of the strong relationships they had negotiated with external aid-providers and they publicised this fact frequently. For example, in its monthly newsletters, the Crisis Centre provided detailed reports of its financial agreements with AusAID, and accounts of Australian diplomats' visits to the Centre's Suva premises. In 2002, the Centre held public meetings at the Australian High Commission in Suva and also displayed the AusAID logo prominently on the billboard at the front of its offices. Similar tendencies were also evident in the activities of the RRRT and the FWRM. Recipient organisations seemed eager to promote their negotiation of funding as something that contributed to their broader political influence and international credibility and differentiated them from other, less well-funded, groups.

Yet, the negative ramifications of these funding arrangements can also be overplayed. As this chapter has shown, important organisational collaborations were also possible during this period and certainly took place during the period of constitutional reform when the FWRM led a domestic coalition of women's groups demanding the abolition of discriminatory citizenship provisions. Moreover, the Women's Prayer Vigil, staged during and after the coup in 2000, was an important pro-democracy initiative which attested to gender activists' willingness to engage in spontaneous collaborative protest against political authoritarianism.

---

29 These included raising awareness on policy issues such as the CEDAW and the Family Law Bill, but also included housing and income-generating projects for single mothers and destitute women (Buksh 2002a; Evening 2002).

30 Alison Van Rooy has argued that 'all too often donor agencies deal with the development NGOs they already know, sidelining other types of civic organizations' (Van Rooy 1998: 67).

It is also important to note that other issues that had caused tension within and between organisations after the 1987 coups were less important in this period. For example, questions pertaining to the ethnicity of gender activists appear not to have caused the same coup-related divisions that they had in the past. The period of constitutional reform and the drafting of a Bill of Rights outlawing racial discrimination suggested the beginnings of a more liberal institutional environment than had prevailed in Fiji since independence. And despite the fact that the post-coup interim government may have done its best to abrogate the 1997 Constitution, the court ruling of 2001 ensured that it remained intact. These developments expanded the civil society space available to groups aiming to challenge communalism and provided local actors such as the ECREA and the CCF with important points of political leverage.

These developments were also significant for the realm of gender politics and saw many women's groups take a much more pronounced stance against communalism than had been evident in 1987. 'We need rainbows, not Rambos', was a key slogan of the pro-democracy movement in Fiji, and it built upon the idea that effective opposition to ethno-nationalist authoritarianism required a collaborative effort from all of the country's ethnic groups. This meant that within secular pro-democracy women's groups such as the FWRM, where there was a much stronger emphasis upon organisational unity than had been apparent in 1987 (FWRM 2001b). These developments were not universal, and groups such as the SSVM continued to respond to local political developments in a more partisan manner.[31] Yet, many women's groups saw the promotion of democracy as a precondition for the recognition of women's rights. Hence, they acted in a determined fashion to ensure that race would not be the point of cleavage amongst gender activists that it had been in the past (Jalal 2002).

These developments once again point to the importance of understanding how the contingencies of the prevailing political environment influenced organisations' negotiations of collectivity during this period. Certainly, questions relating to the ethnic origin of gender activists were less divisive than they had been in the past. This suggests that the mid-1990s period of constitutional reform, and the later post-coup multiracial slogans of the pro-democracy movement, had encouraged many gender activists to resist rather than replicate the communal identifications that were more broadly apparent within civil society in Fiji. Yet, existing tensions amongst women's organisations over funding were also exacerbated at this time as donor institutions sought to increase local engagement with civil society actors across the Pacific. Notwithstanding the instances where important collaborations between women's organisations occurred in this period, in general terms the idea that

---

31   For example, during this period, the SSVM began to articulate a more pro-nationalist line of argument and was supportive of moves to abrogate the 1997 Constitution.

funding levels equated to organisational success encouraged the emergence of hierarchical relationships between women's groups. Better-funded groups were generally perceived to have a level of credibility and influence in gender politics exceeding that of organisations that lived a more 'hand to mouth' existence. Yet, such appraisals also overlooked the important grassroots services provided by less well-recognised groups, particularly the faith-based women's organisations.

Progressive ideas

Speaking in 2002, Imrana Jalal, coordinator of the RRRT, and still an influential board member of the FWRM argued,

> Feminism has become a gentler political engagement … the wisdom now is that you have to engage, even with people who you think are sexist, right wing, fundamentalist because really, if you want to have any influence on the political domain, you've got to engage with people whose politics you don't necessarily agree with…. I engage with all kinds of people that 15 years ago I wouldn't have had a cup of coffee with. I think that is not only part of my own individual political maturation, but the maturation of all of us as a movement (in *fem'Link*, 2002a).

Jalal's reflections clearly indicated how the notion of engagement had become critical to gender activists' understandings of their ability to promote progressive ideas. Yet her statements also included an implicit claim about the effectiveness of political moderation. She suggested that while the provocative style of campaigning that had taken place in the past had given way to a more moderate and politically mature method of political engagement, the ramifications in terms of 'influence on the political domain' had been positive, not negative.

Examinations of the political fortunes of women's organisations in this period provide some level of support for Jalal's position. Certainly the work of the citizenship coalition in the constitutional reform period had paid important dividends for Fiji's women. The FWCC had early success in winning government support for redrafted sexual offences legislation. Additionally, the proposed Family Law Bill which had won support from the Chaudhry government, seemed by 2002 to be again under consideration by the politically conservative, pro-nationalist, Qarase-led government.

Yet, it can also be argued that this project of 'gentle engagement' was shaped in important respects by broader trends within the prevailing domestic and international political environment. Processes of 'dovetailing' were described to me by Claire Slatter as being an important organisational strategy within the prevailing international funding environment, with organisations actively referencing broader themes evident within domestic and international institutional agendas. For example, the juridical emphasis evident within FWRM and FWCC public advocacy in these years was broadly consistent with good governance norms as they were interpreted by institutional donor agencies which placed a high priority upon 'rule of law' and 'law reform' as key means by which to rejuvenate 'state-relations with society' and encourage 'market-led growth' in developing countries (Crook 2001).

AusAID's policies on good governance during this period clearly conformed to this trend, and emphasised the 'primacy of rule of law, maintained through an impartial and effective legal system' (AusAID 2000). Links were also established between rule of law and economic stability; with AusAID policy stating that for markets to function effectively they needed both effective institutional support and the promotion of 'social norms ... that respect contract and property rights' (AusAID 2000). AusAID's 2002 Pacific Regional Strategy reiterated these themes, stating increased support for 'law and justice institutions around the region' (AusAID 2002).

The campaigns undertaken by the FWCC, FWRM or RRRT, which at this time promoted women's human rights in a highly legalistic manner, clearly dovetailed gender equality objectives with broader international norms relating to rule of law and economic good governance. The idea that impartial and effective legal systems can correct the structures which discriminate against women, and increase their opportunities to access the economic benefits of development, was evident in much of the advocacy undertaken by these groups in these years.

For example, the focus upon women's market participation was clearly in evidence in the FWCC's 2002 '16 Days' campaign which drew attention to the economic costs of violence against women. While the broader aim of this campaign was to win government support for proposed reforms in the area of sexual offences law, the emphasis placed upon the economic aspects of gender violence clearly suggested, in part, that government inaction on these issues was obstructing women's market participation and jeopardising women's entrepreneurial capacities. Similarly, the FWRM's post-coup defence of the Family Law Bill was clearly focused upon the economic opportunities that this program would create, empowering women by lifting them out of poverty and improving their access to maintenance provisions. At the regional level, RRRT advocacy for human rights promotion was based upon a similar logic. Here it was argued that a formal recognition of rights could alleviate the lack of opportunity faced by those living in poverty. In a 2002 newsletter published by the RRRT, it was argued that,

> You need to think about what causes poverty in the first place. First you
> need to understand that poverty is not just financial. A person can also

be poor in terms of how much or little access he or she has to resources, like education and information due to a lack of opportunity. Therefore having human rights provides a basis through which people gain access to the resources they have been denied as a result of social, political and legal inequalities. Until every person has access to human rights, the cycle of poverty will not be broken (RRRT 2002b).

This emphasis upon economic opportunity, capacities for market participation and entrepreneurialism contrasted dramatically with the advocacy programs of gender activists in previous periods who tended to adopt the view that local issues of gender subordination could not be understood without coming to terms with the structural sources of inequalities at the global level and the international mechanisms that compromised Pacific Island states' political and economic autonomy. In this later period, this emphasis upon global inequality had come to be seen as a non-progressive, perhaps needlessly 'aggressive' strategy (Jalal, cited in *fem'Link* 2002a). In the more conservative local and international political environment which prevailed in 2002, the strategies employed by women's groups such as the FWCC, FWRM and RRRT suggest that these groups understood there was a strategic value in promoting 'progressive ideas' in a way which dovetailed with the broader tenets of 'law and order' based good governance.

However, while figures associated with the FWRM or RRRT may have viewed this as evidence of political maturation, others were more sceptical, arguing that 'gentle engagement' was not progressive and, in fact, encouraged a narrowing of organisational goals. Organisations such as WAC, who viewed themselves as operating in a way that was far more autonomous and disengaged from the state, regularly articulated progressive advocacy during this period, by outlining objectives in social change terms. Moore frequently expressed the view that empowerment begins with the individual and 'until the inner person feels good, the outer person will not be able to change or survive' (Moore 2002a). The range of programs falling under the WAC umbrella during this period may certainly have had an eclectic quality; however the underlying aim of promoting community empowerment and improving local levels of self-esteem suggests that this organisation was motivated by a very different conceptualisation of progressive ideas than more high-profile groups.

Yet, from a global governance perspective, program outcomes of this sort were much more difficult to measure, and had a far less comfortable fit with broader development paradigms. This helps to explain why WAC's relationships with external donor agencies were consistently of a more ad hoc variety than other more high profile groups.

The extent to which Fiji's Churches provided an enabling forum for women's resistance to the May 2000 coup proved similarly difficult for external actors to conceptualise in global governance terms. Participants in the Women's Peace Vigil described the importance of the emphasis upon 'prayer and action'. They also valued the opportunities the vigil provided for 'networking and creating a movement'. However, donor prioritisation of secular women's groups tended to obscure the importance that this initiative held for local women, and how it allowed them to articulate a collective opposition to the actions of the nationalist insurgents (Bhagwan Rolls 2002a; Buksh 2002a).

Some organisations saw the dovetailing of progressive ideas with institutional agendas—domestic or international—as strategically important and a sign of maturity. These strategies clearly also appealed to donors. By contrast, initiatives that were more disengaged from institutional politics tended not to be recognised by donor agencies as progressive, or as providing evidence of women's political agency, despite being understood as such, in a 'situated sense', by the activists involved. Clearly, women's organisations had widely varying ideas about what could be considered progressive during this period. Yet, institutional aid providers tended only to recognise and give support to those women's organisations whose 'progressive' agendas dovetailed with their own political and economic priorities.

Transnationalism

In 2002, some Fiji-based gender activists were beginning to ask whether the influence of transnational networking was distracting local organisations from attending to the needs of women in the domestic context. In particular, doubts were expressed about the juridical emphasis upon human rights advocacy for women and the increasing emphasis placed upon law reform focused advocacy by high profile organisations. Some argued that while such goals had achieved a transnational legitimacy, there was a disconnect between this type of advocacy and the specific needs of Fiji's most vulnerable women, or the local 'bread and butter issues', as one activist put it (Vere 2002a; Moore 2002a). Others felt that such strategies ignored the fact that Fiji was a developing state and simply did not have the institutional infrastructure to support the proposed programs of law reform that were being advocated, in particular, by the FWRM.[32]

In 2002, the FWRM repeatedly described the Family Law Bill as a mechanism that would improve the conditions of women living in poverty (Jalal, cited in *fem'Link* 2002; Colowai 2002). This group was confident that the predicament

---

32 For an examination of how these same questions have been posed within international agency advocacy circles see Nighat Said Kahn (2002).

of the poor could be alleviated if their rights were recognised and made redeemable through programs of state-based legal reform which would increase protection for women. As I have shown, these strategies dovetailed neatly with international good governance norms, yet some activists also raised concerns relating to the capabilities of individual women—and the extent to which this impeded access to the law. For example, some women claimed that the FWRM's law reform program overlooked the specificities of Fiji's socioeconomic context and, particularly, the extent to which poverty becomes an obstacle that impedes women's access to the law (Moore 2002a, 2002b; Rokotuivuna 2002b).

These questions were increasingly urgent after 2000, due to the fact that women were once again bearing a disproportionate burden of economic hardship as a result of a post-coup national economic downturn. In my discussions with local researchers examining the predicament of female garment workers in Fiji in 2002,[33] I learnt that women earning only FJ$45–50 per week, and generally living in Suva's increasingly crowded squatter settlements, were in such a precarious financial situation that, should their long working hours allow it, paying the extra bus-fare into central Suva to discuss their situation with legal representatives or state welfare authorities represented a costly financial investment with no guarantee of return (see Harrington 2004: 498). When framed in this way, the optimistic promotion of legal literacy as a tool of empowerment for women appeared not to have taken into account the extent to which class and gender can become 'enmeshed', contributing to an intricate and multi-levelled system of 'oppression' (Sen 2002: 147), which requires a range of interventions beyond the confident promotion of legalistic solutions.[34]

Yet, if gender activists' efforts to advance the status of women appeared to be narrowly focused or distracted, it is also clear that their ability to draw attention to the 'bread and butter' needs of women on the domestic and international stage were constrained by broader political trends. After 2000, their energies were engaged once again with the task of lobbying domestically for the restoration of democracy and protection of the 1997 Constitution. 'Every 10 years our attention regularly gets diverted elsewhere,' argued one observer.

At the same time, the domestic political terrain was not conducive to local activists giving prolonged attention to the capabilities of Fiji's poor in anything other than legal terms; a situation that was similar to the post-coup scenario in 1987. In accordance with broader neoliberal orthodoxies, the post-coup government in 2002 had only limited welfare-assistance services in place. These

---

33   I am grateful to Christy Harrington and Claire Slatter for sharing their insights with me on the working and living conditions of Suva's garment workers in 2002 (see Harrington 2004).

34   At the same time, the confident promotion of legalistic measures as a means by which 'poor women' can redeem their rights generally also overlooks the extent to which poverty can be socially disempowering and debilitating to the individual's self-esteem. As Naila Kabeer has noted in the Malaysian context, women in these situations may have limited experience in 'fending for themselves in a public space' or dealing with public officials (Kabeer 1999: 246).

were difficult to access and not well publicised. Even where applicants were considered sufficiently 'destitute' to receive government assistance, average allowance payments of FJ$6.65 per week were much lower than the estimated minimum weekly amount of FJ$45 needed to meet basic household needs. Additionally, the government sought to maintain its revenues through the imposition of a VAT, and indeed increased VAT rates by 25 per cent in 2002, a situation which further compounded post-coup economic disadvantage and consumed a 'disproportionate amount of women's earnings' (Harrington 2004: 504). Yet, local civil society actors' efforts to protest against these policies were subject to state scrutiny and constraint, as I have shown. In this environment, many women's groups appeared reluctant to take a confrontational stand on the issues of women's material disadvantage.

Similar constraints were in operation at the international level. The regressive nature of intergovernmental debate at the Beijing+5 UNGASS, in combination with the tactics employed by conservative religious interests, left little scope for critical international debate on the issue of women's economic status, and no possibility of expanding upon the limited perspectives of this issue within the BPA. As one observer to these deliberations remarked, industrialised member-states were adamant that issues of gender and economic empowerment be articulated in language that emphasised 'economic opportunity' rather than 'economic rights' or fundamental global 'structural change' (electronic communication from Mitra Vasisht UNFPA New York to FWRM 2000). With the focus upon rights and market opportunities, there was limited scope for local activists to draw international attention to the question of how Fiji's women would fare in a liberalised trading environment which threatened the future sustainability of Fiji's export industries.

These same influences also appear to have influenced NGO conduct before the UN CEDAW committee in February 2002. Once again, the contributions made by women's organisations to this process tended to be framed in rights-based language which focused upon state-based legalistic reform but which avoided a broader focus upon more contentious questions of global economic justice or local economic disadvantage. On this occasion, it seems clear that Fiji's women's organisations were responding to an international institutional environment which provided only limited political space to civil society actors aiming to contest broader neoliberal tenets of good governance.

These considerations suggest that although trends within the prevailing political environment encouraged women's organisations to incorporate aspects of the broader institutional good governance agenda into their advocacy, they also diverted activists' attentions away from the material aspects of women's disadvantage on the domestic or international stage. This scenario contrasts significantly with the way such questions were addressed within the sphere of women's organising in earlier periods.

Conclusion

Political developments in Fiji from 1995 encouraged local gender activists to look to the future with some optimism as momentum for political reform became apparent and the space for critical political engagement between civil society and the state expanded. By 2002, however, this mood of confidence had evaporated. The local return to nationalist politics in Fiji, and the severe deterioration in state-civil society relations, challenged the ability of gender activists to draw attention to contentious aspects of women's subordination. At the same time, developments on the international stage also seemed to indicate that this was not the enabling realm for gender advocacy it had been in the past. Internationally endorsed models of development policy-making tended towards an uncritical application of market-participation strategies as the key to women's economic empowerment and discouraged the articulation of region-specific discourses of gender advocacy that had been prevalent in earlier periods. Furthermore, conservative religious lobbies aimed to exclude the issues of sexual orientation and reproductive health from global debate on women's rights. As we have seen, these developments had important implications for the ways in which gender advocates understood their capacity for political agency on the local and international stage.

Certainly, high profile women's groups such as the FWCC and the FWRM maintained a strong commitment towards state, reform-focused advocacy, campaigning for changes to Fiji's Family Law and Sexual Offences Law. In the post-coup context, this was a 'gentle' form of political engagement which saw these groups dovetail their ambitions with domestic and international institutional policy agendas and avoid provocative political confrontation. Amongst other groups, however, there was a level of scepticism about the benefits of this state-focused direction in advocacy. These groups aimed to develop a more grassroots focused style of advocacy that worked towards community empowerment and social change but remained disengaged from the formal sphere of institutional politics. Those groups that followed the path of institutional disengagement continued to view their activities as empowering, political, and posing a provocative challenge to the prevailing status quo. Yet, international donor agencies tended to recognise and support only those groups whose strategies incorporated the prevailing norms that shaped approaches to global governance and development. This mitigated against women's organisations engaging in the type of internationalised, structurally inclined and highly provocative activity that had been discernible in earlier years.

The following chapter considers how the terrain of women's organising fared as Fiji was rocked by yet another coup in 2006. Led by Fiji's military commander, and defended, somewhat ironically in the name of 'good governance', this event ushered in a new era of punitive political authoritarianism. It also became the catalyst for deep divisions within civil society, as individual organisations struggled to agree on questions about Fiji's governance and development priorities into the future. This scenario posed significant challenges for women's organisations. Yet, the fact that Fiji's authoritarian political regime seemed to take great delight in ignoring condemnations made of it by the international community, seemed also to encourage a shift in the local political environment and a newly critical turn in local gender advocacy circles.

As my discussion of this next stage in the history of women's organising in Fiji will show, this set of circumstances seemed, in the long run, to encourage some activist groups to develop their political claims in ways that were reminiscent of the more critical, internationalised and provocative perspectives of women's disadvantage in the Pacific that had been the trademark of earlier periods.

6. 'Working in a Different Way Now': Division and Peacebuilding in the Aftermath of the 'Good Governance' Coup

On 6 March 2009, in the lead up to International Women's Day, the Fiji Women's Rights Movement launched a radio campaign aiming to promote democracy, human rights and rule of law in Fiji. The campaign featured various speakers articulating visions for the future of the country. These included wanting 'a Fiji' with a popularly elected political leadership, 'a Fiji' where equality of opportunity was safeguarded, and 'a Fiji' with a fair and representative legal system. The timing of the campaign was deemed important by the FWRM who argued that women's status could only be improved if democracy, human rights and rule of law were already respected (FWRM 2009a).

Such calls were, of course, entirely consistent with the pro-democracy, human rights agenda which had been promoted by the FWRM since its establishment nearly two decades earlier. Yet, in 2009, these refrains carried a different political weight than they had in previous decades. At this point, the FWRM was operating within a civil society environment newly riven by the fallout of another coup, and widespread disagreement over the appropriateness of democratic models of governance in Fiji.

This chapter examines developments within women's organising in Fiji from 2003 to 2009. In particular it discusses the turbulent nature of gender politics since late 2006 when Fiji again saw its elected government ejected from power by the military. I show that this event has encouraged a trend towards critical organisational self-evaluation and introspection amongst women advocates and an increasing interest in understanding the role that women can play in mending the country's political divisions.

Fiji's fourth coup in two decades, appeared to confirm the prediction that the legacies of 1987 were ongoing and the country was indeed stuck in a 'coup culture' (Madraiwiwi *Radio Australia* 11 March 2009). It ushered in a new era of political authoritarianism in Fiji which forced many women activists to consider the immediate and serious costs of critical political engagement. It also threatened to splinter the women's movement generally, as deep division emerged between activists who opposed the military's assault upon democracy and other women's groups who interpreted the coup as mandated by a broader social justice agenda. Despite such difficulties, these local events, in combination with shifting global political imperatives, also encouraged women's organisations to explore new advocacy directions. This resulted in some groups asking hard questions about the sustainability of their activities and the means by which new leadership could be fostered within the women's movement generally. High-profile groups began to broaden the former narrow focus of their activity to include a more far-reaching emphasis upon peacebuilding. These groups also began to display a renewed interest in 'international' perspectives of women's disadvantage. This saw some women activists develop a more critical attitude towards regional hegemony and the foreign policy agendas being promoted in the Pacific Islands by neighbouring powers.

These shifts were evident within advocacy undertaken by Fiji's women activists on the local, regional and international stage and contrasted in significant ways with the previous decades. But why did such shifts occur at this particular juncture? This chapter will aim to answer this question by, once again, examining the prevailing political context and describing the interplaying global and local political influences which contributed to these trends.

I will demonstrate how discussions about new leadership within women's organisations reflected broader deliberations on inclusiveness and sustainable leadership taking place within the international women's movement. At the local level, concerns were also being raised about the heavy personal toll borne by women activists with long-term experience working within Fiji's volatile political climate. It will also show how increasing disquiet over the divisive nature of civil society relations in Fiji prompted some women activists to shift the focus of their advocacy away from previously predominant law and order concerns to engage more explicitly with issues related to relationship mending and community peacebuilding. It will also demonstrate how the increasingly isolationist international posture adopted by Fiji's self-appointed military regime appeared to open the way for some women's groups to also develop their own critical stance on questions of international significance—such as regional free trade and regional governance.

As Fiji entered a new era of military rule in 2006, many regional observers of Pacific affairs made gloomy predictions for the country's future. Yet, despite the political instability introduced in the wake of the December 2006 coup, the military violence used to quell critical voices in the months which followed, and the contending visions for Fiji's future which divided civil society, the vibrancy of the women's movement remained undimmed. In the pages which follow, this vibrancy will become fully evident as deeper consideration is given to the activity undertaken by women's groups in Fiji on local, regional and international stages and the prevailing influences which shaped their work. This discussion will be followed, as in the previous chapters, by a more thematically driven consideration of how women's organisations negotiated collectivity, progress and transnationalism in this period.

Local developments

In the previous chapter of this book, I demonstrated how the political forces unleashed during the 2000 coup continued to shape the prevailing political environment in the years directly following this event, bringing to power a pro-nationalist regime that frequently displayed hostility towards those actors within civil society that challenged its political sympathies or policy agenda. As the years passed, and the Qarase regime held on to power, little had changed in this regard. Women's groups did successfully promote reform in some areas at this time; the most noteworthy instance being parliamentary endorsement of the Family Law Bill. In general terms however, the climate for advocates aiming to promote political and social change was a challenging one and, as I will show, only became more volatile as the years passed.

For many activists, and particularly the Fiji Women's Rights Movement (FWRM), October 2003 was the high point of this period; a date which saw Fiji's parliament finally pass the Family Law Bill. This was the culmination of a process begun some thirteen years previously, spear-headed by Imrana Jalal who was a key member of both the FWRM and the Fiji Law Reform Commission, and someone who ensured that the momentum needed to sustain the campaign for gender equity in law did not wane. Despite the many levels of consultation on the Bill that had taken place in the years prior, it remained controversial even after being passed into law. Some political and religious figures feared that the impact of the new laws would enable easier procurement of divorce, or the equitable distribution of matrimonial property following such an event. They argued that the changed family law framework undermined indigenous conceptions of leadership, property rights and inheritance and threatened the religious sanctity of marriage (Kanailagi cited *Radio New Zealand* 24 October 2003).

Despite such public misgivings, the government maintained its commitment to the new Family Law Act. Delays occurring during the implementation phase, which required Fiji to establish a new family law court, meant that it was two more years before the law officially came into effect. Finally, in 2005, Fiji's new Family Law Court was opened by Fiji's Vice President and former High Court judge, Ratu Joni Madraiwiwi (Madraiwiwi cited *Government of Fiji*, 2 November 2005).

Fem'Link exhibited a strong degree of organisational growth in this period as AusAID, the IWDA and the Global Fund for Women provided crucial sources of funding to support its programs promoting women's media presence. This enabled the organisation to move from its temporary and somewhat makeshift office space, located in the foyer of the Caines Jannif Building in Central Suva, to its own premises. By 2009, the organisation had secured its own 'community media centre', occupying a whole floor of a small building at the edge of Suva's town centre. Organisational ranks had also swollen beyond the two original members of fem'Link's staff—Sharon Bhagwan Rolls and her video producer Peter Sipeli—to a much larger cohort in 2009. This enabled fem'Link to continue its community video projects, but also expand into areas such as community radio broadcasting and 'suitcase' radio transmission which saw the organisation use a portable transmitter to create radio programs in regional locations. The aim of these small-scale media projects was to increase the voice of rural and semi-urban women 'whose stories and issues' according to Bhagwan Rolls, 'do not make the news or even dissemination through NGO information networks' (Bhagwan Rolls 2007: 18). Fem'Link had also developed a media training scheme for young women entitled 'Generation Next', which aimed to increase the radio broadcasting skills of participants. As of 2007, the project had trained twenty young women who were charged with running fem'Link's weekend broadcasts from the Suva offices (Bhagwan Rolls 2007: 21).

The fortunes of the Fiji Women's Crisis Centre (FWCC) were also boosted in these years thanks to the continued support of AusAID which agreed to fund the construction of a new headquarters for the organisation. While the FWCC had operated out of an unassuming, small timber building only a short distance from central Suva since 1993 (a property originally purchased with AusAID's assistance), working conditions had become cramped as the years passed and the organisation grew. Hence, AusAID was again approached by the FWCC and asked to help finance a new building project on the same land. The completed structure opened in November 2006. Comprising three stories, painted a dramatic shade of lilac, and hung with banners promoting women's human rights, it was a far more imposing presence than the former premises and testimony to the local, regional and international profile of the organisation and its continued efforts to combat violence against women across a range of Pacific Island nations. Not since the 1970s and the heady days of the Fiji YWCA's expansive youth training, education and advocacy programs had such a grand headquarters for a women's organisation been constructed in Suva. This was something that fellow women activists across the country openly recognised and celebrated (fem'Link 2006).

Figure 6.1. Fem'Link's expanded operations in 2009.

Source: Photograph by Nicole George.

Figure 6.2. New FWCC premises opened in 2006 and constructed with AusAID funding.

Source: Photograph by Nicole George.

Although these types of achievements gave women's activists cause to celebrate, this period was also sadly marked by the death of long-time feminist activist and YWCA member Amelia Rokotuivuna in 2005. She had battled continued ill-health for some time but remained to the end of her life an important, if always unconventional, figure within activist circles across the Pacific. Before her death she had been recognised internationally for her life-long contribution to peacebuilding by the Swiss-based, Peace Women Across the Globe. This organisation was established with the aim of increasing global awareness of women peace builders and, in 2005, launched a campaign to have a list of 1000 women from around the world awarded the Nobel Peace-Prize. Amelia Rokotuivuna and Sharon Bhagwan Rolls from fem'Link were both included on this list (Peace Women Across the Globe, 2005).

Rokotuivuna's funeral on 9 June 2005 saw women from across the Pacific converge on Suva to celebrate her life and remember with fondness and admiration her unwavering efforts to promote equality and justice for Pacific peoples. Her commitment to multiculturalism and the value of religious diversity was evident even at the end of her life, with her funeral combining Christian and Hindu elements (Goodwillie 2005b). Her death also focused renewed attention upon some of the hallmark themes that had defined her advocacy. In the days following Rokotuivuna's funeral, Ruth Lechte addressed a group of twenty young women who had recently taken part in a FWRM program designed to promote leadership skills. Lechte described how Amelia had always 'dared to be different', often shocking fellow Fijians with her political viewpoints 'not just for the sake of it, but ... to effect change in addressing injustice and improving the situation of women' (Goodwillie 2005a).

Certainly, this was a period when questions relating to justice and equality were thrown into sharp national focus in Fiji, as political divisions deepened over the government's efforts to promote various pieces of legislation that many felt catered too heavily to the interests of indigenous nationalists. The most contentious of these was the government's Reconciliation, Tolerance and Unity (RTU) Bill.[1] The Qarase government defended this piece of legislation, arguing that it would help uncover the truth behind the earlier civilian-led coup of 2000. It established state mechanisms to administer compensation to those who suffered loss as a result of the coup and amnesty claims lodged by those found guilty of coup-related offences. The government used cultural arguments to justify these provisions arguing that such measures reflected principles of restorative justice that were built into Fijian culture and reinforced by a belief in

---

1   The second piece of contentious legislation was known as the Qoliqoli Bill and aimed to return control of Fiji's foreshore areas and offshore waters (currently under government control) to local communities. If passed into law, traditional owners would decide who might access these areas, how they might be used and the level of reparations paid by outsiders using these areas for fishing or tourism activities.

unconditional forgiveness held by Fijian Christians (Bhim 2007). Many rejected such arguments, however, and felt that the government was simply pandering to hardline ethnonationalists in order to win their support in up-coming national elections, scheduled for mid-2006. The Bill was seen to offer little in terms of national reconciliation and, in fact, was viewed as a measure with the potential to reignite racial tensions within the country that had simmered since 2000 (Bhim 2007).

From the outset, Fiji's military, and most notably its commander Commodore Voreqe Bainimarama, voiced strong opposition to the RTU Bill. As the government continued to stand behind the Bill, Bainimarama adopted an increasingly belligerent position and made many strong statements publically criticising Prime Minister Qarase. At certain critical points in this debate, uniformed soldiers were also sent in significant numbers to Fiji's parliamentary complex; a portentous sign that the military could, and would, intervene politically should it so choose (Bhim 2007; *Fiji Sun* 28 March 2006).

The government won the 2006 elections convincingly. With his mandate secured, and little debt owed to the nationalists, Qarase appeared to adopt a more conciliatory attitude towards opponents of the RTU Bill, choosing to soften many of its most contentious provisions. Bainimarama rejected these concessions, however. He continued to voice his dissatisfaction with the government's alleged communalist politics and repeatedly made threatening statements regarding his intention to lead a military intervention should efforts to promote the RTU Bill, in any shape, continue.

By late 2006, a climate of political brinkmanship emerged as Prime Minister Qarase and Military Commander Commodore Frank Bainimarama appeared to harden their positions and began to trade accusations and threats in the media. Civil society figures urged the parties to end the standoff and come to some form of agreement, while foreign governments attempted to broker peace between the government and military camps. But local and international efforts to bring the leaders to agreement and avert political upheaval ultimately floundered. Fiji's military seized power in December 2006 and made good on a threat that had hovered over the country for the previous eighteen months.

Bainimarama invoked notions of good governance as he sought to defend his decision to eject the Qarase government from power. He decried what he alleged was a 'silent coup' waged on Fiji by the Prime Minister through 'bribery, corruption and the introduction of controversial bills' (Bainimarama 2006). While he further stated that the military had observed 'with concern and anguish the deteriorating state of our beloved Fiji,' he also sought to assure Fiji's citizens that '[a]fter a proper census and electoral system is in place,' the caretaker government would 'facilitate democratic national elections' (Bainimarama

2006). These statements were, however, accompanied by a warning for those contemplating opposition that might disrupt 'peace and harmony' or pose a threat to what was termed the 'life of the state'. On 7 December, the army followed up on this warning by declaring a state of emergency and suspending sections of the constitution which protected civil rights in the areas of freedom of expression, freedom of association and assembly, and individual rights to liberty (*Fijilive* 7 December 2006).

In the days following the military takeover, a broad spectrum of civil society groups, ranging from the Fiji Public Service Association, the Fiji Nursing Association and the National Farmers Union, to the Fiji Council of Churches and the right-wing Assembly of Christian Churches, pleaded with the military to return to barracks and return the country to democracy (*Daily Post* 8 December 2006; *Fiji Times* 8 December 2006; Waqairatu 2006). Some high-profile women's groups were also at the forefront of these debates, with figures such as Imrana Jalal of the Regional Rights Resource Team, Virisila Buadromo from FWRM and Shamima Ali from the FWCC all vigorously promoting a pro-democracy agenda through press-releases and general media commentary. These groups ignored the military's warnings of the serious consequences that would be faced by those it deemed to be inciting dissent. They were soon to learn that the military meant what it said. Reprisals against anyone taking a public stand against the military were swift and violent and resulted in members of civil society organisations, as well as media representatives, former politicians, lawyers and business figures being detained by the military 'for questioning'. Before long, allegations of serious human rights violations were being made against the military by detainees upon their release.[2]

Buadromo gained a firsthand understanding of the military's uncompromising response to criticism when she was taken for questioning to the military barracks in late December 2006 with five other pro-democracy activists. At this time, she was allegedly subject to verbal intimidation and physical abuse ending with a forced ten kilometre walk through the rainy streets of Suva in the early morning of Christmas Day (Buadromo cited SBS 2007). The military also placed Buadromo on a list of people banned from undertaking international travel. At a later date, the army also placed a travel ban on the coordinator of the FWCC, Shamima Ali.

---

2   For early documentation of this situation see the 'Monitoring human rights abuses Fiji Coup 2006,' document circulated via electronic networks and also known as 'Monitoring Framwork [sic] of the violation of the freedom from arbitrary arrest and detention and freedom from cruel or degrading treatment by the Reprublic [sic] of Fiji Military Forces (RFMF) since its Coup d' etat of 5th December 2006', updated 26th January 2007 in *Defending Women, Defending Right*s, URL: http://www.defendingwomen-defendingrights. org/pdf2007/Updated260107Monitoring_FijiCoup2006_Shortversion.pdf accessed 21 May 2010; also SBS 2007, *Fiji Times*, 14 December 2006, 26 February 2006, 8 March 2007; *Fijilive*, 17 July 2007.

As the army's campaign of intimidation increased and appeared to take on a more indiscriminate quality, with a series of unexplained deaths in custody coming to public attention (SBS 2007), pro-democracy groups began to adopt a more subdued posture of quiet and cautious observation. They called for all efforts to be geared towards finding a peaceful solution to the political crisis and condemned the military's alleged human-rights abuses, but they also desisted from acting in a way that would provoke military hostility (Yabaki cited *Fiji Times* 18 January 2007; Suva-based activist, personal communication February 2007). A cautious approach was judged to be the most sensible course of action in this environment. Women activists were even discouraged from staging peace vigils, similar to those that had been organised amidst the chaos of the 2000 coup, for fear such activities might invite hostile military reaction. This cautious political stance also helped distance pro-democracy activists from the vocal pro-Qarase, Fijian nationalist camp who, in something of an ironic and uncomfortable twist, had now also chosen to promote themselves as guardians of democracy in Fiji.[3]

Yet, opposition to the coup was not universal within Fiji's civil society. A number of organisations also sought to challenge the pro-democracy campaigners; key amongst them the Fiji Human Rights Commission (FHRC), an independent, constitutionally-established body designed to uphold the human rights of Fiji's citizens since 1997. This organisation, directed by Shaista Shameem, challenged those who described the military regime as unlawful. Instead it raised doubts over the assumed legality of the previous Qarase regime which had come to power in the wake of the 2000 coup—an event which it claimed had abruptly halted the incumbency of the legitimately elected Chaudhry government (Shameem 2007). It was also highly critical of non-government organisations (NGOs) promoting a pro-democracy stance, alleging that these groups' political outlook had become compromised by their close relationship with 'interventionist' governments such as Australia and New Zealand (Shameem 2007). Describing this scenario as a 'conflict of interest', Shameem offered a negative appraisal of NGOs' ability to independently assess the political situation in Fiji and respond in a way that served the interests of Fiji's people (Shameem 2007: 24–26).[4]

---

3   The 2000 coup had been a catalyst for these individuals' political ascendancy and, in the ensuing years, they had consistently voiced scepticism about the appropriateness of democracy in Fiji. In the changed political circumstances of late 2006, these same figures now rallied against the military, and espoused sentiments which indicated a recently found appreciation for democratic principles of governance.

4   Shamima Ali, as the only 'legally and constitutionally appointed commissioner' of the FHRC at the time of the coup, sought the assistance of a group of 'highly respected senior lawyers' (FHRC 2007: 1) to commission a response to these claims. This report, also published on FHRC letterhead, rejected Director Shameem's allegations regarding the illegality of the Qarase government but failed to engage fully with the substance of criticisms made against the NGO community in Suva, other than branding them as 'baseless' and 'derogatory' (FHRC 2007).

Other civil society representatives including, most notably, members of ECREA, questioned the value of democracy for Fiji, arguing that although Qarase's SDL party had been democratically elected to govern the country in 2006, this regime had hardly demonstrated a policy track record which served the interests of all Fiji's people in any inclusive or responsible way (Casimera 2006). Ecumenical Centre for Research Education and Advocacy (ECREA) representatives were also critical of the seemingly flippant manner in which democracy was being discussed in the post-coup environment, and warned against pro-democracy NGOs becoming co-opted into an insincere ethno-nationalist platform which camouflaged narrower and more self-serving political aims (Casimera 2006; Barr 2007). According to this argument, the military's aims to 'clean up' Fiji's politics were built around social justice ambitions. The coup was defended as an opportunity to resolve issues such as the 'explosive mix of fundamentalist religion and extreme nationalism' that shaped the policy agendas of the previous government, as well as economic programs that were alleged to have intensified poverty and created 'two Fiji's' (Barr 2007)

Longstanding figures within the women's movement such as WAC's Peni Moore, were also prominent within this broader group. Deeply dissatisfied with the Qarase government, they put their faith in Bainimarama's stated vision for a more socially just and inclusive Fiji and committed to engage with the military's efforts to establish a National Council for Building a Better Fiji (Moore 2007).[5] They also voiced some disappointment in their colleagues who had adopted a more antagonistic stance towards the regime. They argued that deeper complexities underlay the current challenges faced by the country. According to this view, the achievement of a sustainable and enduring peace in Fiji required more than an unswerving faith in democracy (Academic and activist, personal communication, Suva 2007).

In the weeks and months which followed, the military regime began to move away from its earlier statements regarding Fiji's future return to democracy and became more non-committal on how or even when it might begin these reform processes. At the same time, there was growing evidence that the military's violent intimidation of its critics was continuing unchecked. While concern over the military's human rights violations of detainees spanned the pro-military, pro-democracy divide within Fiji's civil society, there was also a growing appreciation amongst all civil society actors that a dramatic shift had occurred within the prevailing political environment, significantly contracting the space

---

5   This Council sought to develop a People's Charter for Change, Peace and Progress which would provide a future roadmap for Fiji, enabling it to become a more 'culturally vibrant, and united, well-governed and truly democratic nation' that observed the principles of 'merit-based equality of opportunity, justice and mutual observance of everyone's human rights' (NCBBF 2008). The process was launched in September 2007 and a 45-member council was appointed to develop a draft report reflecting working group deliberations and findings from community consultations. The report was delivered in August 2008.

for critical political comment. In this climate, neighbouring countries' calls for Fiji's citizens to engage in strategies of civil resistance against the military (Downer cited *Fiji Times* 13 December 2006) were locally viewed as dangerous and meddlesome. Long-time activists within the women's movement, who had previous experience of similar circumstances in 1987, privately voiced the view that only the politically naïve or irresponsible would choose to pursue anything other than a moderate public agenda in such a climate.

One particular organisation bucked this trend, however, and made a bold stand against the military regime. The Fiji Nursing Association's struggle for fair pay and conditions in 2007 brought it into headlong confrontation with the interim government—but seemed to elicit unqualified support from women's groups around the country, bringing a brief moment of unity to a movement that was otherwise deeply divided at this time.

This strike was a continuation of a dispute that had begun under the Qarase regime and seen nurses demand pay rises in accordance with agreements signed in 2003 that had never been fulfilled. However, if the FNA was 'definitely not' supportive of the Qarase government, it was also highly critical of the coup and newly established military regime (Lutua 2009). The Association was particularly dismayed by Mahendra Chaudhry's decision, acting as the regime's interim finance minister, to impose an across the board 5 per cent pay cut on the Public Service. For the nurses, this was simply more evidence to confirm their view that 'coups equal salary reductions' (Lutua 2009). Dissatisfaction simmered within the nursing association throughout the early months of 2007 but became more serious in July of that year when the Health Minister, Dr Jona Senilagakali, and the Public Services Minister, Poseci Bune, refused to move beyond an initial offer of a 1 per cent raise for nurses (*Fiji Times* 26 July 2007; Lutua 2009). Dissatisfied with the government's seemingly 'stubborn' rejection of negotiation or formal arbitration, the Association voted to stop work indefinitely from midnight on 24 July 2007 (*Fiji Times* 25 July 2007).

Many women's groups, including the FWCC, the NCW, fem'Link, and the SSVM, expressed strong support for the nurses' action. They called upon the government to desist from blaming nurses for the breakdown in national health services in the wake of the strike and, instead, work towards a resolution of the crisis (FWCC 2007; fem'Link electronic communication, PACWIN 25 July 2007; Lutua, personal communication February 2009). They were also highly critical of the government request that police physically remove striking nurses from their hospital-based, or rural, health-centre living quarters.[6]

---

6   FNA General Secretary Kuini Lutua rejected some communities' offers of assistance and housing for evicted nurses, arguing that she did not want to put these communities at risk of government retaliation.

As the strike continued, the FNA devised a new strategy to gain government attention. On 6 August, nurses gathered at the makeshift picket that had been maintained at the FNA offices since the beginning of the strike. Here they decided to stage a public protest at Suva's Government offices where an interim Cabinet meeting was due to be held that morning. Lutua recounted to me how the action was planned and preceded,

> I said 'I need 20 volunteers and I want you to know that we will be arrested. We will be arrested.' There were lots of tears that day. But we had to stand up to them—as mothers, as women of Fiji—we had to tell them they were wrong.... I rang the head of CID who is a friend of mine and told him what we were planning. I felt safer if the police got to us before the military. He was cross and told me to stop, but by that time we were almost there [at the government offices]. Within half an hour we were outside the cabinet meeting and right in front of TV1 [national television station]. We were the face of 1400 nurses. I told the nurses to stand in twos twenty meters apart. I knew if we stood together we could be arrested for protesting. But if we stood apart it could not be called a protest. Luckily the police got us first. But the charges against us were dropped. I had read the Public Order Act and knew that we had not broken the law. We were just given a warning (Lutua 2009).

After this 'successful' action (viewed as such for the fact that it captured media and government attention), the FNA decided to end the strike and pursue the matter through the courts. Rather than seeing the strike episode as a 'bitter defeat' (Fraenkel 2008: 455) for the fact that the FNA had failed to win widespread support from key unions or win concessions from the government, Lutua described these events in positive terms. She argued that the strike and later protest action made the nurses' grievances clear, elicited a strong level of public support and demonstrated the weakness of the military regime and its inability to make a decision on the wage claims (Lutua 2009). In the months which followed, the validity of the FNA's grievances was again recognised. Within the judicial sphere, the FNA won a court case against the minister of Labour, whose initial refusal to take the matter to arbitration was deemed illegal. The FNA was awarded FJ$18,000 in compensation but the government later appealed this decision and the matter remains before the courts.

While the strike generated broad support amongst women activists for its challenges to the government, such moments of apparent unity amongst women activists were not long lasting. As the lines of division within the movement began to harden, groups such as the FWRM began to ask themselves if their own adversarial style of advocacy was counterproductive and in fact contributing to Fiji's ongoing political difficulties. In 2009, FWRM coordinator, Virisila Buadromo, described to me an important discussion which had taken place within her organisation a year earlier. Suggesting that some members were becoming more self-critical about the tone and substance of their advocacy, she stated,

> Last year we sat down and asked ourselves why do we keep getting into this situation? Not only the country but we, as an organisation. We had to be critical of ourselves and ask if we were contributing to the situation. FWRM is adversarial. We're right and you're wrong and this is what needs to be done to change. But we realise we have to work in a different way now (Buadromo 2009).

This more critical approach to adversarial forms of advocacy prompted the FWRM to investigate the utility of developing peacebuilding programs involving other civil society actors. Buadromo argued that while the military were disinclined to involve civil society organisations such as hers in national consultative processes, and indeed remained highly critical of groups it accused of promoting 'irrationally senseless confrontation' (Driti cited *Fiji Times* 30 March 2009), civil society actors themselves had to work to heal the divisions that had emerged in the wake of the 2006 coup. In early 2009, the FWRM was therefore proposing a series of civil society dialogues aimed at peacebuilding and had approached a neutral facilitator to coordinate these sessions across the country. In our discussions Buadromo admitted that this more negotiated form of advocacy emphasising peacebuilding departed in significant ways from the highly legalistic focus of activity undertaken by the organisation in the past. She stated,

> FWRM is a 'rule of law' organisation—and for us, if we saw law and order we expected peace—we saw law and order as equalling peace. But we now realise that it's more complex than that. There's many dimensions to peacebuilding (Buadromo 2009).

Such introspection suggests that the fallout from the 2006 coup had generated a far more self-critical process of policy formulation within the FWRM than had been evident in previous periods and a broadening of the organisations' advocacy focus. This was revealed in the organisation's shifting approach to peacebuilding but also in other aspects of the FWRM's activity related to trade and economic development.

At this time the FWRM had formed a close relationship with the regional organisation Pacific Network on Globalisation, or PANG, a group that was committed to promoting awareness of economic and trade issues in the Pacific Islands. PANG's advocacy called attention to the negative implications of Pacific

Island States' accession to trade agreements under negotiation with the EU, under the Cotonou Agreement provisions, and with Australia and New Zealand, under PACER.

The impact of this collaborative relationship began to influence the ways in which the FWRM examined regional trade-related issues in its own advocacy. This was clearly reflected in the FWRM quarterly bulletins, entitled *Balance*, which began to include critical articles on trade justice (FWRM 2008a), Australian and New Zealand efforts to 'fast-track' negotiations on free-trade negotiations within the Pacific Islands Forum (FWRM 2009b), and the gendered implications of current global trade negotiations under the Monterrey Consensus (FWRM 2008b). Such inclusions suggest that FWRM members were developing a more critical understanding of how developments within the international trade environment might impact upon local communities.

As the opening paragraphs of this chapter demonstrate, the FWRM's consideration of regional trade-related issues and the organisation's broader approach to peace making did not completely displace the 'rule of law' focus that had long been the organisation's trade-mark area of political engagement. Neither did this move away from highly adversarial forms of advocacy result in the FWRM desisting from criticism of the interim government altogether. Nonetheless, as I have shown, these more 'typical' agendas were being complemented, at this time, with varieties of political activity that reflected a considered approach towards organisational self-evaluation and a new-found awareness that the agendas so keenly pursued in the past could have unanticipated and divisive consequences.

The FWCC and fem'Link sought to maintain pressure on the interim government, but in a way which respected the potentially divisive consequences of their public advocacy (Bhagwan Rolls 2009). Both organisations were particularly careful to avoid references to democracy in their advocacy and became more inclined to point out the gendered social impacts of the military government's actions and policies.

For example, Shamima Ali argued that increased militarisation in Fiji had allowed discrimination against women to flourish (*Fiji Times* 25 February 2009). She claimed the military's seizure of government had sanctioned a patriarchal form of authority which deprived women of a public voice. In particular, she was critical of the dissolution of the national parliament and, later, local councils—events which Ali argued had seen women deprived of access to the 'places where they could speak out' (*Radio Australia* 24 February 2009). At the same time, Ali also argued that militarism in Fiji was contributing to an increase in violence against women as men combated generalised feelings of social powerlessness and disenfranchisement by punishing the women in their lives. Ali claimed this to be a strong pattern replicated after each coup in Fiji, whereby men were prompted to 'take it out on the most vulnerable' when they felt their 'manhood had been taken away' *Radio Australia* 24 February 2009).[7]

Fem'Link's critique of the military regime also emphasised its patriarchal bias, demonstrated by an unwillingness to engage with women NGO representatives and community leaders. Bhagwan Rolls stated that this was particularly evident in the wake of the serious flooding which had occurred in Fiji's Western Division in late January 2009. The military had established a flood rehabilitation task force but had, according to Bhagwan Rolls, failed to capitalise on the expertise and local knowledge that women had gained working at the forefront of informal disaster response efforts (*Fiji Times,* 15 February 2009).

Like Ali, Bhagwan Rolls also lamented what she described as the 'continuum of violence in our communities', from the military violence perpetrated at the national level, both symbolic and actual, to the domestic flow-on effects of this violence within families. She argued that as 'women and as mothers in this country', there was a need to 'stand up and ... say that enough is enough' (*Radio Australia* 24 February 2009).

During this period, the coordinators at WAC were also paying close attention to the political consequences that might follow from their actions. In contrast to the groups mentioned previously, WAC had signalled a willingness to work with the regime. In 2007, Peni Moore was appointed to the military-sponsored National Council for Building a Better Fiji, and charged with establishing future guidelines for national governance. By 2009, however, WAC was also becoming dissatisfied with certain aspects of the administration's policy. At this time, WAC was particularly disturbed by the actions of the military-appointed police commissioner, Esala Teleni, who had earned a prominent place in the media for his ethnically motivated public criticisms of Indo-Fijian police officers, accused of disloyalty to his command (*Fiji Times* 18 February, 20 February 2009). While the WAC members were dismayed at Teleni's racially divisive outbursts, they were also careful to avoid public criticism of his actions that could invite potentially incendiary consequences. The organisation's coordinators, instead, considered how they might make their complaints to the regime through their personalised government contacts rather that voicing them in the public domain (Moore 2009).

---

7   These assertions, indicating a level of latent stress within society, were also backed up in a newspaper report appearing in the *Fiji Times* around the same time discussing the Fiji Ministry of Health Figures that showed a highly elevated suicide rate for the first months of 2009—14 cases of suicide and 28 cases of attempted suicide in 51 days (*Fiji Times* 21 February 2009).

Such considerations demonstrate the complex nature of the challenges navigated by women's organisations in the years since the 2006 coup. On the one hand, activists were forced to contend with a regime that displayed a low tolerance for criticism and a continuing disregard for the rights of those it deemed to be inciting dissent. On the other hand, the military's seizure of power had produced deep divisions within the movement as individual activists and organisations re-engaged with the now decades-long debate about the institutional structures that would afford the country just, fair and inclusive governance.

Yet, such challenges did not detract from the vibrancy of the movement. In important instances, the 2006 coup appeared to encourage some new directions in advocacy. A strong inclination towards self-evaluation and consequentialist thinking within individual organisations perhaps explains this scenario. Fears about isolation from other civil society groups prompted members within the FWRM to consider how the organisation might broaden its advocacy from the narrower rule of law focus to better address the need for peacebuilding within the associational realm. At the same time, the trend towards selfevaluation prompted this same organisation to consider the divisive consequences of adversarial styles of advocacy and how these might be contributing to ongoing political crisis in Fiji.

Of course there were women's organisations such as the FNA, whose advocacy issued far more provocative challenges to the interim regime. Yet, this activity was undertaken in a calculated and practically-minded way so as to minimise negative consequences. As I have shown, Fiji's activist nurses were fully cognisant of the risks their protest actions would entail. Although they were not dissuaded from engaging in public protest, their General Secretary had clearly thought long and hard about how these risks might be minimised.

As the following pages will demonstrate, this trend towards introspection and consequentialist organisational self-assessment did not simply impact upon how women's groups operated locally but also shaped their advocacy on the regional and international stage. Indeed, this trend towards selfevaluation appeared to encourage a return to a more internationally provocative form of advocacy that had not been evident since the pioneering days of the women's movement in Fiji in the 1960s.

Regional developments

Despite the locally restrictive nature of Fiji's political environment, and the fractured nature of civil society relations generally, Fiji's women's organisations continued their regional engagement during this period and looked to extend the local focus of their programs to other Pacific Island contexts. Fem'Link's regional activity centred upon efforts to promote the provisions of United Nations Security Council Resolution 1325 on women and peacebuilding. This involved lobbying to advance the implementation of the Women, Peace and Security agenda within Pacific Island countries and also within regional institutions such as the Pacific Islands Forum and was conducted in association with women's groups located in Tonga, Solomon Islands and Bougainville (*fem'Link* 2008). The FWCC's collaborative work with organisations across the Pacific aiming to combat violence against women also continued, as did the RRRT's efforts to promote the regional ratification and implementation of CEDAW. While this activity was generally an extension of locally focused programs and, in some cases, a continuation of regional agendas developed in the preceding years, other Fiji-based women's groups established new regional programs with a significantly altered advocacy focus.

These developments were clearly in evidence at the SPC-sponsored 10th Triennial Conference for women convened in Noumea in late May 2007 which I attended as an observer and rapporteur. The theme of the conference was 'Stepping up the Pace to 2010' and many of the presentations urged state representatives at the conference to follow through on their rhetorical commitments to gender equality in ways that saw actions match words. Not surprisingly perhaps, this meant a great many conference sessions were devoted to regional recognition of CEDAW and the challenges faced by Pacific Island states in achieving CEDAW ratification or fulfilling reporting requirements to the UN CEDAW Committee.

The SPC policy on gender also came under scrutiny, however, when it was announced that the PWRB would be disbanded and a gender focus mainstreamed across the SPC's Human Development program (Mann 2007). This decision had come after an external review of the SPC's human development program and was a victory for those who promoted the more bureaucratic aim of institutional efficiency. The SPC representatives argued that they were aiming to 'concentrate on a few things and doing them well' (Petersen 2007). Yet, representatives from the state delegations to the meeting complained that the SPC's ability to focus in a concentrated way upon Pacific women's needs and interests would be lost with this administrative change. Some argued that the SPC was already showing a waning commitment to programs for women and there was a risk that gender issues would be marginalised within the program overall. Many also voiced concern that the SPC had taken this decision without consulting SPC-member countries.[8]

Despite these dissatisfactions, the planned changes were agreed to by state delegations without further controversy. However, the mood of polite deliberation was 'shaken-up' not long after as NGOs began to have greater

---

8   Delegates from Fiji and Samoa and Tonga were the most vocal on these points.

input into the sessions. This change of mood was particularly apparent during a session led by the region's gender activists which was entitled 'Building a Women's Movement' which aimed to demonstrate how women's organisations were able to advance the women's agenda within Pacific Island countries.

From the outset, a defiant tone became apparent as the first speaker, FWRM coordinator, Virisila Buadromo, confidently asserted her identity as a 'feminist Fijian woman'. Buadromo then described her organisation as concerned with critical feminist analysis which involved investigation of the 'multiple levels of oppression' endured by Pacific women (Buadromo 2007). She went on to describe the evolution of the women's movement in Fiji. While her discussion discounted the early contributions to Pacific feminism by women active in organisations such as the Fiji YWCA during the 1960s and 1970s, her examination of later developments within the women's movement accurately and honestly considered the challenges faced by NGOs that enter into close relationships with international funding agencies or policy-making institutions. Buadromo hinted at the potential for organisational cooptation when she asked, 'are we shaped by the institutions we engage with?' (Buadromo 2007). She also spoke of her own organisation's difficulties in keeping the local community level engaged as the FWRM had become more involved in regional and international gender-advocacy networks. She stated that the FWRM had strayed from community engagement at the local level but was conscious of this and aimed to maintain that connection more effectively in the future. Buadromo was also honest about the divisions currently challenging the women's movement in Fiji. Disrupting the idea of an activist 'sisterhood' with a note of understatement, she remarked, 'We're not one big happy family.'

Anna Padarath, also from the FWRM, contributed to this discussion by examining the role that younger women in Fiji played within the women's movement more broadly. Again, this discussion raised some provocative questions regarding the evolution of Pacific feminism, as well as the participatory nature of the women's movement more generally.

Padarath described her own participation at a workshop jointly convened by DAWN Pacific and the FWRM in the preceding year (Padarath 2007). These workshops typically involved asking young women to think critically about Pacific women's disadvantage. For example, one session involved placing a can of tuna before the participants and then asking them to think about the local, regional and international factors involved in this product's production and how these might have gendered implications. Consideration was given to the position of local women working in foreign-owned fish canneries, the circumstances of local sex workers meeting the demands of foreign fishing fleets docked in Pacific Island harbours, the environmental impacts of Pacific Ocean fish-stock depletion, and the ability of Pacific Island states to negotiate fair compensation for access to this ocean resource within the international trade environment.[9] These types of exercises sought to provide participants with an understanding of the benefits of feminist analysis and its capacity to expose the interlinked phenomena, local and global, that may threaten the security of Pacific women (Padarath 2007).

Padarath's presentation to the SPC women's conference also critiqued the participatory nature of the Pacific women's movement. In particular she questioned the willingness of older women activists to engage in what she termed 'intergenerational dialogue' rather than sending the younger women to the kitchens to 'make the tea and do the dishes' (Padarath 2007).[10] Padarath urged the current generation of organisational leaders to think about delegating their authority. While she conceded that women leaders feared that the younger members of their organisations might 'mess things up' she also urged them to have more confidence. 'You have nothing to fear,' she stated, 'we've learnt from you and you've done your job well' (Padarath 2007).

Other Fiji-based activists took part in these discussions but their view-points demonstrated a less self-critical perspective. Shamima Ali, from the FWCC, adopted a narrower view of feminism, although one entirely consistent with her organisation's public advocacy approach, when she defined her feminism as committed to the promotion of 'women's human rights' (Ali 2007). Her assessments of the FWCC's contributions to the forging of a women's movement did not display the same self-questioning position adopted by her compatriots. Ali spoke confidently of the FWCC's regional network confronting violence against women as the most vibrant in the Pacific and argued that locally women had been at the forefront of opposition to the military's human rights abuses (Ali 2007).

While these types of presentations offered varying, and indeed challenging, perspectives on feminism they were not accepted by the main body of conference delegates at the SPC without some discussion. One male representative from the Cook Islands echoed concerns first heard in the 1970s when he stated that feminism was not a term that sat comfortably in the Pacific and that the women who had participated in this session needed to think more carefully about the

---

9   This account of the FWRM/DAWN Pacific Young Feminist Advocacy Training Workshop can be found on the FWRM website http://www.fwrm.org.fj/index.cfml?go+view&pgID+29 accessed 10 March 2009.

10   In some ways, Padarath's observations were highly ironic. During the course of this research I have encountered many Pacific women activists who have said the same thing about their male family members, and who have been critical of the expectation that women will opt out of family decision-making and instead stay 'in the kitchen making tea'.

social and cultural implications of this type of language. His concerns were greeted by many women in room with supportive applause. Shamima Ali responded by stating that such concerns made her feel that little had changed in nearly twenty-five years, when Pacific women activists were condemned by some as feminist radicals intent on 'burning their bras'. She went on, 'At that point many of us didn't even have money to buy a bra let alone think about burning it.' This comment was greeted with an even stronger round of supportive applause from the conference participants.

The conference delegates' mixed responses to this type of debate is indicative of the contention that still surrounds the term feminism in the Pacific Islands. The women who spoke were evidently untroubled by the idea of belonging to a women's movement and firmly committed to advocacy agendas promoting women's advancement. Yet, for some in the audience, the term feminism continued to be viewed as an imported ideology that was difficult to embrace. It is telling that the final conference session which was devoted to finalising a set of draft conference resolutions, to be presented to the SPC-member countries' ministerial delegations, saw all delegates vote to remove references to feminism in the conference document.

The SPC had, somewhat unusually, provided the space for women's NGOs to address the regional conference and explain to government delegations their role and political potential. Nonetheless, state delegations had the final word on the shape of conference resolutions. For these parties, feminist language was deemed unnecessarily contentious. While this indicates continued regional resistance to the term feminism, it also demonstrates, once again, the restrictions placed on the SPC's regional policy-making by Pacific Island state representatives, who expect the organisation to formulate programs which reflect their views.

International developments

The local obstacles that impeded critical political dialogue in the aftermath of the 2006 coup saw many of Fiji's women's organisations place renewed emphasis upon the importance of international engagement. In the early post-coup period, the military had sought to clamp down on this activity by placing intermittent international travel bans on those it termed 'dissidents' and restricting their ability to voice international criticism of the regime. The fact that these travel bans were ultimately withdrawn suggests that, in the longer term, the military regime realised that it drew more negative international publicity from applying the travel bans than was generated when opponents to the regime made their criticisms heard on the international stage (*Radio NZ* 14 February 2007, 17 July 2007; *ABC Pacific Beat* 17 July 2007).

Even when they could not travel internationally, Fiji's women's groups were still able to make an impact internationally through their advocacy network connections. They often called upon sister women's organisations operating in other countries to lobby their own governments to put pressure on Fiji to return to democracy. Virisila Buadromo described how the FWRM had sought to enlist the support of transnational advocacy networks to promote greater awareness of political developments in Fiji. The Fiji Nursing Association had also called upon organisations such as Public Servants International, the International Council of Nurses, and the Commonwealth Nurses Federation to write letters of support for striking nurses to Fiji's President and the Interim Prime Minister. These transnational strategies had a local and international significance. While they enabled women's groups to publicise their predicament internationally, they also ensured that a level of critical pressure was maintained upon the regime without local women's groups themselves becoming the direct targets of further violent military intimidation. The US State Department's decision to honour Buadromo with a Woman of Courage award in 2008 also increased the international exposure of the FWRM and placed Fiji's military regime under increased international scrutiny.[11]

Where they could, Fiji's women activists also used their involvement in international events and conferences taking place during this period to assert the place of Pacific women in the Asia Pacific region. As previous chapters of this book have shown, since the early 1970s, Pacific women activists attending international events such as the UN-sponsored conferences for women had felt disgruntled by the fact that they were generally grouped regionally with activists from the broader Asia Pacific. They argued that their voices were being marginalised thanks to the numerical superiority of delegates from much larger Asian countries. The result, they claimed, was that Pacific women's concerns were overlooked or downplayed in broader regional debates on gender issues.

To combat this situation a concerted effort was made to challenge what was regionally termed 'the silent P' (silent Pacific) within the international terrain of gender politics. In this period, Pacific activist women sought to increase their international visibility by attending international events in number, armed with professional and sophisticated presentation material. This endeavour was also recognised as important by international donors such as AusAID and UNDP, who provided assistance in the form of funding and technical training for international activity. This enabled Pacific women to make an important impression upon debate at events such as the triennial conference convened by the Association for Women's Rights in Development (AWID) in Cape Town

---

11 Buadromo recounted that she was heavily criticised by colleagues within the women's movement for accepting this award from a world power whose militarised approach to foreign policy was resisted by many feminists.

in 2008 and the annual United Nations Commission on the Status of Women held in New York in March of 2009. At these events, the trend towards a selfevaluation of organisational life continued, with Fiji-based spokeswomen foregrounding the importance of inclusive participation within the women's movement generally. Critical responses to issues of an international orientation such as climate change, and the 2008/09 global economic crisis, also became a more prominent part of Pacific women's advocacy on the international stage at this time.

AWID Conference Cape Town 2008

At the end of 2008, a large group of Pacific women attended the AWID Conference convened in Cape Town, South Africa. While this group aimed to demonstrate the vibrancy of women's organising in the region, they also offered a self-critical analysis of how the women's movement had evolved in the preceding decades. Fifty delegates from Pacific Island countries attended this meeting, with representatives from Fiji including Sharon Bhagwan Rolls and Veena Singh Byar from fem'Link, Virisila Buadromo, Tara Chetty and Michelle Reddy from the FWRM and Noelene Nabulivou from WAC. To ensure that the Pacific delegations were coordinated and clearly visible at this meeting, a great deal of preliminary networking and organisation had taken place, largely instigated by Noelene Nabulivou and Tara Chetty. Aside from viewing the Cape Town conference as an opportunity to put the Pacific back on the advocacy map, Pacific delegates also voiced the hope that it might help 'rejuvenate the movement' by enhancing solidarity between older and younger generations of activists, and eliciting new interest in the feminist basis of women's advocacy (Buadromo cited Lahari electronic post to PACWIN email list 14 November 2008).

On this occasion, a Pacific Woman was invited to make the opening address to the conference plenary. Lynnsay Rongokea, a Cook Islander with a long history of involvement with women's organisations in that setting, but now working as the coordinator of the Thai-based regional organisation, Asia Pacific Forum on Women Law and Development, gave a deeply thoughtful and honest response to the conference theme, 'The Power of Movements'. Echoing discussion that had occurred at the SPC regional conference held in Noumea eighteen months earlier, an event she had also attended, she urged activists to examine the nature of collectivity within the women's movement and to act to break down what she described as the 'hierarchies of personalities and small cliques within our organisations … and the power play among the handful who make decisions' (Rongokea 2008). Rongokea also examined the question of intergenerational exchange, urging her colleagues to 'open up spaces for new voices, mentor, partner, empower those we speak for, including the younger generation and encourage them to speak for themselves' (Rongokea 2008).

This introspective address set the tone for the FWRM's activities at the conference which also examined the nature of women's movements in the Pacific, the challenges which threaten collectivity and the sustainability of Asia-Pacific regionalism amongst the activist community. One FWRM-organised session entitled 'Tok Talk: Nourishing an Asia Pacific Women's Movement' examined how younger and more senior activists might collaborate to address the challenges facing the region and how 'power sharing' within the women's movement is shaped by an individual's age, class and social status. Video clips were combined with panel presentations and audience discussion. The session was filmed to be used for a joint FWRM-APFWLD DVD project also entitled 'Tok Talk' (FWRM 2008c). In another session, Buadromo described the challenges being faced by the women's movement in Fiji in the prevailing political climate. Buadromo again used this occasion to firmly state her commitment to feminism, and challenge the tendency for Pacific communities to negatively respond to this term as the 'f-word' (Buadromo, cited FWRM 2008c). This was an issue that Buadromo also addressed in a more personalised fashion through her decision to wear a t-shirt boldly emblazoned with the word 'feminist'.

Ultimately, Pacific delegates to the AWID conference described the experience in highly positive terms as energising and contributing to a personal reawakening to the feminist project. The meeting was said to have generated new interest in developing critical regional collaboration around the issue of regional free trade issues, particularly negotiations on a regional structure for Pacific free trade (PACER-PLUS) and the development of feminist networks (Nabulivou electronic communication to PACWIN email list, 28 November 2008). 'I feel like a walking light bulb, shaking with power,' wrote one euphoric Pacific correspondent as she reflected upon the personal experience of connecting with women from diverse settings and cultures (Lahari-Williams electronic post to PACWIN email list, 15 November 2008).

This positive momentum carried through into early 2009, when a number of Pacific women NGO representatives travelled to New York to attend the UN's annual Commission on the Status of Women sessions in early March. In the preceding months, the UNDP Pacific Centre had designed a program aiming to train representatives from Pacific women's organisations in the skills they would require to become lobbyists at the CSW sessions and also to assist them financially to attend. This program aimed, once again, to increase the international visibility of Pacific women within the UN and to counter the poor levels of Pacific representation at CSW sessions in the preceding years (SPC 2008). Selection for participation at the 2009 session was on a competitive basis and representatives from four of the region's women's organisations were chosen to undergo training to attend. Sharon Bhagwan Rolls and Veena Singh Byar represented fem'Link alongside representatives from the Pacific Disability

Forum, Samoa AIDS Foundation, Cook Islands Women's Counselling Service, Tonga National Centre for Women and Children, and a women's organisation from Palau called Voices. These groups came together in September 2008 for a training session designed to assist them in developing country action statements to be presented to the Pacific government delegations. The issues they considered included the recognition of women's unpaid work in the domestic realm, women's participation in decision-making, the regional prevalence of gender-based violence and the needs of Pacific women living with disabilities.

While the delegates travelling to New York in March 2008 found the intricacies of the UN Commission procedures a challenge to negotiate, they also valued the insights they were able to gain into international policy-making processes. Pacific Island States were represented at the commission through a collective delegation sent from the Pacific Islands Forum Secretariat and chaired by Niue's Minister for Health and Women's Affairs, O'Love Jacobsen. Some Pacific Island states also sent their own formal delegations comprising both institutional and civil society representatives. But the aforementioned UNDP-sponsored women's representatives were not accredited to government delegations. This meant that their efforts to have input into the CSW deliberations relied on their ability to effectively lobby the officially recognised CSW participants. As such the group was required to spend long hours poring over official documents to find where Pacific Island governments and regional intergovernmental institutions had made statements on issues related to the concerns identified by NGO representatives. This 'agreed' language was then put forward as a legitimate inclusion in the final regional and individual country statements to be delivered to the Commission. The culmination of this process saw the Forum delegation give an important and well-supported statement which covered themes such as the gendered impacts of climate change, gender-based violence, the need for temporary special measures to increase women's parliamentary representation and the impacts of the global economic crisis (Guttenbeil-Likiliki electronic post to PACWIN email list 11 March 2009; fem'Link 2009).

While the efforts had been painstaking, the final outcomes were viewed by the women's NGO delegation as a triumph for the Pacific Island region as a whole. The region's government delegations successfully argued for the CSW to include references to the gendered impacts of climate change in its final declaration. These were listed as including women's 'displacement from income-generating activities' and dependence upon 'sustainable ecosystems' that sustain 'livelihood and daily subsistence'. In addition, the Pacific Island delegations put forward a statement on the negative impacts of the global economic crisis which was also accepted. This statement reminded states to recognise and respond to women's and girls' increasing economic vulnerability and called upon states to continue their financial commitments to gender-equality programs despite the looming economic uncertainty (SPC 2009).

NGO representatives from the Pacific Islands interpreted these inclusions as a demonstration of their capacity to shape international negotiations and draw global attention to the specific nature of challenges facing the Pacific. Ofa Guttenbeil-Likiliki, an NGO representative with the Tongan delegation, summed up this idea when, after a nightlong session of negotiations on the CSW Agreed Conclusions, she stated, 'It just goes to show that no matter how small the Pacific may be, amidst a room full of powerful people ... WE CAN MAKE A DIFFERENCE' (emphasis in the original, electronic post to PACWIN email list, 13 March 2009).

These international developments indicate the beginnings of a changed direction of gender advocacy in the Pacific. Echoing agendas promoted by YWCA women in the 1960s and 1970s, new themes in advocacy began to emerge which challenged the centrality of the human rights discourse that had dominated Pacific women's advocacy in the preceding decades. At the same time, there was also a renewed interest in examining the women's movement from a more critical perspective than had been evident in previous decades. This involved close examination of collectivity within the movement and how a more inclusive participatory ethos might be encouraged. At the same time, renewed attention was also focused on feminism as a strategy that might provide the basis for greater solidarity within the movement.

In the following section of this chapter, I will provide a more analytical account of the events described here by concentrating upon Fiji-based activists' negotiation of collectivity, progressive ideas and transnationalism. As in previous chapters, I will show how this activity was shaped by local political instabilities as well as shifting political influences prevailing globally.

Collectivity

This chapter has highlighted the turbulence shaping civil society relations in the wake of Fiji's 2006 coup. It has also discussed the divisions which had become deeply felt amongst activist women who were, at one level, nominally committed to the cause of gender equality, but also in strong disagreement over broader-ranging questions relating to Fiji's political future, and the legitimacy of the military government and its proposed agendas of reform.

My discussions with women activists in these years indicated that groups that had formerly collaborated closely now operated in a more isolated manner

(Buadromo 2009). There were some who expressed puzzlement over this situation. They were confounded by the fact that they no longer enjoyed close relationships with former allies and struggled to understand how they had come to occupy opposing sides of this post-coup political gulf (Moore 2009). There were others who accepted these difficulties philosophically, perhaps reflecting the fact that women's groups have been constantly challenged by authoritarianism and intra-movement disagreement since the 'pioneering' days of the 1960s.

Activists associated with the Fiji Women's Rights Movement, adopted a less accepting line, however. Recognising that while overt challenges to the military were unwise and dangerous, divisions within civil society could be acted on and not allowed to further harden. Concerns about organisational isolation seemed to prompt this move, as the FWRM coordinator explained,

> We were becoming isolated. It was different to earlier coups where other groups would have been saying the same things as us. Now we felt like we were the only ones. Civil society was split this time. We were isolated by civil society organisations and by other women's groups. Even by members of our families who took a different position to us. At present CSOs are ignoring each other or when they get together they're simply not talking about the elephant in the room. (Buadromo 2009).

To address the divisions within civil society or as Buadromo described it, 'the elephant in the room', the FWRM was therefore proposing a series of civil society dialogues aimed at mending relationships and achieving a more conciliatory civil society environment.

The women's movement was not the only sector within civil society to experience such discord, as I learnt while interviewing Kuini Lutua about the FNA strike undertaken in July 2007. While Lutua had conceded that the nurses' strike had generated a brief moment of unity within the women's movement, this unity was not replicated within the labour movement more generally. In particular, Lutua felt that the strike action had cost the FNA support from formerly close union allies such as the Fiji Public Service Association and the Fiji Teachers Association.

Speculating upon why this shift in support might have occurred, Lutua stated that a fear of military retaliation played a big part, again reiterating the idea that activists within civil society were making conscious decisions about the possible consequences of their actions. Lutua recounted her own experience of attempted coercion during this period, stating that aside from anonymous threats directed towards the organisation, she had also been subject to personal intimidation and threats for her strike activity. Lutua advised those who threatened her that she 'would not be stopped' but she also conceded that there were many within the union movement who were disinclined to stand up to the regime and had generally become 'accepting of what is dished out' (Lutua 2009).[12]

These types of developments clearly put questions about the nature of collectivity within Fiji's women's movement into sharp focus. But the emphasis was not solely placed upon the challenges of political division. As the previous discussion has indicated, a stronger trend towards introspection seemed also to encourage debate on the need for new leadership and the role younger women might play as advocates. This was apparent within the FWRM, as my discussion of Anna Padarath's presentation to the SPC conference of June 2007 has indicated. Here Padarath raised important concerns regarding the participatory nature of the women's movement, in particular emphasising the issue of generational leadership. Padarath was critical of the older generations of women activists who tended to maintain positions of seniority within women's groups while also dismissing the contributions that younger women might make to the organisation as inconsequential. Padarath's references to young women being sent to the kitchen to 'make the tea and do the dishes' illustrated this point with eloquence.

Certainly, as one of the more established women's organisations, the FWRM had demonstrated a willingness to bring young women into the organisation and assist them in forging their own public profiles as defenders of women's rights. Since 1987, the FWRM had also changed organisational leadership several times. This tendency was less apparent within the FWCC where Shamima Ali had maintained the position of coordinator and principal media spokesperson for over twenty years. Ali's dominant presence within the FWCC had provided the organisation with continuity in leadership and advocacy focus over the preceding two decades. But this also meant the absence of the participatory ethos that was evident at the FWRM—a situation which perhaps raises doubts about the FWCC's long-term sustainability, particularly if Ali were to retire in the near future.

Similar organisational challenges were also faced by WAC in this period. From the time of its foundation, WAC's organisational structures reflected a strong participatory ethos, with the organisation welcoming new faces and

---

12   In a public address to the ACS alumni in 2008, Wadan Narsey, a USP academic and vocal critic of the regime, echoed these sentiments, lamenting the fact that so few civil society figures had dared express their views candidly for, or indeed, against the regime since 2006. He also speculated that if the former ACS head student Amelia Rokotuivuna had still been alive, no-one would be in doubt of her views on the current regime. Remembering with admiration her vehement articulation of political principle, regardless of what this cost her personally, Narsey asked why there were presently 'so few Amelias' in Fiji's public life (*Fiji Sun* 14 November 2008).

younger members to assume part of the ever increasing workload. However, even though WAC was administered by a management collective, there was a strong tendency for members of this collective to defer to the organisation's coordinator, Peni Moore, a charismatic personality, who seemed to command a natural authority over the group. In 2005, this situation changed with creation of a new organisational structure which divided the task of coordination between two individuals. While Moore became the organisation's creative coordinator concerned principally with the management of the WAC Theater, Noelene Naboulivou, was appointed as advocacy coordinator—a position that drew upon her skills and experience gained through community development and advocacy work in Fiji and Australia. This appointment enabled WAC to take a much more engaged stance on a range of policy issues and raised the profile of the organisation generally. It also indicated that WAC was thinking about leadership succession and the consolidation of organisational structures that would enable younger women to assume positions of authority within the organisation.

This was a concern that Moore had raised with me during our interviews in earlier years, as she speculated on the ongoing challenges facing civil society organisations in Fiji and the personal energy required to remain politically active on questions of principle in an uncertain future. In the wake of the 2006 coup, similar concerns also became evident within the FWRM. Buadromo's experiences of military intimidation demonstrated to the organisation the high personal costs borne by activists committed to engaging in provocative forms of public debate. In the following year, the FWRM had begun to discuss the need for activists to take time out to protect their health and wellbeing and to work more collaboratively to ensure that the burden of their work was shared (FWRM 2008b).

In summary, it is clear that Fiji's military coup of 2006 had important ramifications for the way women activists' negotiated collectivity within their own particular organisations and the women's movement more generally. In the first instance, this event encouraged the emergence of differing views within the movement regarding the legitimacy of the military's takeover and the ensuing regime's long-term vision for Fiji's future. In some cases, these differences hardened over time creating distance between groups, feelings of isolation and, to some extent, confusion within individual organisations. Yet, although such developments might have been cause for pessimism, the coup also appeared to encourage a mood of introspection within some high profile women's groups which had positive ramifications. This mood saw organisations such as the FWRM become more critical about the impact of their advocacy and act to broaden their approach to peacebuilding so that civil society rifts that had emerged since the military take-over might be repaired. At the same time, these developments also threw into sharp focus the high personal costs borne by those engaged in public advocacy on questions of political principle. Some organisations therefore began to see the benefits of harnessing the energies of new generations of women activists to their cause. And this scenario also opened the way for individual advocates to challenge the cultural protocols that tended to confer authority upon senior members of women's groups and discount the political importance of young women's political contributions.

It can therefore be argued that while the fallout from the 2006 coup posed important challenges to collectivity within the women's movement it also encouraged women activists to critically engage in open debate on this question; a shift which augured well for the sustainability of key women's groups and the overall vibrancy of Fiji's women's movement into the future.

Progressive ideas

Between February 2007 and February 2009, I made a number of trips to Fiji and was struck by the extent to which women's organisations in Suva seemed to develop an increasing interest in peacebuilding as a progressive aspect of their broader advocacy agenda in this period. While organisations such as fem'Link had, since 2001, developed a strong focus upon peacebuilding in their advocacy program and, through their lobbying, to promote increased awareness of UN Security Council Resolution 1325, this emphasis became more generalised within other organisations in the years following the 2006 coup. In this context, peacebuilding seemed to represent a progressive means by which to address the phenomena that compounded gender inequity in Fiji and, in many ways, seemed to displace other forms of advocacy that, up to this point, had been more prominently focused upon the promotion of women's human rights.

Women's organisations approached the task of peacebuilding in various ways however. As I have shown, the FWRM was particularly concerned about rifts within civil society in Fiji and sought to develop a national program of civil society dialogue which might ease the tensions which had created isolation and division since 2006. Buadromo recognised that this more negotiated style of peacebuilding signalled an important new shift in the FWRM's advocacy agenda and, as I have previously shown, an appreciation of the fact that the achievement of peaceful social relations required more than a strictly defined emphasis of 'law and order' issues (Buadromo 2009).

In the previous ten years, WAC had been highly critical of the limited reach of advocacy focused on 'law and order'. Yet, in this later period, this organisation also sought to broaden its approach to peacebuilding. This meant that in addition to the advocacy around stress and trauma healing that had already been a strong aspect of WAC's community theatre activities for many years, WAC became deeply involved in advocacy around conflict resolution and community mediation. This focus saw the organisation develop education programs that aimed at promoting peer mediation amongst young adults and school age children. The aim was to develop a nation-wide network of young mediators interested in how the principles of restorative mediation and justice could be used to achieve peace (WAC 2009).

Such broad interest in peacebuilding amongst activist women also paved the way for the establishment of a new organisation in 2008 specifically devoted to the promotion of peace. Led by Koila Costello-Olsen (who had formerly been associated with ECREA), the Pacific Centre for Peacebuilding (PCP) sought to work locally in Fiji and regionally to promote peaceful conflict resolution and train communities in mediation practices.

The newly placed emphasis upon peacebuilding within the women's movement was generated by strongly held concerns about the divisive impact of Fiji's apparent coup cycle (Costello-Olsen 2009). At the same time, international donor agencies active within the Pacific Islands region were also increasing the emphasis they placed upon peacebuilding as part of their own development programs. This focus was particularly evident within AusAID which, in 2002, had released an important policy statement on the development implications of peacebuilding and conflict prevention. In this document, AusAID stated its intention to increase program support for local processes of dialogue that aimed to resolve conflict and to give particular prominence to the peacebuilding skills of women (AusAID 2002). At the same time, donors were also incorporating peace and conflict sensitivity analysis into their programs; a shift which required them to consider how their own programs may in fact be contributing to community tension and unrest which may escalate into more serious conflict. According to Costello-Olsen, AusAID's work in this area had prompted local organisations to also consider how their work might contribute to conflict and how they might better engage in peacebuilding processes, either working individually or through collaboration (Costello-Olsen 2009).

Figure 6.3. WAC Theater member working with pupils of Veuto Primary School on conflict management.

Source: Photograph by Nicole George.

This meant that while local women's organisations were responding to the 'on the ground' challenges to peace that had recently become evident in the wake of the 2006 coup, they were also being encouraged to engage in peacebuilding dialogue by international donor agencies. However, if the need for peacebuilding was foremost in the minds of Fiji's women activists, as a result of local and international influences, there were also interesting debates taking place within activist circles about who should be included in such programs and whether engagement with the military was appropriate.

WAC gave strong approval to the military leaders' vision for a more inclusive Fiji. As a result, the organisation became more closely aligned with the military regime than other civil society groups, and Moore became directly involved with the 'people's charter' process. According to Moore, the WAC's willingness to engage with the military reflected an inclusive approach to conflict mediation. She argued that while efforts to build peace usually involved groups who were generally liked and respected, the participation of actors who were less well regarded, or seen to 'oppose or oppress' such as the 'military, [those] in prisons or violent offenders', was also necessary (WAC 2009).[13]

Other women's groups seemed to be also motivated by this idea. Fem'Link was opposed 'in principle' to the military's intervention but also committed to 'undertake conciliatory dialogue with all parties to conflict', with the particular aim of seeing such processes result in the local implementation of SCR 1325 and the increased participation of women in crisis resolution measures. Bhagwan Rolls also argued that her advocacy program required her organisation to engage at the community level and relay her findings back to policy makers operating at the national level, and that this work could only continue, safely and efficiently, when fem'Link remained in communication with the military powers. While fem'Link's donors were not entirely pleased with the fact that the organisation maintained a commitment to dialogue with the military regime, Bhagwan Rolls pointed out that the military regime would remain in power for at least three to five years and that fem'Link's involvement in peacebuilding could only be maintained through a process of engagement (Bhagwan Rolls 2009).

The benefits of constructive engagement were also reiterated by PCP members. Costello-Olsen argued that although her organisation had been required to justify its decision to engage with the military to potential donors, the broader goal of peacebuilding necessitated dialogue rather than provocational forms of criticism and opposition. When asked if this commitment towards engagement with a militarised regime undermined her organisation's ethical commitment to peace advocacy in any way, Costello-Olsen was quick to point out that engagement did not mean organisational cooptation. 'We challenge them,' she stated. 'You bet we do' (Costello-Olsen 2009).

As I have shown, organisations such as the FWRM and the FWCC initially counted as some of the most strident pro-democracy voices in 2006 and early 2007, and they refused to consider engaging with the regime at any level. This gained them a great deal of local and international media exposure but, as we have seen, individual members such as Virisila Buadromo also paid a heavy personal price for publicly upholding such a tough oppositional stance.

By early 2009, however, the hardline attitudes of two years earlier had begun to dissipate to some extent. While the FWCC continued to rule out any engagement with the interim government, arguing that it was 'wrongly appointed' and therefore would not be offered the assistance of the FWCC (*ABC Radio National* 24 February 2009), the FWRM had begun to rethink the utility of this approach.

---

13   Moore had not argued this in earlier interviews conducted with her in 2002, however. On these occasions, she defended her desire for the WAC to operate at a distance from the ethno-nationalist Qarase regime as a matter of political principle.

This was indicated to me personally by Virisila Buadromo who expressed some misgivings about the impact of continued criticism of the military regime by organisations. 'If you're too critical you're backing the regime into a corner,' she stated. 'It's got no allies and that's dangerous' (Buadromo 2009). Here she seemed concerned that the FWRM was provoking the military in ways that produced aggression and hostility and undermined the broader prospects of Fiji achieving any kind of peace into the future. At other points, Buadromo's observations suggested that the FWRM was looking to modify its stand towards the military. While she stated that the FWRM was committed to the 'rule of law' and would therefore not be able to work directly with the military government, she also seemed interested in the possibility of developing a more forward-looking form of engagement with the regime. She stated, 'We realised that we can't keep being critical without providing solutions.' This suggested again that the FWRM was becoming less averse to the idea of engagement with the regime at some level and perhaps more inclined to follow the lead of other women's organisations that had shown some readiness to work with the regime in the interests of promoting peace.

As the previous chapter has demonstrated, women activists in Fiji had been giving increasingly close consideration to the utility of broad-based political engagement in the preceding years. Even in the wake of the 2000 coup, figures such as Imrana Jalal seemed more critical of the provocative forms of advocacy that had been so emblematic of the women's movement in Fiji's independence era. In this later period, this debate continued, with activists now considering how engagement and negotiated forms of peacebuilding could move Fiji forward from the cycle of coups that marked its recent political past. For international donor agencies such as AusAID, peacebuilding was also viewed as a progressive aspect of development policy at this time, and a project they were happy to support across the Pacific in a bid to avert dire predictions of a regional decline into political crisis and instability (Borgu 2002; Henderson 2003; May 2003; Windybank and Manning 2003; Wainwright 2003; Reilly and Graham 2004).

While women's organisations employed varying peacebuilding methodologies, it is also clear that activists' views on the importance of forging a peacebuilding agenda that engaged with the military began to converge. By 2009, many activists had became more sensitive to the social and political costs of a continued adversarial opposition which was seen to only harden lines of division within civil society and to risk provoking further military aggression. Accepting that these scenarios did little to enhance the long-term prospects for peace in Fiji, even those groups which had formerly been highly critical of the military's actions now began to consider how strategies of engagement might help to advance the peacebuilding agenda and, by extension, progress the long-term interests of Fiji's women.

Transnationalism

Transnational engagement continued to be an important part of women's advocacy during this period and, indeed, took on a special significance when women activists were placed under travel bans or involved in activity which might incite hostile reaction from the post-coup regime. As I have shown, both the FNA and the FWRM used their contacts within broader transnational networks to publicise their concerns and to write letters in support of their claims to Fiji's political and military leaders.

This activity was also complemented by another variety of transnational engagement which more squarely focused upon global developments and how they were contributing to Pacific women's disadvantage. This trend towards a globally engaged form of transnational political activity was particularly evident on the occasions when Fiji's women activists sought to increase debate about how feminism might be defined in the Pacific context.

Raising this issue was a bold move on the part of the activists involved, for it was a question that had not received a sustained level of regional attention since the discussions led by Vanessa Griffen in the mid 1980s. And, as my discussion of the responses to Buadromo's statements at the SPC forum in 2007 has demonstrated, the term feminism was still contentious in Pacific policy-making circles. This debate touched on questions relating to the local authenticity of feminist ideals and provoked a fear that such ideals were in conflict with the socio-cultural protocols regulating behaviour in the Pacific Islands. However, in these years, this discussion also indicated that some Pacific women activists were becoming dissatisfied with articulations of feminist goals that tended to emphasise legal reform, human rights or violence against women. There seemed to be growing interest in the ways in which feminist advocacy could offer broader insight into the multiple influences that contributed to Pacific women's disadvantage.

This shift did not occur within all organisations. As I have shown, influential women activists, such as the FWCC's Shamima Ali, continued to define feminism in a way which privileged the idea of women's human rights. As previous chapters have demonstrated, this advocacy focus tended to result in a localised focus of activity that avoided examination of how global, political and economic structures compounded Pacific women's subordination. However, during this period, these perspectives on feminism were also broadened. As we have seen, this involved Fiji's women activists voicing concern about the local impacts of changing international regimes governing foreign aid distribution, international negotiation on free trade and the regional implications of climate change.

In many ways, the more internationalised focus of transnational engagement echoed themes that characterised women's advocacy in the 1960s and 1970s but had been more difficult to discern in the later decades. As the later chapters of this book have demonstrated, 'gentler' forms of political engagement tended to prevail in the restrictive local and global political environment of the 1980s and 1990s and during the first years of the new millennium. It may, therefore, seem counter-intuitive that this more contentious form of gender advocacy would emerge during a period where Fiji's advocacy community was operating within a political environment marked by an even greater level of authoritarianism than in previous decades. Nonetheless, a careful examination of the local political environment prevailing at this time provides the key to understanding why such a shift in the construction of feminist advocacy occurred.

Although the local political environment was even more authoritarian than it had been under the ethno-nationalist Qarase regime, Bainimarama's interim administration also developed a far less compliant international posture. This seems to have opened the way for women's organisations in Fiji to take a more provocative stance towards the policies being promoted in the region by states such as Australia and New Zealand.

For example, Fiji's military regime had, since the coup, developed an increasingly antagonistic posture towards states neighbouring the region and even other Pacific Island leaders, arguing that Fiji's problems were Fiji's to solve and not the subject for international or regional commentary (Finin 2009).[14] As criticism mounted from countries such as Australia, New Zealand, the United Kingdom, the United States and even some key Pacific Island Forum states, the interim government increasingly responded with a 'tough talking' and strongly isolationist rhetoric. While this prompted many external observers of Pacific Island affairs to predict that Fiji's uncooperativeness would see it become the '"Burma" of the Pacific' (Lal 2009), this international recalcitrance appeared, somewhat ironically, to open the way for local civil society actors to, themselves, adopt a more critical posture on issues of international political consequence. Hence, women activists began to voice strong criticism of the allegedly heavy-handed role played by Australia and New Zealand in promoting PACER-PLUS (FWRM 2009b, 2008a). In so doing, they were moving away from the more accepting position they had taken on questions of Fiji's economic development in the past, particularly on the local impacts of foreign aid conditionality and structural adjustment programs (see Chapters 4 and 5).

Local political conditions also encouraged this shift. Activists making critical appraisals of international political developments and their regional ramifications did so safely, with no threatened backlash from Fiji's highly sensitive and

---

14 Bainimarama's attack on the Samoan Prime Minister, Tuilaepa Sailele Malielegaoi, who spoke out in opposition to the Fiji military in February 2009, was interpreted as a violation of the longstanding political protocol that has seen Pacific Island leaders desist from making public criticisms of each other (Finin 2009).

increasingly volatile post-coup regime. Indeed, this activity coincided in interesting and perhaps unintended ways, with the interim government's own attempts to discredit regional institutions, such as the Pacific Island Forum, that had repeatedly called for Fiji's return to democracy. In the government's view, this regional body was working under the hegemonic influence of the region's dominant powers, Australia and New Zealand, and no longer operating to serve the interests of Pacific Island countries.

Such activity also sidestepped some of the more difficult questions challenging and indeed dividing the movement in this period, as women's groups struggled to reconcile their opposing views on the legitimacy of the military's intervention with their collective broader vision regarding women's advancement and the achievement of gender equality. Defining feminist politics in a way that engaged with questions of international economic significance, therefore, provided women activists with a less locally divisive focus of activity and an area where their views might more easily come into alignment.

Of course, as I've shown, this more internationalised perspective did not displace the formerly dominant human rights focus of Fiji-based activists' transnational activity; something that was clearly evident when Shamima Ali described her own vision of Pacific women's feminism at the SPC women's conference in 2007. Nonetheless, as the previous discussion demonstrates, this emphasis upon human rights was also being challenged by new discussions amongst women activists keen to see feminist engagement extend beyond the narrow concerns that had predominated in earlier decades. This newly emergent critical interest in global phenomena such as international trade liberalisation, climate change and the 2008/9 financial crisis, echoed themes that had characterised the advocacy undertaken by the pioneering generation of women activists in the 1960s and 1970s. It suggested the emergence of new perspectives challenging the sectionalised and issue-specific approach to women's advocacy that had predominated across the previous twenty years.

Conclusion

The Easter weekend of 2009 saw the military further entrench its control over Fiji. In reaction to a High Court ruling, which declared the military's seizure of power and subsequent efforts to establish a government to be illegal (9 April), the regime moved, with the support of President Iloilo, to abrogate the 1997 Constitution, sack the country's judiciary and suspend democratic elections until 2014 (*Fijilive* 11 April 2009).

In the following days, the military acted with haste to quell potential sources of dissent. Media outlets were warned against publishing critical material that might negatively depict the situation. Subsequently, members of the discipline forces were placed in all media premises to ensure that no material inciting 'disorder ... or public alarm' was published (*Fijilive* 12 April 2009). Later, the military went further, shutting down the local radio transmitter carrying broadcasts from Radio Australia and deporting a number of foreign journalists from Australia and New Zealand for their alleged critical reporting of these events. Amid intense speculation over the extent of the military's media scrutiny, the advocacy community became nervous about the security of email communications and seemed to shy away from making any public comment on the court ruling and subsequent military actions. Regional electronic discussion sites that had, in the previous years, served as important venues for the transfer of information during political crises, and which had also carried statements of support for Pacific women caught up in such events, now 'went dark', with almost no discussion of the 2009 developments. Even those women activists who had articulated a strongly adversarial line against the regime in the past, and used these forums to make their positions known internationally, now recognised that such activity might place them in a situation of extreme vulnerability.

Internationally, these events saw Fiji become further isolated and economically imperilled. In May 2009, Fiji was expelled from the Pacific Islands Forum. With the economy in severe downturn, the Reserve Bank moved to devalue the Fiji Dollar by 20 per cent (*Fiji Times* 16 April 2009) and introduced measures to halt the outflow of capital (Lal 2009). Such developments appeared to confirm the many dire predictions made by observers of Pacific affairs regarding Fiji's future.

There is no doubt that the current outlook for Fiji has few points of light, but women activists in Fiji have continued to meet these challenges philosophically. Certainly, there are those who have lamented the military's decision to tear up yet another of Fiji's constitutions, questioning how this act can assist its supposed 'good governance' agenda. Others have sought to justify the military's action, arguing the regime had little alternative. Such differences of opinion have been evident in the wake of each of Fiji's former coups. But, as this chapter and indeed this book demonstrate neither Fiji's coups nor the differences they provoke within civil society prove fatal to the realm of gender advocacy. Fiji's women activists are now well used to dealing with division, repression, expulsion and recession. They have continually shown their capacity to work within and around all that the ever volatile local *and* global political environment throws at them.

Certainly, Fiji's changed political circumstances suggest that, presently, there is only a remote possibility of the country returning to constitutional democracy. But for Fiji's women activists, projects continue to run and questions about leadership, peacebuilding and definitions of feminism continue to receive close attention.

The international community may wring its hands over Fiji's repeated tendency to 'disappoint'. It may also lament the apparent divisions emerging within civil society in the wake of the 2006 coup. For Fiji's women activists, however, a 'life goes on' attitude seems currently to prevail (FWRM electronic posts to PACWIN April/May 2009; WAC 2009; Bhagwan Rolls cited *ABC Radio National* 15 April 2009). Continued despair and blaming is, for them, useless and provides no-one inside or indeed outside Fiji with a pathway forward. This perhaps explains why many of Fiji's women activists have begun to place an increasing emphasis on the utility of constructive and non-adversarial engagement with the military regime. Some may judge this as an abandonment or betrayal of liberal political ideals. Others may describe it as evidence of civil society cooptation. But such views are mistaken. In Fiji, women activists' determination to maintain a political presence has relied upon their ability to decide upon viable courses of action in an always-changing political environment. This capacity is, in many ways, their hallmark. It has allowed them to continue operating through periods of intense political upheaval and has not undermined their broad-based commitments to women's advancement. For these reasons, we should not be surprised when the courses of action they decide upon demonstrate their determination to work within a complex local and global political environment. This has been a well-established pattern within the realm of women's organising over the past forty years.

Gender Politics and Circumstance: Some Contingent Conclusions

What is the relationship between political circumstance and women's political agency? This central question lies at the heart of my analysis of gender politics in Fiji and informs my development of a 'situated' history of women's organising in this setting. This book has demonstrated the limitations of standard 'cliff-top' approaches to the study of women's organising which assess political agency in terms of how well activities conform to ideal-type reform- or resistance-oriented benchmarks. In contrast, this study gives extended consideration to the shifting socio-cultural, political and economic currents or contingencies which, at particular historical junctures, have shaped the political agency of women's organisations operating in Fiji.

The history of women's organising which has been charted in the preceding chapters describes the complex and, at times, seemingly contradictory aspects of women's political engagement. Eschewing the idea that women's groups only appear 'successful' if their activities suggest a uniformity of purpose, this is a story that emphasises neither reform-oriented paths of increasing institutional gain, nor resistance-oriented paths of institutional disengagement. Rather, it is a history which is mapped with sensitivity to the contingent nature of civil society activity and the currents that have shaped domestic and transnational associational life in more general terms. Further, it seeks to explain how these currents have influenced the local, regional and international political engagements of Fiji-based women's groups at various historical junctures.

To achieve these aims, the methodology employed in this study blurs the lines that distinguish the historical from the contemporary, the global from the local, and the disciplines of academic enquiry. As I have shown, a clear conceptualisation of the ways that colonial legacies configure political life in Fiji in the contemporary context has been critical to my attempts to demonstrate the contingent nature of gender politics in this setting and it has allowed me to demonstrate the historical basis of tensions which continue to shape the realm of gender advocacy some forty years after Fiji gained its formal independence. Similarly, sensitivity to the interplay between global and local spheres of political life has been crucial for my examination of the differing advocacy strategies that have been undertaken by women's organisations on domestic, regional and international stages, as they have negotiated repeated episodes of local political upheaval and shifting international political trends.

The emphasis placed upon contingency in this study has not resulted in a postmodern deconstruction of gender advocacy, however. Rather, I have used the term contingency here to signify the conjuncture of events and political circumstances which influence the political strategies employed by Fiji-based women's organisations, at particular points in time, and within particular arenas of political activity. As such, I have developed a conceptual middle path which avoids reductionism and idealised conceptualisations of political agency but which, at the same time, does not go to the extremes of Foucauldian genealogy which emphasises 'flux and discord' and denies the possibility of 'any order "out there" to be discovered' (Ferguson 1991: 327).

Therefore, while my construction of the history of gender politics in Fiji has been 'situated' to the extent that it has been able to accommodate flux and variation, the nuances that are captured here are also 'translated' in ways which are relevant to broader intellectual debates on the nature of representativeness and participation in world politics; a question that will be considered in the final sections of this conclusion.

Before exploring the broader implications of this research, however, I will demonstrate the significance of applying a contingent perspective to the study of women's political agency. I do this by returning to the themes of collectivity, progressive ideas and transnationalism; three aspects of women's organisational behaviour that have featured throughout this book as characteristics conventionally understood to enhance women's political agency. At this point, it is important to consider how the material I have presented might have been treated if a more standard cliff-top analytical approach, emphasising reform or resistance, had been applied to these themes, and to demonstrate what has been gained by utilising a 'situated' perspective.

Collectivity

When viewed from a reform-oriented perspective, it could certainly be argued that horizontal collectivity has been an important characteristic of women's organising in Fiji and the region more broadly. With varying degrees of success, groups such as the YWCA in the 1960s and 1970s, and in later periods, the FWCC, the FWRM and WAC, have attempted to develop organisational structures that have avoided traditional and customary hierarchical lines of authority and encouraged horizontal cooperation amongst individual members, even across communal divides. At the inter-organisational level, collaborations between larger, high-profile women's organisations and smaller, cultural or faith-based women's groups have also increased, particularly on projects related to violence against women and the promotion of legal literacy. Equally, the success of collaborative initiatives such as the campaign for ratification of CEDAW in the early 1990s, or the joint-effort to raise the issue of Fiji's discriminatory citizenship law before the 1997 Constitutional Review commission hearings, attest to the spirit of collective effort which has been evident within the sphere of women's organising in Fiji.

At the regional and international levels, there have also been many instances where gender activists based in Fiji and the Pacific Islands have joined their efforts to campaign for institutional reform or to demand greater regional and international recognition of the challenges they face locally. The staging of the first regional conference for women in 1975, the protest action challenging the lack of women's representation within the SPC in 1980, the collaborative effort which brought political leaders and gender activists from the region together at the UN women's conference in Copenhagen in 1980, and the many regional initiatives on issues related to nuclear testing, decolonisation, violence against women, women in politics and women's legal literacy, can all be viewed as indicative of the strong level of regional cooperation and collective action that has been evident within the sphere of women's organising in this setting.

On the other hand, when considered from a resistance-oriented perspective, there is also evidence which suggests that horizontal collectivity has been difficult to sustain, particularly as engagement between women's organisations and formal political institutions has increased, and continued crises within the local political environment in Fiji have created more generalised political divisions. For example, it might be argued that in certain instances, horizontal collectivity within Fiji-based women's organisations has been undermined, most recently as a result of different perspectives on the military coup of 2006, or as a result of earlier ethno-nationalist extremism which saw a general hardening of communal allegiances in Fiji. As we have seen, this situation had particularly divisive ramifications for some women's groups in the wake of the 1987 coup. At the same time, the experiences of women involved in organisations such as the FWCC and the FWRM would suggest that, in certain instances, the issue of race has been exploited by some activists to cast doubt about the representativeness of particular women's groups or as a means by which to bolster the legitimacy of certain groups; especially as important funding relationships with external aid providers have been negotiated.

The nature of funding arrangements may also be viewed as contributing to the emergence of hierarchical relationships between organisations. As has been demonstrated at many points in this book, funding relationships can generate a spirit of competitiveness between women's groups, not only creating an environment of 'turfiness' (see Chapter 5), but also reinforcing the more general idea that those organisations which have negotiated strong relationships with external aid providers are more 'successful' or have a political authority which outweighs that of other groups. The success of the FWRM and the FWCC in this regard has meant that when these groups have been involved in regional collaborative efforts such as the Pacific Women's Network Against Violence Against Women or initiatives aimed at increasing women's political participation, they have frequently been viewed as the lead or 'agenda-setting' organisations. Such findings might therefore easily be used to substantiate the claim that, as the groups' institutional engagement increases, horizontal collectivity between women's organisations becomes more difficult to maintain.

When viewed from a situated perspective, both the reform- *and* resistance-oriented positions on the issue of horizontal collectivity become more difficult to sustain, however. Certainly collaborative efforts between women's organisations have accrued some institutional gains. These gains need also to be understood in context. The creation of women's machineries within the Fijian Government in 1987 or the regional SPC in 1982 certainly came about as a result of sustained collaborative campaigns waged by women's groups at the domestic and regional levels. However, as I have shown, the Fiji Ministry for Women has often operated in a way which has reflected the partisan policy agenda favoured by the indigenous Fijian establishment. Likewise, the creation of the regional women's machinery, the PWRB, was shown ultimately to have been an office that was never able to push beyond the broader institutional limitations of the SPC and, since 2007, was officially disbanded.

From a situated perspective, issues of ethnicity can also be seen to have caused divisions within the domestic sphere of women's organising in Fiji, and certainly to have disrupted gender activists' ability to maintain horizontal relationships. This scenario is not presented as a failing of women's organising. Rather, it is understood to reflect the broader historical contingencies that have 'racialised' many aspects of political, economic and social life in Fiji. From this perspective, the politics of race is not viewed as 'intruding' into the realm of gender politics in Fiji, but, instead, is treated as a pervasive and powerful local idiom which, since colonial times, has influenced institutional, political conduct and the internal operations of women's groups, while also configuring the spaces available to women's organisations within the broader realm of Fiji's associational life.

Equally, from a situated perspective, the ways in which institutional funding arrangements alter relationships within and between women's organisations, and potentially contribute to the emergence of inter-organisational hierarchies, are viewed as a development that neither compromises the legitimacy of women's organising, nor undermines the capacity of women's groups to differentiate themselves from the realm of institutional politics. Rather, such developments are scrutinised in relation to the broader local and global political environment where emerging ideas about 'good governance' have translated into increased support for, and engagement with, civil society organisations. And, as my discussion of the events of 2001 and 2002 demonstrates, it is possible to over-emphasise the negative aspects of these funding relationships and overlook the extent to which representatives from a wide variety of women's groups in Fiji collaborated their efforts in spontaneous support of the Women's Prayer Vigil and pro-democracy campaigns staged in the wake of the 2000 coup.

While accounts of women's organising performed from a cliff-top perspective tend to insist upon horizontal collectivity as a characteristic that enhances women's political agency, such claims become more problematic when the analysis is performed from a more situated perspective. As I have shown, conventional reform- or resistance- oriented analyses of women's organising fails to take full account of the way that contingencies within the prevailing local, regional or international political environments shape the ways in which relationships are negotiated within and between women's groups and has difficulty in accounting for the inconsistencies and apparent contradictions that are also part of this terrain.

Progressive ideas

When considered from a reform-oriented perspective, there is clearly a strong body of evidence to suggest that Fiji's women's organisations have played an important role in promoting progressive ideas and campaigning for progressive change for women. Since the early 1960s, women's organisations have raised questions about gender violence, women's institutional representation, women's participation in politics, legal literacy and women's human and reproductive rights. Campaigns undertaken by women's groups have led to the establishment of women's machineries in domestic and regional institutions, and encouraged institutional support for programs of law reform in the area of family law, sexual offences law and citizenship law. The efforts of women's groups have meant that Fiji was the first Pacific Island country to ratify CEDAW (1995) and to deliver a country report to the UN CEDAW Commission (2002). Additionally the development of collaborative projects with domestic state bureaucracies has occurred at various points. While some projects have followed the more conventional path of awareness raising on issues such as gender violence or the promotion of women's political participation, other projects, and particularly those undertaken by WAC within Fiji's prison and education system, have been of a more unconventional and creative style. When the evidence is mapped in a way which privileges organisations' reform-oriented activities, the conclusion that women's organisations have played an increasingly important role over the decades in promoting progressive ideas which challenge the gender discriminatory status quo appears easily supportable.

Resistance-oriented analysis would undoubtedly examine these developments in a more critical and contrastive light, however. Here descriptions of political activity would emphasise the provocative campaigns waged by women's organisations in the independence era, and their willingness to challenge the prevailing status quo. This would be contrasted with organisations' seemingly compliant relationships with donor agencies in later periods, and their apparent wariness of entering into overt confrontation with domestic authoritarian regimes. In the post-2006 coup context, questions might be asked about the extent to which debate about engagement with an anti-democratic regime could be construed as progressive. Undoubtedly, from this perspective, the trajectory of women's political agency would be plotted in a way that suggested a regressive rather than progressive history.

Yet, when appraised from a 'situated' perspective, closer consideration can be given to the contingent factors within the prevailing political environment which have influenced activists' understandings of viable courses of action at particular junctures. From this perspective, the locally provocative focus of political activity undertaken by the YWCA in the 1960s and 1970s is also shown to have been enabled within an independence-era political environment where civil society organisations responded to the idea that they were operating on a new frontier and were confident of their ability to challenge prevailing social, political and religious protocols. By contrast, in later and more tumultuous political periods, the political restrictions faced by women's groups are shown to have encouraged a more cautious approach to gender advocacy, as organisations came to terms with a political environment increasingly marked by communalism, the rise of indigenous ethno-nationalism and, recently, a more extreme form of authoritarianism. This climate has hardly been conducive to women's groups promoting the same types of provocative challenges to local sites of authority that featured in the advocacy of the past. Hence, I have shown how shifts in the prevailing political environment inclined women's organisations to gravitate towards a more issue-specific and legalistic variety of advocacy. This said, as the last chapter of this book also demonstrates, recent developments occurring in Fiji and particularly the current regime's tendency towards a more isolationist international posture do seem, ironically, to have opened the way for women advocates to take a more critical perspective on the international political economy. In the current context there does seem to be at least a peripheral interest in re-engaging with some of the themes that motivated gender activists in the post-independence period.

I have also provided a 'situated' analysis of how the relationships between institutional benefactors and women's organisations impact upon activists' abilities to promote progressive ideas. It is certainly recognised that in the more contemporary period, certain types of donor support have encouraged women's groups to 'dovetail' their agendas to those of their benefactors, resulting in a 'gentler political engagement'. From a situated perspective, however, the idea that this scenario equates to the more general cooptation of gender politics in Fiji is problematic.

On the one hand, this tendency is not universal, and certainly groups such as WAC continue to pursue unconventional and creative advocacy strategies. And, as the events taking place in the wake of the 2000 coup demonstrate, even the more high-profile women's groups such as the FRWM, have been prepared to engage in provocative political activity upholding constitutional democracy. On the other hand, the troubled engagements between pro-democracy women's groups and the military regime in the immediate aftermath of the 2006 coup demonstrate that there has also been strong suspicion and some hostility shown towards non-government organisations that access support from external benefactors while also engaging in strident critique of local political leaders. Where women's organisations advertise donor support of this type they have often been accused of employing advocacy strategies or promoting agendas that are inauthentic to the local socio-cultural context, even when they are careful to frame their advocacy of women's rights in ways which seek to accommodate local cultural or religious sensitivities.

These considerations suggest that organisations' capacities to promote progressive ideas are influenced in complex and contradictory ways and that this nuance is not easy to appreciate from a cliff-top analytical position. While there is little doubt that the relationships negotiated between women's groups and formal political institutions influence the tenor and direction of campaign strategies employed by women's groups, this book sets out to explain the complex interplay of global *and* local political influences which shapes activists' own understandings of what progressive advocacy might be, and how viable it is to pursue at a particular historical juncture.

Transnationalism

When appraised from a cliff-top perspective, transnationalism clearly emerges as an important aspect of women's organising in Fiji since the early 1960s. Representatives of women's organisations have been active and energetic participants on the international stage, both shaping and drawing inspiration from the directions that international debate on gender disadvantage has followed. Hence, from a reform-oriented perspective, it could be argued that through their direct participation within international forums, representatives from Fiji-based women's groups have contributed in significant ways to the emergence of consensual norms and a multilayered transnationalism within international feminism (Pettman 1996; Yuval Davis 2006). Certainly, Fiji-based gender activists had early misgivings about the dominance of western and first world voices within international feminist networks. However, they also logged some early success in drawing international attention to the particular kinds of structural disadvantage faced by Pacific Island women. During the early years of the UN Decade for Women, for example, Fiji-based gender activists, in coalition with women from around the Pacific Island region, successfully used their access to international and regional conferences to promote awareness about nuclear testing in the Pacific Island region, the struggles for decolonisation waged by Pacific Island communities, and the neo-colonial aspects of economic engagement in the Pacific from near, and more powerful, regional neighbours.

In later periods, Pacific gender activists' mistrust of the universalising aspects of international feminism began to give way, as a more issue-specific approach to gender disadvantage became predominant. This development allowed for global consideration to be given to common phenomena contributing to women's disadvantage such as violence against women, while at the same time accommodating recognition that these scenarios might be lived by women differently according to their context. Certainly, the local adoption of human-rights focused gender advocacy frameworks in relation to issues such as gender violence by the FWCC, or economic justice by the FWRM, could be viewed as evidence of a flexible and creative approach to this type of advocacy which is attentive to the importance of accommodating prevailing cultural, religious, political and even economic sensitivities. Such practices could certainly be viewed as consonant with the idea of a multilayered, transversal feminist politics accommodating of local specificities (Yuval Davis 2006).

On the other hand, a resistance-oriented perspective of gender politics in Fiji might suggest that as engagement has increased between local women's organisations and international institutions, the nature of transnational engagement has become more conservative. Hence, the gravitation from structurally inclined and internationalised forms of advocacy in the 1960s and 1970s towards more issue-specific, human rights-oriented forms of advocacy might be presented as an ongoing consequence of global power politics allowing continued western dominance of discussion about the causes of gender disadvantage. It might be argued that for too long, transnational feminisms have been disinclined to confront the idea that there is an inescapable link between the unequal distribution of global economic and political power and the economic, physical and social vulnerability of women in developing contexts, a scenario which suggests that the consequences of an enduring western feminist hegemony have not been diminished.

When appraised from a 'situated' perspective, however, these developments are shown to reflect broader global and local contingencies. I have shown how the internationalised and structurally inclined focus of advocacy undertaken by women's organisations on the global stage in the 1960s and 1970s was enabled by a prevailing Third Worldism evident within global politics in this period. I have argued that the prevalence of redistributive themes in world politics increased the transnational space in which Pacific women could protest against prevailing international structures, political (colonial) and economic (neo-colonial) which led to disempowerment and alienation within their communities in general terms. Further, I have shown how this political climate also enabled women from the Pacific to draw international attention to the unique ways in which global economic and political power imbalances were manifest in local contexts and contributed to the subordination of women.

In more contemporary periods, the shift towards issue-specific forms of advocacy which privileged human rights ideals, and which were frequently articulated in legalistic terms, has also been described in a manner that has drawn attention to broader domestic and international political circumstances. Hence I have described how activists' abilities to focus upon the 'bread and butter' aspects of women's disadvantage in an ongoing manner were distracted by domestic political crises and the continued requirement to confront questions related to the democratic future of Fiji. At the same time, I have shown how the transnational space available to women's groups aiming to promote a structurally inclined critique of global economic or political relations was severely reduced within a global political climate governed by neo-liberal orthodoxies, which have tended to emphasise the capacities of the individual and their ability to create their own market *and* political opportunities. As chapter five of this book demonstrates, efforts to liberalise trade in the Pacific Island region will necessarily have serious economic ramifications for Fiji's women in the future, and undoubtedly increase the economic vulnerability of many Pacific women. Yet, in a global and domestic political environment where the language of economic governance emphasises economic opportunity over economic redistribution or structural change, the political space available to women's organisations aiming to contest this scenario has been extremely limited. Of course, overplaying this narrative also ignores the evidence presented in the final chapter of this book. Here I suggested that domestic political conditions may have encouraged the pendulum to 'swing back' a little with some women activists showing more interest in challenging regional moves to develop a more liberalised trade environment.

Ultimately, my efforts to develop a 'situated' analytical perspective of women's political agency have resulted in a more nuanced account of gender activists' transnational political engagements than would have been possible from either a reform- or resistance-oriented perspective. Leaving aside the contest of ideas which promotes international feminism either as a terrain of consensual norms, or as a realm of enduring western feminist hegemony, I have instead given closer consideration to the ways that the transnational strategies employed by women's groups in Fiji have been shaped by contingent factors. As such, I have demonstrated how the circumstances of the prevailing political environment, local and international, have configured the political space available to women's organisations enabling more provocative forms of advocacy in certain contexts and discouraging women's groups from contesting the political and economic status quo in later periods.

In sum, analysis of women's political agency that emphasises contingency is clearly a complex undertaking and requires a detailed understanding of political circumstance, past and present. Yet, as this brief resume of some of the key findings presented in this book suggests, a sensitivity to context and the situated experience of gender activists certainly enables a fuller understanding of what has been achieved, and what is possible in particular political circumstances, than investigations of women's organising which are framed in more ideal-typical reform- or resistance-oriented terms. While such observations have an important relevance for the broader academic analysis of women's organising and women's political agency, they are also pertinent to a more generalised discussion about the nature of political participation in world politics.

Civil society and global politics

Many scholars working in this area are concerned about the lack of representativeness within formal structures of global governance and the normative orientation of policy-making activity. They describe widespread public disenchantment with formal models of political organisation, and a pervasive 'capital driven style of politics' (Falk 1998: 102) or 'turbo-capitalism' (Keane 2003: 65) which is alleged to have eroded institutional accountability (Falk 1995: 1; Held 1995, 1998; Archibugi 1998; Keane 2001, 2003; Kaldor 2003). The formulation of 'new social, political and economic' relationships (Keane 2003) is needed, it is argued, which might underpin systems of governance built upon principles that are democratic, participatory, non-violent and humane. Increased recognition and participation of civil society within global governance is viewed by many as the way forward (Falk 1995, 1998; Held 1995, 1998; Archibugi 1998; Kaldor 2003).

However, civil society is conceptualised in many of these accounts in highly idealised terms. Seen to be a realm of 'bottom-up' political engagement, it is understood to provide a site in which those who are marginalised by prevailing local or global political structures are able to 'mount their protests and seek alternatives' (Cox 1999: 10). From an international perspective, the transnational networks of civil society actors are seen to provide a sphere for counter-hegemonic political engagement, with the capacity to complement or reshape international institutions and contribute to a more participatory and just system of global governance (Falk 1995, 1998; Held 1995, 1998; Archibugi 1998; Kaldor 2003). Put bluntly, civil society features here unproblematically as a benign force for the good (Howell 2005); a sphere with the capacity to increase democratic representativeness and normative accountability within the structures of global governance.

The findings presented in this book tell a different story and coincide with a more critical vein of civil society scholarship which challenges such idealised perspectives of civil society capacity (Hulme and Edwards 1997; Van Rooy 1998; Howell and Pearce 2001; Khilnani 2001; Chandoke 2002, 2003). These accounts have all drawn attention to the contextual factors which influence the conduct of civil society actors in domestic and transnational spheres but they are usually overlooked in much of the international relations scholarship on civil society which tends more often to construct positive ideal-type representations of this realm as progressive and naturally reform-oriented.

The Fiji case clearly demonstrates how a complex interplay of socio-cultural protocols, religious values, colonial legacies and geo-political influences have configured the domestic realm of associational life in specific ways at certain historical junctures. In many instances, these influences have clearly shaped the conduct of women's organisations. For example, socio-cultural protocols relating to social rank or ethnicity have frequently influenced the way relations are negotiated between gender activists, and they have often made for tension or division within the sphere of women's organising more broadly. In other instances, communal identifications or broader political allegiances have prompted some women's organisations to lend their support to the divisive political agendas promoted by Fiji's political leaders. This type of activity is clearly antithetical to the liberal norms assumed by many to motivate civil society actors. It is argued that global governance structures should be broadened to enable these actors' participation on the basis of their capacity to promote these liberal values. Yet, in Fiji, such partisanship within civil society is entirely consistent with the local terrain of political life where, since colonial times, divisions have raged over the legitimacy of proposed models of governance for the country and the values systems that they should reflect. Moreover, as I have also demonstrated, trends within international politics also configure the spaces available to women activists and place some significant constraints upon their ability to push for a normative reorientation of global governance. As has been made clear, recent trends in development policy-making have encouraged closer engagement between institutions and civil society in order that program delivery can be made more participatory and responsive to the needs of grass-roots communities. Nevertheless, as the final chapters of this book also demonstrate, the broader policy paradigms relating to good governance and market liberalisation have in many ways come to define how engagements between civil society and international institutions are structured and have often placed limitations upon how far civil society activists are able to question these global trends.

International relations' scholarship that celebrates the emergence of a global civil society and anticipates that this presence in world politics will contribute to a re-orientation of global governance structures, making them more just, participatory and accountable, clearly presents an illustration of future possibilities which is highly appealing. Yet it may also be overly hopeful. As this study has shown, when the political agency of civil society actors is examined from a 'face to face' perspective which allows for an increased sensitivity to circumstance, it becomes possible to appreciate activists' 'situated' appraisals of what has been achieved and what is possible at various political junctures. Studies of the role to be played by civil society actors in world politics would therefore benefit from less idealised conceptualisations of these actors' political agency and a closer scrutiny of the ways that political engagement is shaped by circumstance.

Bibliography

Ackerly, B.A., 2001. 'Women's human rights activists as cross-cultural theorists,' *International Feminist Journal of Politics*, 3(3): 311–46.

ACWIN (Action Centre for Women in Need), 1983. *Rape in Fiji: A Preliminary Report Prepared by the Action Centre for Women in Need* (ACWIN) (Suva: ACWIN, January).

Adinkrah, M., 1995. *Crime, Deviance and Delinquency in Fiji* (Suva: Fiji Council of Social Services).

Agarwal, B., 1996. 'From Mexico 1975 to Beijing 1995,' *Indian Journal of Gender Studies*, 3(1): 21–35.

Al-Ali, N.S., 2003. 'Gender and civil society in the Middle East,' *International Feminist Journal of Politics*, 5(2): 216–32.

Alexander, M.J. and C.T. Mohanty, eds, 1997. *Feminist Genealogies, Colonial Legacies, Democratic Futures* (New York and London: Routledge).

Ali, A., 1978. 'Fiji Indian politics,' *Journal of Pacific Studies*, 4: 1–26.

Ali, I., 2002. Interview with author, Suva, 14 November.

Ali, S., 1987. 'The women's crisis centre in Suva, Fiji,' in *Women, Development and Empowerment: A Pacific Feminist Perspective, Report of a Pacific Women's Workshop*, Naboutini, Fiji, 23–23 March 1986, ed. V. Griffen (Kuala Lumpur: Asian and Pacific Development Centre), pp. 37–44.

—— 2002. Interview with author, Suva, 25 March.

—— 2007. 'Fiji women's crisis centre,' paper presented at the 10th Triennial Conference of Pacific Women, *Pacific Women, Pacific Plan: Stepping Up the Pace to 2010*. Noumea, 27–31 May.

Alvarez, S., 1999. 'Advocating feminism: The Latin American feminist NGO "boom",' *International Feminist Journal of Politics*, 1(2): 181–209.

Amnesty International, 2000a. 'Women's Rights are Human Rights. Commitments Made by Governments in the Beijing Declaration and the Platform for Action.' Online: http://www2.amnesty.se/wom.nsf/f64b3a7cOpenDocument Accessed 27 August 2005.

—— 2000b. 'Beijing plus five not minus five,' Press Release, 9 June 2000. Online: http://web.amnesty.org/library/Index/ ENGACT770102000?open&of=ENG—373 Accessed 29 August 2005.

Amratlal, Jyoti, Eta Baro, Vanessa Griffen, Geet Bala Singh J., 1975. *Women's Role in Fiji* (Suva: South Pacific Social Sciences Association).

Anheier, H., M. Glasius and M. Kaldor, 2001. 'Introducing global civil society,' in *Global Civil Society2001*, ed. H. Anheier, M. Glasius and M. Kaldor. (Oxford: Oxford University Press), pp. 3–22.

Antrobus, P., 2004. *The Global Women's Movement: Issues and Strategies for the New Century* (London: Zed Books).

—— 1984. 'Reaching beyond university walls,' *Development: Seeds of Change* 1984(4) 45–9.

Archibugi, D., 1998. 'Principles of cosmopolitan democracy,' in *Re-imagining Political Community: Studies in Cosmopoliian Democracy*, ed. D. Archibugi, D. Held and M. Köhler. (Stanford: Stanford University Press), pp. 198–232.

Arya, K., 2002. Interview with author, Suva, 15 April.

Ashwin, R., 1981. '1980 UN Mid-Decade Conference for Women,' in *Office of Women's Affairs, Copenhagen and Beyond: Perspectives on the World Conference and NGO Forum for the UN Decade for Women*, Copenhagen, Denmark, July 1980 (Canberra: Australian Government Publishing Service).

AusAID, 2000. *Good Governance: Guiding Principles for Implementation* (Canberra: Commonwealth of Australia).

—— 2002. *AusAID Pacific Regional Strategy 2002–2006* (Canberra: Commonwealth of Australia).

Bainimarama, V., 2006. 'Statement of Fiji Commander Bainimarama (12/5/06).' Available from: http://archives.pireport.org/archive/2006/december/12-12-st1.htm Accessed 14 May 2009.

Baro, E., 1975. 'Lolohea Akosita Waqairawai,' in J. Amratlal, *et al.*, *Women's Role in Fiji* (Suva: South Pacific Social Sciences Association), pp. 33–9.

Barr, K., 2007. 'Solutions before democracy,' *Fiji Times*, 14 May.

Basu, A., 1986. 'Reflections on Forum '85 in Nairobi, Kenya: voices from the international women's studies community,' *Signs: Journal of Women in Culture and Society*, 10(3): 603–5.

Beneath Paradise, 1994. *Beneath Paradise: See Us, Hear Us, Beijing '95: Grassroots Women's NGOs of the Pacific, Documenting Women's Life Stories, Strengths, Achievements, Needs and Struggles* (Melbourne: International Women's Development Agency).

—— 1995. *Report from Beneath Paradise, Beijing '95: Grassroots Women's NGOs of the Pacific* (Melbourne: Beneath Paradise).

Bergeron, S., 2003. 'The post-Washington consensus and economic representations of women in development at the World Bank,' *International Feminist Journal of Politics*, 5(3): 397–419.

Berkovitch, N., 1999. 'The emergence and transformation of the international women's movement,' in *Constructing World Culture: International Non-Government Organizations since 1875*, ed. J. Boli and G.N. Thomas (Stanford: Stanford University Press), pp. 100–26.

Bernstein, A., 1986. 'Reflections on Forum '85 in Nairobi, Kenya: voices from the international women's studies community,' *Signs: Journal of Women in Culture and Society*, 10(3): 606–8.

Bhagwan Rolls, S., 2000. 'Gender and the role of the media in conflict and peacemaking: the Fiji experience,' *Development Bulletin*, 53(November): 62–4.

—— 2002a. Interview with author, Suva, 8 April.

—— 2002b. Interview with author, Tavuya, 30 October.

—— 2002c. Interview with author, Suva, 6 December.

——2007. 'Women's media: challenging the status quo,' *Pacific Journalism Review* 13(2): 17–27.

—— 2009. Electronic communication with author, 3 April.

Bhagwati, J., 1977. 'Introduction,' in *The New International Economic Order: The North South Debate*, ed. J. Bhagwati (Cambridge, MA: MIT Press), pp. 1–20.

Bhim, M., 2007. 'The impact of the promotion of Reconciliation, Tolerance and Unity Bill on the 2006 election,' in *From Election to Coup in Fiji: the 2006 Campaign and its Aftermath*, ed. J. Fraenkel and S. Firth (Canberra: ANU E Press), pp. 111–43.

Bickham Mendez, J., 2002. 'Creating alternatives from a gender perspective: transnational organising for Maquila workers' rights in Central America,' in *Women's Activism and Globalization: Linking Local Struggles and Transnational Politics*, ed. N. Naples and M. Desai (New York: Routledge), pp. 121–41.

Bishop, A., 1997. 'Poverty,' in *Back to Basics from Beijing: An Australian Guide to the International Platform for Action*, ed. S. Mitchell and R.D. Pradhan (Canberra: ACFOA), pp. 10–13.

Booth, K.M., 1998. 'National mother, global whore, and transnational femocrats: the politics of AIDS and the construction of women at the World Health Organisation,' *Feminist Studies*, 24(1): 115–39.

Borgu, A., 2002. *Beyond Bali: ASPI's Strategic Assessment 2002*, Canberra: Australia Strategic Policy Institute.

Boserup, E., 1970. *Women's Role in Economic Development* (London: Allen and Unwin).

Boseto, P., 2000. 'Melanesian women, mothers of democracy,' in 'Women and governance from the grassroots in Melanesia,' *State, Society and Governance in Melanesia Discussion Paper 00/2*, ed. B. Douglas (Canberra: SSGM Project, Australian National University), pp. 8–10.

Bradley, C., 1997. 'Why violence against women is a development issue: reflections from Papua New Guinea,' in *Women and Violence*, ed. M. Davies, (London: Zed Books, 2nd ed.), pp. 10–28.

Brown Thompson, K., 2002. 'Women's rights are human rights' in *Restructuring World Politics: Transnational Social Movements, Networks and Norms*, ed. S. Khagram, J.V. Riker and K. Sikkink (Minneapolis: University of Minnesota Press), pp. 96–122.

Buadromo, V., 2002. Interview with author, Suva, 10 April.

—— 2007. 'Fiji women's rights movement,' paper presented at the 10th Triennial Conference of Pacific Women, *Pacific Women, Pacific Plan: Stepping Up the Pace to 2010*, Noumea 27–31 May 2007.

—— 2009. Interview with author, Suva 17, February.

Bulbeck, C., 1998. *Reorienting Western Feminisms: Women's Diversity in a Post-Colonial World* (Cambridge: Cambridge University Press).

Bunch, C., 1990. 'Women's rights as human rights: towards a re-vision of human rights,' *Human Rights Quarterly*, 12(4): 486–98.

Buksh, N., 2002a. Interview with author, Suva, 28 March.

—— 2002b. Interview with author, Suva, 15 November.

Çağatay, N., C. Grown and A. Santiago, 1986. 'The Nairobi women's conference: toward a global feminism?,' *Feminist Studies*, 12(2): 401–12.

Caine, B., M Gatens, E. Graham, J. Larbalestier, S. Watson and E. Webby, eds, 1998. *Australian Feminism: A Companion* (Melbourne: Oxford University Press).

Carling, M., 2002. Interview with author, Suva, 14 November.

—— and C. Peacock-Taylor, 2001. *Study of the Impacts of the Political Crisis on Children and Families in Fiji* (Suva: UNICEF Pacific).

Carrillo, R., 1992. *Battered Dreams: Violence Against Women as an Obstacle to Development* (New York: UNIFEM).

Casimera, A., 2006, electronic communication to Fiji Human Rights NGO Coalition, 14 December.

CCF (Citizens' Constitutional Forum), 2001. 'What is the Citizens' Constitutional Forum' (Suva: CCF).

—— 2005. 'Constitutional renewal in the Pacific Islands: an international conference and workshop.' Online: http://www.ccf.org.fj/artman/publish/printer_339.shtml Accessed 1 April 2005.

Chandhoke, N., 2003. 'The 'civil' and the 'political' in civil society,' in *Civil Society and Democracy: A Reader*, ed. C. Elliot (Oxford: Oxford University Press), pp. 238–62.

—— 2002. 'The limits of global civil society,' in *Global Civil Society*, ed. M. Glasius, M. Kaldor and H. Anheier (Oxford: Oxford University Press), pp. 35–53.

—— 2001. 'The 'civil' and the 'political' in civil society,' *Democratization*, 8(2), pp. 1–24.

Chappell, D., 2005. 'Africanisation in the Pacific: blaming others for disorder in the periphery,' *Comparative Studies in Society and History*, 47: 286–317.

Chappell, L., 2006, 'Contesting women's rights: charting the emergence of a transnational conservative counter-network,' *Global Society*, 20(4): 491–520.

Chattier, P., 2005. 'Understanding poverty from a gender perspective,' *Journal of Fijian Studies*, 3(2): 249–76.

Chew, C., 1985a. 'We're represented by a man,' *Fiji Sun*, 14 July.

—— 1985b. 'Pacific women unhappy,' *Fiji Sun*, 16 July.

—— 1985c. 'Woman slams "White Gods",' *Fiji Sun*, 20 July.

—— 1985e. 'Pacific people are being used, woman says,' *Fiji Sun*, 25 July.

—— 1985f. 'Our women aim to continue message,' *Fiji Sun*, 6 August.

Chung, M., 2002. Interview with author, Suva, 20 November.

Clark, J., 1997. 'The state, popular participation and the voluntary sector,' in *NGOs, States and Donors: Too Close for Comfort*, ed. D. Hulme and M. Edwards (London: Macmillan), pp. 43–58.

Colowai, A., 2002. Interview with author, Suva, 11 October.

Connors, J., 1996. 'NGOs and the human rights of women at the United Nations,' in *The Conscience of the World: The Influence of Non-Governmental Organisations in the UN System*, ed. P. Willetts, (London: C. Hurst and Co.), pp. 147–80.

Costello-Olsen, K., 2002. Interview with author, Suva, 22 November.

—— 2009. Interview with author, Suva 19 February.

Cretton, V., 2004. 'Cakobau's sisters: status, gender and politics in Fiji,' Working Paper No. 11 (Canberra: Gender Relations Centre, Australian National University).

Crook, R., 2001. 'Editorial introduction,' *International Development Studies Bulletin*, 32(1): 1–6.

D'Costa, B., 2006. 'Marginalized identity: new frontiers of research for IR?' in *Feminist Methodologies for International Relations*, ed. B.A. Ackerly, M. Stern and J. True (New York: Cambridge University Press), pp. 129–52.

Dakuvula, J., 1973. 'Development for whom?' in *Fiji: A Developing Australian Colony*, ed. A. Rokotuivuna (North Fitzroy, VIC: International Development Action), pp. 10–17.

Danielsson, B., 1980. 'Pacific women speak out in Copenhagen,' *Pacific Islands Monthly*, October: 21–22.

—— 1990. 'Poisoned Pacific: the legacy of French nuclear testing,' *Bulletin of the Atomic Scientists*, 46(2): 22–31.

Danielsson, M-T. and B. Danielsson, 1981a. 'A chorus of female voices,' *Pacific Islands Monthly*, January: 18–19.

—— 1981b. 'Seminar on a circular track,' *Pacific Islands Monthly*, September: 20–21.

Davies, J.E., 2005. 'Ethnic competition and the forging of the nation-state in Fiji,' *The Round Table*, 94(1): 47–76.

Dé Ishtar, Z., 1994. *Daughters of the Pacific* (North Melbourne: Spinifex Press).

Denoon, D., 1997. 'New economic orders: land, labour and dependency,' in *The Cambridge History of the Pacific Islanders*, ed. D. Denoon, *et al.* (Cambridge: Cambridge University Press).

Department of Women and Culture, Fiji, 1994. *Women of Fiji, A Statistical Gender Profile* (Suva: Government of the Republic of Fiji).

Dirlik, A., 1992. 'The Asia-Pacific idea: reality and representation in the invention of a regional structure,' *Journal of World History*, 3(1): 55–79.

—— 1993. 'Introducing the Pacific,' in *What is in a Rim? Critical Perspectives on the Pacific Region Idea*, ed. A. Dirlik (Boulder, CO: Westview Press), pp. 3–11.

Douglas, B., 1998. 'Traditional individuals? Gendered negotiations of identity, Christianity and citizenship in Vanuatu,' *State, Society and Governance in Melanesia DiscussionPaper 98/6* (Canberra: SSGM Project, Australian National University).

—— 1999. 'Provocative readings in intransigent archives: finding Aneityumese women,' *Oceania*, 70: 111–29.

—— 2000a. 'Conflict, gender, peacemaking, and alternative nationalisms in the Western Pacific,' *Development Bulletin*, 53(November): 10–13.

—— 2000b. 'Hearing Melanesian,' in 'Women and governance from the grassroots in Melanesia,' *State, Society and Governance in Melanesia Discussion Paper 00/2* (Canberra: SSGM Project, Australian National University).

—— 2002. 'Christian citizens: women and negotiations of modernity in Vanuatu,' *Contemporary Pacific*, 14(1): 615–50.

—— 2003. 'Christianity, tradition, and everyday modernity: towards an anatomy of women's groupings in Melanesia,' *Oceania*, 74(1/2): 6–23.

Dureau, C., 1993. 'Nobody asked the mother: women and maternity on Simbo, Western Solomon Islands,' *Oceania*, 64(1): 18–35.

Durutalo, S., 1985. 'Buccaneers and chiefly historians,' *Journal of Pacific Studies*, 11: 117–56.

Elliot, C., 2003. 'Civil society and democracy: a comparative review essay,' in *Civil Society and Democracy: A Reader*, ed. C. Elliot (Oxford: Oxford University Press), pp. 1–39.

Elshtain, J., 1981. *Public Man, Private Woman: Women in Social and Political Thought* (Princeton, NJ: Princeton University Press).

Elson, D., 1995. 'Male bias in macro-economics: the case of structural adjustment,' in *Male Bias in the Development Process*, ed. D. Elson (Manchester: Manchester University Press, 2nd ed.).

Emberson-Bain, A., 1992. 'Women poverty and post-coup pressure,' in *Tu Galala: Social Change in the Pacific*, ed. D. Robie (Annandale: Pluto Press Australia), pp. 145–62.

—— ed., 1994. *Sustainable Development or Malignant Growth* (Suva: Marama Publications).

—— 1997. 'Dust to dust, ashes to Phoenix,' in *With Heart and Nerve and Sinew: Post-coup Writing From Fiji*, ed. A. Griffen (Suva: Christmas Club), pp. 275–92.

—— 2001. *In the Name of Growth: A Story of Fisheries Development, Indigenous Women and Politics* (Suva: Infocus Productions).

—— and C. Slatter, 1995. *Labouring Under the Law: A Critique of Employment Legislation Affecting Women in Fiji* (Suva: Fiji Women's Rights Movement).

Evening, S., 2002. Interview with Author, Lami, 9 April.

Fairbairn, T., 1977. 'Foreign aid for Pacific Islands development,' *Pacific Perspectives*, 6(1): 33–40.

Fairbairn-Dunlop, P., 2005, 'Gender, culture and sustainable development – the Pacific Way,' in *Culture and Sustainable Development in the Pacific*, ed. A. Hooper (Canberra: Asia Pacific Press 2nd ed.), pp. 62–75.

—— 2000. 'Gender, culture and sustainable development: The Pacific way,' in *Culture and Sustainable Development in the Pacific*, ed. A. Hooper (Canberra: Asia Pacific Press) pp. 62–75.

Falk, R., 1995. *On Humane Governance: Toward a New Global Politics* (Cambridge: Polity Press).

—— 1998. 'Global civil society: perspectives, initiatives, movements,' *Oxford Development Studies*, 26(1): 99–111.

—— and M. Blasius, 1976. 'State of the globe report: International Women's Year,' *Alternatives*, 2: 262–6.

FCRC (Fiji Constitutional Review Commission), 1997a. *Fiji in Transition: Research Papers of the Fiji Constitutional Review Commission*, 1 (Suva: University of the South Pacific).

—— 1997b. *Fiji and the World: Research Papers of the Fiji Constitutional Review Commission*, 2 (Suva: University of the South Pacific).

fem'Link, 2000. *Mothers in Dialogue* (Suva).

—— 2001. *Fem'talk, Not Just Sweet Talk*, (Suva).

—— 2002a. Transcript of Interview with Imrana Jalal, October, Suva, unpublished.

—— 2002b. *Keeping Watch* (Suva).

—— 2006. Electronic communication with author, 11 November.

—— 2008. *femLINK Pacific Annual Report 2008*. Online: http://www. femlinkpacific.org.fj/_resources/main/files/femLINKPACIFIC%20 ANNUAL%20REPORT%202008.pdf Accessed 14 May 2009.

—— 2009. 'femLINK Pacific Postcards from the 53rd UN Commission of the Status of Women,' [Press Release], 25 February. Online: http://www. femlinkpacific.org.fj/_resources/main/files/femLINKPACIFIC%2520at%252 0the%2520Commission%2520of%2520the%2520Status%2520of%2520Wo men%2520Meeting.pdf Accessed 26 February 2009.

Ferguson, K., 1984. *The Feminist Case against Bureaucracy* (Philadelphia: Temple University Press).

—— 1991. 'Interpretation and genealogy in feminism,' *Signs: Journal of Women in Culture and Society*, 16(1): 322–39.

FHRC (Fiji Human Rights Commission) 2007. 'A response to the Fiji Human Rights Commission Directors Report on the Assumption of Executive Authority by Commodore J.V. Bainimarma, Commander of the Republic of Fiji Military Forces,' Suva. January. [circulated privately via email networks].

Field, M., 2002. 'Pacific mainline Christianity succumbing to new influences,' *Agence France Press*, Auckland, 11 June.

Fiji Islands Bureau of Statistics, 2005. 'Facts and figures as at July 2005,' *Fiji Islands Bureau of Statistics*. Online: http://www.statsfiji.gov.fj/FjFacts&Figs05.pdf Accessed 6 February 2006.

Fiji Ministry of Women and Culture, 1998. *The Women's Plan of Action 1998–2008,* (Suva: Ministry of Women and Culture, October).

—— 1999a, *Women and Culture: Annual Report for the Year 1998, Parliamentary Paper 42* (Suva: Parliament of Fiji).

—— 1999b, *National Report on the Implementation of the Beijing Platform for Action,* 3 September (Suva: Fiji Ministry of Women and Culture).

Fiji Mission to the UN, 2002. *The Republic of Fiji Islands Presentation to the Twenty-Sixth Session of The Committee on the Elimination of All Forms of Discrimination Against Women,* United Nations, New York, 16 January.

Fiji YWCA, 1965a. *Programme for Term 1* (Suva: Fiji YWCA).

—— 1965b. *Programme for Term II* (Suva: Fiji YWCA).

—— 1965–1991. *Management Committee Record Books* (Suva: Fiji YWCA).

—— 1965–1994. *Program Committee Record Books* (Suva: Fiji YWCA).

—— 1967a. *Application for Grant in Aid, Building Project Proposal* (Suva: Fiji YWCA).

—— 1967b. 'The role of voluntary societies in social welfare' (Suva: Fiji YWCA).

—— 1968–1984. *Public Affairs Committee Record Books* (Suva: Fiji YWCA).

—— 1970a. *First National Convention, March 14 1970. Natabua High School, Lautoka, Fiji,* Report of the Proceedings and Minutes of the Convention.

—— 1970b. *Annual Report 1970* (Suva: Fiji YWCA).

—— 1973. *Annual Report July 1972–December 1973* (Suva: Fiji YWCA).

—— 1976. *Third National Convention, September 10–13,Community Resource Centre, Sukuna Park, Suva, Fiji,* Report on the Work of the YWCA of Fiji.

—— 1979–1994. *National Executive Committee Minute Books* (Suva: Fiji YWCA).

Finin, G., 2009. 'Oppression finds new paradise in Fiji,' *Far Eastern Economic Review* 172(4): pp. 55–7.

Finin, G. and T. Wesley-Smith, 2000. 'Coups conflicts and crises: the new Pacific way?,' East-West Center Working Papers No. 13 (Honolulu: East-West Center, June).

Firth, S., 1997. 'Colonial administration and the invention of the native,' in *Cambridge History of the Pacific Islanders,* ed. D. Denoon, et al. (Cambridge: Cambridge University Press), pp. 253–88.

—— 2000. 'The Pacific Islands and the globalization agenda,' *Contemporary Pacific*, 12(1): 178–92.

Fraenkel, J., 2000. 'The clash of dynasties and rise of demagogues; Fiji's Tauri Vakaukauwa,' *Journal of Pacific History*, 35(3): 295–308.

—— 2004. 'The coming anarchy in Oceania? A critique of the 'Africanisation' of the South Pacific thesis,' *Commonwealth and Comparative Politics*, 42(1): 1–34.

—— 2008. 'Fiji: issues and events 2007,' *The Contemporary Pacific*, 20(2): 450–60.

Fraser, A., 1987. *The UN Decade for Women: Documents and Dialogue* (Boulder, CO: Westview Press).

Friedman, E., 1999. 'The effects of "transnationalism reversed" in Venezuela: assessing the impact of UN global conferences on the women's movement,' *International Feminist Journal of Politics*, 1(3): 357–81.

Fry, G., 1979. 'South Pacific regionalism: the development of an indigenous commitment,' Unpublished Masters Thesis, Department of International Relations, Australian National University, Canberra.

—— 1994. 'International cooperation in the South Pacific: from regional integration to collective diplomacy,' in *The Political Economy of Regional Cooperation: Comparative Case Studies*, ed. W.A. Axline (Pinter: London).

—— 1997. 'Framing the islands: knowledge and power in changing Australian images of "the South Pacific",' *Contemporary Pacific*, 9(2): 305–44.

—— 2000. 'Political legitimacy and the post-colonial state in the Pacific: reflections on some common threads in the Fiji Islands and Solomon Islands coups,' *Pacifica Review*, 12(3): 295–304.

FWCC (Fiji Women's Crisis Centre), 1995. *Pacific Women against Violence*, 1(1).

—— 1996. *Fiji Women's Crisis Centre: Report on the 2nd Regional Meeting on Violence Against Women in the Pacific, Bergengren House Suva*, Fiji (Suva: FWCC).

—— 1998a. *Breaking the Silence* (Suva: FWCC).

—— 1998b. 'Address to the National Congress on Women,' Suva. Online: http://www.fijiwomen.com/index.php?id=1305 Accessed 2 December 2005.

—— 1999a. *Newsletter*, April.

—— 1999b. *National Research on Domestic Violence and Sexual Assault* (Suva: FWCC). Online: http://www.fijiwomen.com/index.php?id=1282 Accessed 2 December 2005.

—— 2000. *Pacific Women Against Violence*, 5(4) September.

—— 2001a. *Pacific Women Against Violence*, 6(3) April.

—— 2001b. *Pacific Women Against Violence*, 6(4) June/July.

—— 2007. 'Nurses' strike,' [Press Release], 31 July.

FWRM (Fiji Women's Rights Movement) 1995. *Balance: Newsletter of the Fiji Women's Rights Movement*, September–October.

—— 1996. '10th anniversary edition,' *Balance: Newsletter of the Fiji Women's Rights Movement*.

—— 1999. *Balance: Newsletter of the Fiji Women's Rights Movement*, April–June.

—— 2000a, *Herstory: A Profile of the Fiji Women's Rights Movement* (Suva: FWRM).

—— 2000b, *Balance: Newsletter of the Fiji Women's Rights Movement*, July–September.

—— 2001a, *FWRM 1986–2001* (Suva: FWRM).

—— 2001b, *Balance: Newsletter of the Fiji Women's Rights Movement*, July–December.

—— 2002. *Presentation of the NGO Shadow Report to the CEDAW Committee of the United Nations in New York*, 15 January 2002, Suva.

—— 2008a. *Balance: Newsletter of the Fiji Women's Rights Movement 1/2008*, June.

—— 2008b. *Balance: Newsletter of the Fiji Women's Rights Movement 2/2008*, September.

—— 2008c. 'Tok talk: nourishing an Asia Pacific feminist movement,' paper presented at the AWID International Forum on Women's Rights and Development, The Power of Movements. Cape Town, 14–17 November.

—— 2009a. Electronic communication to PACWIN of Campaign Press Release, 8 March.

—— 2009b. *Balance: Newsletter of the Fiji Women's Rights Movement 1/2009*, April.

FWRM, *et al.*, 2002. *NGO Report on the Status of Women in the Republic of the Fiji Islands* (Suva: FWRM, 12 January).

Galey, M., 1986. 'The Nairobi Conference: the powerless majority,' *PS*, 19(2): 255–65.

—— 1995a. 'The United Nations and women's issues,' in *Women, Gender and World Politics: Perspectives, Policies, and Prospects*, ed. P.R. Beckman and F. D'Amico (Westport, Conn.: Bergin and Garvey), pp. 131–40.

—— 1995b. 'Women find a place,' in *Women, Politics and the United Nations*, ed. A. Winslow (Westport, Conn: Greenwood Press), pp. 11–28.

Garner, K., 2003. *Precious Fire: Maud Russell and the Chinese Revolution* (Amherst: University of Massachusetts Press).

George, N., 2011. 'Pacific women building peace: a regional perspective,' *The Contemporary Pacific* 23(1): pp. 37–71.

Goetz, A-M., ed., 1997. *Getting Institutions Right for Women in Development* (London: Zed Books).

Gokal, S., 1985. 'World more aware of disadvantaged women,' *Fiji Times*, reprinted in D. Goodwillie, *United Nations World Conference for Women 1985: What Happened at Nairobi?* (Nadi: Ofis Blong Ol Meri).

Goodwillie, D., 1985. *United Nations World Conference for Women 1985: What Happened at Nairobi?* (Nadi: Ofis Blong Ol Meri).

—— 2005a. Interview with author, Sydney, 13 August.

—— 2005b. Electronic post to PACWIN, 15 June 2005.

—— and J. Kaloumaira, 2000. 'Fiji women's rights movement: innovative exemplars project: women's coalition for women's citizenship rights,' November, unpublished.

—— and R. Lechte, 1985. 'Women and development programs in the Pacific,' in *From Rhetoric to Reality? Papua New Guinea's Eight Point Plan and National Goals after a Decade*, ed. P. King, W. Lee and V. Warakai (Port Moresby: University of Papua New Guinea Press), pp. 58–65.

Grant, R., 1991. 'The sources of gender bias in international relations theory' in *Gender and International Relations*, ed. R. Grant and K. Newland (Indianapolis: Indiana University Press), pp. 8–26.

Greer, G., 1970. *The Female Eunuch* (London: MacGibbon and Kee).

Gregg, R., 1981. 'UN decision-making structures and the implementation of the NIEO,' in *Political and Institutional Issues of the New International Economic Order*, ed. E. Laszlo and J. Kurtzman (New York: Pergamon Press), pp. 103–32.

Grewal, I. and C. Kaplan, eds., 1994. *Scattered Hegemonies: Postmodernity and Transnational Feminist Practices* (Minneapolis: University of Minneapolis Press).

Griffen, V., 1975a. *Women Speak Out! A Report of the Pacific Women's Conference, October 27–November 2* (Suva: Pacific Women's Conference).

—— 1975b. 'Two Fijian women,' in *Women's Role in Fiji*, ed. J. Amratlal, *et al.* (Suva: South Pacific Social Sciences Association), pp. 41–59.

—— 1984. 'The Pacific Islands: all it requires is ourselves,' in *Sisterhood is Global: The International Women's Movement Anthology*, ed. R. Morgan (New York: Anchor Books), pp. 517–24.

—— ed., 1987. *Women, Development and Empowerment: A Pacific Feminist Perspective, Report of a Pacific Women's Workshop, Naboutini, Fiji, 23–23 March 1986* (Kuala Lumpur: Asian and Pacific Development Centre).

—— 2005. 'YWCA mourns death of outspoken feminist, activist,' *Pacific Beat*, Australian Broadcasting Commission, 9 June.

Guest, K.J., 1997. 'Activist,' in *Back to Basics from Beijing: An Australian Guide to the International Platform for Action*, ed. S. Mitchell and R.D. Pradhan (Canberra: Australian Council for Overseas Aid), pp. 110–14.

Haraway, D., 1991. 'Situated knowledges: the science question in feminism and the privilege of partial perspective,' in *Simians, Cyborgs, and Women: The Reinvention of Nature*, ed. D. Haraway (New York: Routledge), pp. 183–201.

Harrington, C., 2000. 'Fiji's women garment workers: negotiating constraints in employment and beyond,' *Labour and Management in Development Journal*, 1(5): 2–22.

—— 2004. '"Marriage" to capital: the fallback positions of Fiji's women garment workers,' *Development in Practice*, 14(4): 495–507.

Hart, J.A., 1983. *The New International Economic Order: Conflict and Cooperation in North-South Economic Relations* (New York: St Martin's Press).

Hau'ofa, E., 1994. 'Our sea of islands,' *Contemporary Pacific*, 6(1): 148–61.

—— 1998. 'The ocean in us,' *Contemporary Pacific*, 10(2): 392–410.

Held, D., 1995. *Democracy and the Global Order: From the Modern State to Cosmopolitan Governance* (Stanford: Stanford University Press).

—— 1998. 'Democracy and globalization,' in *Re-imagining Political Community: Studies in Cosmopolitan Democracy*, ed. D. Archibugi, D. Held and M. Köhler (Stanford: Stanford University Press), pp. 11–27.

Henderson, J., 2003. 'The future of democracy in Melanesia: what role for outside powers,' *Asia-Pacific Viewpoint*, 44(3): 225–41.

—— 2005. 'Introduction: Pacific conflict – how much and why?' in *Securing a Peaceful Pacific*, ed. J. Henderson and G. Watson (Christchurch: Canterbury University Press), pp. 3–12.

Hill, N., 1980. 'Pacific women and the United Nations,' *New Zealand International Review*, 5(6): 25–8.

Houng Lee, G., 2002. Interview with author, Suva, 4 April.

Howell, J., 2003. 'Women's organisations and civil society in China: making a difference,' *International Feminist Journal of Politics*, 5(2): 191–215.

—— 2005. 'Gender and civil society' in *Global Civil Society Yearbook 2005/2006*, ed. M. Glasius, M. Kaldor and H. Anheir (London: Sage).

—— and D. Mulligan, eds., 2005. *Gender and Civil Society: Transcending Boundaries* (New York: Routledge).

—— and J. Pearce, 2001. *Civil Society and Development: A Critical Exploration* (Boulder, CO: Lynne Rienner).

Hughes, H., 2003. 'Aid has failed in the Pacific,' *Issue Analysis, Center for Independent Studies*, 7 May. Online: http://www.cis.org.au/ Accessed 12 January 2005.

Hulme, D. and M. Edwards, eds., 1997. *NGOs, States and Donors: Too Close for Comfort?* (New York: St Martin's Press in Association with Save the Children).

Hultman, T., 1986. 'Reflections on Forum '85 in Nairobi, Kenya: voices from the international women's studies community,' *Signs: Journal of Women in Culture and Society*, 10(3): 589–93.

Jalal, I., 1997. 'The status of Fiji women and the constitution,' in *Fiji in Transition: Research Papers of the Fiji Constitution Review Commission, 1*, ed. B.V. Lal and T. Vakatora (Suva: School of Social and Economic Development, University of the South Pacific), pp. 80–104.

—— 2002. 'Gender issues in post-coup d'etat Fiji: snapshots from the Fiji Island (A short history of life in the feminist trenches),' paper delivered to International Women's Conference, Townsville, Australia, 6 July.

Jaquette, J., 2003. 'Feminism and the challenges of the 'post-cold war' world,' *International Feminist Journal of Politics*, 5(3): 331–54.

Joachim, J., 1999. 'Shaping the human rights agenda: the case of violence against women,' in *Gender Politics in Global Governance*, ed. E. Prügl and M.K. Meyer (Lanham, MD: Rowman and Littlefield), pp. 142–60.

—— 2003. 'Framing issues, seizing opportunities: The UN, NGOs and women's rights,' *International Studies Quarterly*, 47(2): 247–74.

Jolly, M., 1996. 'Woman ikat raet long human raet o no?: women's rights, human rights and domestic violence in Vanuatu,' *Feminist Review*, 52(1): 169–90.

—— 1997. 'Women-nation-state in Vanuatu: women as signs and subjects in the discourses of *kastom*, modernity and Christianity,' in *Narratives of Nation in the South Pacific*, ed. T. Otto and N. Thomas (Amsterdam: Harwood Academic Publishers), pp. 133–62.

—— 1998. 'Other mothers: maternal "insouciance" and the depopulation debate in Fiji and Vanuatu 1890–1930,' in *Maternities and Modernities: Colonial and Postcolonial Experiences in Asia and the Pacific*, ed. K. Ram and M. Jolly (Cambridge: Cambridge University Press), pp. 177–212.

—— 2000. 'Woman ikat raet long human raet o no? women's rights, human rights, and domestic violence in Vanuatu,' in *Human Rights and Gender Politics: Asia-Pacific Perspectives*, ed. A-M. Hilsdon, M. MacIntyre, V. Mackie and M. Stivens (New York: Routledge), pp. 120–42.

—— 2003. 'Epilogue,' *Oceania*, 74(1/2): 134–47.

—— 2005a. 'Beyond the horizon? Nationalisms, feminisms and globalization in the Pacific,' *Ethnohistory*, 52(1): 138–66.

—— 2005b. 'Epilogue: multicultural relations in Fiji – between despair and hope,' *Oceania*, 75(4): 418–30.

—— and M. MacIntyre, eds., 1989. *Family and Gender in the Pacific: Domestic Contradictions and the Colonial Impact* (Cambridge: Cambridge University Press).

Kabeer, N., 1999. 'Resources, agency, achievements: reflections on the measurement of women's empowerment,' *Development and Change*, 30(3): 435–64.

Kahn, C., 1980. 'draft report of the sub-regional follow-up meeting for Pacific women on the World Conference of the United Nations Decade for Women, Suva, Fiji, 29 October to 3 November, 1980' (South Pacific Regional Development Office, United Nations, ESCAP).

Kahn, N.S., 2002. 'The impact of the global women's movement on international relations: Has it happened? What has happened?' in *Common Ground or Mutual Exclusion*, ed. M. Braig and S. Wölter (London: Zed Books).

Kaldor, M., 2003. *Global Civil Society: An Answer to War* (Polity Press, Cambridge).

Kamikamica, E., 1982. 'Fiji women on the move,' *Pacific Perspectives*, 11(2): 40–4.

——— 1985. 'Problems of women's education in Fiji,' in *Women in Development in the South Pacific: Barriers and Opportunities: Papers Presented at a Conference held in Vanuatu from 11 to 14 August 1984* (Canberra: Development Studies Centre, Australian National University), pp. 71–87.

Kanailagi, cited in 'Fiji Government Senator attacks Family Law Bill,' *Radio New Zealand International*, 24 October 2003. Online: http://www.rnzi.com/pages/news.php?op=read&id=7080 Accessed 12 June 2009.

Kaplan, T., 1997. 'The sources of gender bias in international relations theory,' in *Gender and International Relations*, ed. R. Grant and K. Newland (Indianapolis: Indiana University Press), pp. 8–26.

Karides, M., 2002. 'Linking local efforts with global struggle,' in *Women's Activism and Globalization: Linking Local Struggles and Transnational Politics*, ed. N. Naples and M. Desai (New York: Routledge), pp. 156–71.

Karl, M., 1995. *Women and Empowerment: Participation and Decision Making* (London: Zed Books).

Keane J., 2001. 'Global civil society?,' in *Global Civil Society 2001*, ed. H. Anheier, M. Glasius, and M. Kaldor (Oxford: Oxford University Press), pp. 23–47.

——— 2003. *Global Civil Society?* (Cambridge: Cambridge University Press).

Keck, K. and M. Sikkink, 1998. *Activists Beyond Borders* (Ithaca: Cornell University Press).

Keith-Reid, R., 1976. 'Teeth and talons bared at Suva "Y",' *Pacific Islands Monthly*, September: 16–17.

Kelly, J.D. and M. Kaplan, 2001. *Represented Communities: Fiji and World Decolonisation* (Chicago: University of Chicago Press).

Kenny, M., 2003. 'Global civil society: a liberal-republican argument,' in *Governance and Resistance in World Politics*, ed. D. Armstrong, T. Farrell and B. Maiguashca (Cambridge: Cambridge University Press), pp. 119–44.

Khagram, S., J.V. Riker and K. Sikkink, 2002. 'From Santiago to Seattle: transnational advocacy groups restructuring world politics,' in *Restructuring World Politics: Transnational Social Movements, Networks, and Norms*, S. Khagram, J. V. Riker and K. Sikkink (Minneapolis: University of Minnesota Press), pp. 3–23.

Khilnani, S., 2001. 'The development of civil society,' in *Civil Society: History and Possibilities*, ed. S. Kaviraj and S. Khilnani (Cambridge: Cambridge University Press), pp. 11–32.

Knapman, C., 1986. *White Women in Fiji 1835–1930: The Ruin of Empire?* (Sydney: Allen and Unwin).

Labra, A., *et al.*, 1981. 'The sovereignty of states,' in *Political and Institutional Issues of the New International Economic Order*, ed. E. Laszlo and J. Kurtzman (New York: Pergamon Press), pp. 3–13.

Lal, B. V., 2002. 'Making history, becoming history: reflections on Fiji's coups and constitutions,' *Contemporary Pacific*, 14(1): 148–67.

—— 2003. 'Fiji's constitutional conundrum,' *The Round Table*, 92(372): 671–85.

—— 2005. Personal communication with author, Canberra, 15 October.

—— 2009. 'One hand clapping: reflections on the first anniversary of Fiji's 2006 coup' in *The 2006 Military Takeover in Fiji: A Coup to End all Coups?*, ed. S. Firth, J. Fraenkel and B.V. Lal (Canberra: ANU E Press), pp. 425–48.

Lamont, C., 1959. 'Fiji women eager for progress,' *South Pacific Commission Quarterly Bulletin*, October: 40.

Lang, S., 1997. 'The NGOization of feminism,' in *Transitions, Environments, Translations: Feminisms in International Politics*, ed. J.W. Scott, C. Kaplan and D. Keates (New York: Routledge), pp. 101–20.

Larmour, P., 1998. 'Introduction,' in *Governance and Reform in the South Pacific*, ed. P. Larmour (Canberra: National Centre for Development Studies), pp. 1–20.

Lateef, S., 1990. 'Rule by the Danda: domestic violence among Indo-Fijians,' *Pacific Studies*, 13(3): 43–62.

Lawson, S., 1991. *The Failure of Democratic Politics in Fiji* (Oxford: Clarendon Press).

—— 1996. *Tradition Versus Democracy in the South Pacific: Fiji, Tonga and Western Samoa* (Cambridge: Cambridge University Press).

Lechte, R., 1978. 'Women's role in development,' in *Paradise Postponed*, ed. A. Mamak and G. McCall (Sydney: Pergamon Press), pp. 157–71.

—— 2005. Interview with author, Suva, 13 August.

Leckie, J., 2002. 'The complexities of women's agency in Fiji,' in *Gender Politics in the Asia-Pacific Region*, ed. B. Yeoh, P. Teo and S. Huang (New York: Routledge), pp. 156–79.

—— 2000a. 'Women in post-coup Fiji: negotiating work through old and new realities' in *Confronting Futures in Fiji*, ed. A.H. Akram (Canberra: Asia Pacific Press), pp. 178–201.

—— 2000b. 'Gender and work in Fiji: Constraints and re-negotiation,' in Bitter Sweet: Indigenous Women in the Pacific, ed. A. Jones, P. Herda and T. Suaalii (Dunedin: University of Otago Press), pp. 73–92.

—— 1997. 'Gender and work in Fiji: constraints to re-negotiation,' *Women's Studies* Journal 13(2): pp. 127–53.

—— 1992. 'Industrial relations in post-coup Fiji: a taste of the 1990s,' New Zealand Journal of Industrial Relations 17(1): 5–21

Lovel, H. and M.-T. Feuerstein, 1985. 'Women, poverty and community development in the third world,' *Community Development Journal* 20(3) (July): 156–62.

Lukere, V., 1997. 'The native mother,' in *The Cambridge History of the Pacific Islanders*, ed. D. Denoon, *et al.* (Cambridge: Cambridge University Press), pp. 280–87.

Lutua, K., 2009. 'The Fiji nurses' strike' in *The 2006 Military Takeover in Fiji: A Coup to End all Coups?* ed. S. Firth, J. Fraenkel and B.V. Lal (Canberra: ANU E Press), pp. 253–66.

Mackie, V., 2001. 'The language of globalization, transnationality and feminism,' *International Feminist Journal of Politics*, 3(2): 180–206.

Mair, L., 1986. 'Women: a decade is time enough,' *Third World Quarterly*, 8(2): 583–93.

Malua, M., 2004. 'Globalisation and trade and the impact on Pacific women,' *Women Today – Pacific* (SPC) June, (1) 1.

Mann, R. 'Human development programme report card' paper presented at the 10th Triennial Conference of *Pacific Women, Pacific Women, Pacific Plan: Stepping Up the Pace to 2010*, Noumea, 27–31 May 2007.

March, A., 2002. Presentation made by AusAID to workshop on strengthening government and non-government cooperation for effective poverty reduction in the Pacific, Australian Council for Overseas Aid, Deakin ACT, 13 September.

Marchand, M.H. and A.S. Runyan, eds, 2000. *Gender and Global Restructuring: Sightings, Sites, and Resistance* (London: Routledge).

Marques-Periera, B. and B. Siim, 2002. 'Representation, agency and empowerment' in *Contested Concepts in Gender and Social Politics*, ed. B. Hobson, J. Lewis and B. Siim (Aldershut: Edward Elgar), pp. 170–94.

Martin, S., 1985a, 'Pacific women's lobby,' *Forum 85*, 11 July.

—— 1985b, 'Pacific women pull together,' *Forum 85*, 18 July.

—— 1985c, 'What is feminism,' *Forum 85*, 18 July.

Marx-Ferree, M., 2006. 'Globalization and feminism: opportunities and obstacles for activism in the global arena' in *Global Feminism: Transnational Women's Activism, Organizing, and Human Rights*, ed. M. Marx-Ferree and A.M. Tripp (New York: New York University Press), pp. 3–23.

Masina, S., 2002. 'New Zealand, Pohiva and Tonga's silent majority,' *Pacific Islands Report*, 25 February. Online: http://archives.pireport.org/archive/2002/february/02-25-03.htm Accessed 7 March 2005.

Masura, F., 2002. Interview with author, Suva, 4 April.

May, R., 2003. 'The military in Papua New Guinea: a "culture of instability?"' in *"Arc of Instability"? Melanesia in the Early 2000s*, ed. R. May (SSGM & University of Canterbury).

McConaghy, M-J., 1975. 'Trials at the Tribune,' *Ms*, 4(5): 101–4.

McKenzie Aucoin, P., 1990. 'Domestic violence and social relations of conflict in Fiji,' *Pacific Studies*, 13(3): 23–41.

Meggitt, M.J., 1989. 'Women in contemporary Central Enga Society, Papua New Guinea,' in *Family and Gender in the Pacific: Domestic Contradictions and the Colonial Impact*, ed. M. Jolly and M. MacIntyre (Cambridge: Cambridge University Press), pp. 135–55.

Mera Molisa, G., 1991. *Women Ikat Raet Long Human Raet O No? Convensen Blong Stopem Evri Kaen Diskrimineisen Agansem Ol Woman* (Port Vila: Black Stone/Sun Productions).

Merry, S.E., 2003a, 'Human rights law and the demonization of culture (and anthropology along the way),' *Political and Legal Anthropology Review*, 26(1): 55–77.

—— 2003b, 'Rights talk and the experience of law: implementing women's human rights to protection from violence,' *Human Rights Quarterly*, 25(2): 343–81.

____ 2006a. 'Transnational human rights and local activisim: mapping the middle,' *American Anthropologist*, 108(1): 38–51.

—— 2006b. *Human Rights and Gender Violence: Translating International Law into Local Justice* (Chicago: Chicago University Press).

Mohanty, C., 1984. 'Under western eyes: feminist scholarship and colonial discourses,' *Boundary 2*, 12(3) / 13(1): 338–58.

Moore, K., 1975. *Report: United Nations International Women's Year Conference and Tribune: June–July 1975 Mexico City* (Canberra: Australian Council for Overseas Aid).

Moore, P., 2002a. Interview with author, Suva, 29 October.

—— 2002b. Interview with author, Suva, 5 November.

—— 2003. 'Rehabilitation for change in Fiji: a women's initiative,' in *A Kind of Mending: Restorative Justice in the Pacific Islands*, ed. S. Dinnen, with A. Jowitt and T. N. Cain (Canberra: Pandanus Books), pp. 123–38.

—— 2007. Interview with author, Suva, 6 February.

—— 2009. Personal communication with author, Suva, 19 February

—— and M. Desai, eds., 2002. *Women's Activism and Globalization: Linking Local Struggles and Transnational Politics* (New York: Routledge).

Naples, N. and M. Desai, eds, 2002. *Women's Activism and Globalization: Linking Local Struggles and Transnational Politics* (London: Routledge).

Narayan, J., 1984. *The Political Economy of Fiji* (Suva: South Pacific Review Press).

Narsey, W., 2007. *Gender Issues in Employment, Underemployment and Incomes in Fiji* (Suva: Vanuavou Publications).

NCBBF 2008. 'NCBBF role and responsibility' in *People's Charter for Change, Peace and Progress.* Online: http://www.fijipeoplescharter.com.fj/ncbbf2. htm Accessed 26 May 2009.

NCW (National Council of Women), 1981. *Fiji Women's United Nations' Mid-Decade Plan of Action 1981–1985* (Suva: NCW).

—— 1982. *Seminar Report: Fiji Women in Development, 25–27 October 1982* (Suva: Marama Publication).

Niukula, P., 1997. 'Religion and the state,' in *Fiji in Transition: Research Papers of the Fiji Constitution Review Commission, 1,* ed. B.V. Lal and T. Vakatora (Suva: School of Social and Economic Development, University of the South Pacific), pp. 53–79.

Norton, R., 2000. 'Reconciling ethnicity and nation: contending discourses in Fiji's constitutional reform,' *Contemporary Pacific,* 12(1): 83–122.

Nussbaum, M., 2002. 'Women's capabilities and social justice,' in *Gender Justice, Development and Rights,* ed. M. Molyneux and S. Razavi (Oxford: Oxford University Press), pp. 45–77.

O'Barr, J.F., 1986. 'Reflections on Forum '85 in Nairobi, Kenya: voices from the international women's studies community,' *Signs: Journal of Women in Culture and Society,* 10(3): 584–6.

Ogashiwa, Y., 1991. *Microstates and Nuclear Issues: Regional Cooperation in the Pacific* (Suva: Institute of the Pacific Studies, University of the South Pacific).

O'Hare, U.A., 1999. 'Realizing human rights for women,' *Human Rights Quarterly,* 21(2): 364–402.

Oloka-Onyango, J. and S. Tamale, 1995. 'The personal is "political," or why women's rights are indeed human rights: an African perspective on "international feminism",' *Human Rights Quarterly,* 17(4): 691–731.

Omomo Melen Pacific, 1995. *Omomo Melen Pacific: Women from the Non-Self Governing Territories and Colonies of the Pacific, Beijing, August 1995* (Christchurch: IWDA).

Otto, D., 1996. 'Non-governmental organisations in the United Nations System: the emerging role of international civil society,' *Human Rights Quarterly*, 18(1): 107–41.

Padarath, A., 2007. 'Young women's leadership programme,' paper presented at the 10th Triennial Conference of Pacific Women, *Pacific Women, Pacific Plan: Stepping Up the Pace to 2010*, Noumea, 27–31 May 2007.

Paini, A., 2003. '"The kite is tied to you": custom, Christianity and organization among Kanak women of Drueulu, Lifou, New Caledonia,' *Oceania*, 74(1/2): 81–97.

Pande, R., 2002. Interview with author, Suva, 5 March.

Papanek, H., 1975a, 'Women in South and Southeast Asia: issues and research,' *Signs: Journal of Women in Culture and Society*, 1(1): 193–213.

—— 1975b, 'The work of women: postscript from Mexico City,' *Signs: Journal of Women in Culture and Society*, 1(1): 215–16.

Pareti, S., 2002. 'Affirmative action … an illusion or a recipe for success?,' *Pacific Islands Business*, July.

Parkinson, S., 1961. 'Girls club formed in Suva,' *South Pacific Bulletin*, April: 60–4.

Parpart, J. and M. Zalewski, 2008. *Re-thinking the Man Question: Sex, Gender and Violence in International Relations* (London: Zed Press).

Patton, C.G., 1995. 'Women and power: the Nairobi Conference, 1985,' in *Women Politics and the United Nations*, ed. A. Winslow (Westport, Conn.: Greenwood Press), pp. 61–76.

PCC (Pacific Council of Churches), 1979. *Women in Development: Report of the First PCC Women's Consultation* (Suva: Lotu Pasifika Productions).

PCRC (Pacific Concerns Resource Centre), 2002. *Pacific News Bulletin*, November/December.

—— 2005. *Pacific New Bulletin*, January.

Peace Women Across the Globe, 2005. *1000 PeaceWomen*. Online: http://www.1000peacewomen.org/eng/friedensfrauen.php Accessed 18 May 2009.

Petersen. L., 2007. 'Pacific women's bureau/human development report card' paper presented at the 10th Triennial Conference of Pacific Women, *Pacific Women, Pacific Plan: Stepping Up the Pace to 2010*, Noumea, 27–31 May 2007.

Peterson, V.S., ed., 1992. *Gendered states: Feminist (Re)Visions of International Relations Theory* (Boulder, CO: Lynne Rienner).

Peterson, V.S. and A.S. Runyan, 2010. *Global Gender Issues in the New Millennium* (Boulder, CO: Westview Press, 3rd ed.).

Pettman, J., 1996. *Worlding Women: Feminist International Politics* (London: Routledge).

Pietilä, H. and J. Vickers, 1996. *Making Women Matter: The Role of the United Nations* (London: Zed Books, 3rd ed.).

Pukui, M.K., 1983. *'Olelo No'eau: Hawaiian Proverbs and Poetical Sayings* (Honolulu: Bishop Museum Press).

Pulea, M., 1982. 'Women, employment and development,' *Pacific Perspectives*, 11(2): 18–23.

Rai, S.M., 2002. *Gender and the Political Economy of Development: From Nationalism to Globalization* (New York: Polity Press).

Ralston, C., 1989. 'Changes in the lives of ordinary women in early post-contact Hawaii,' in *Family and Gender in the Pacific: Domestic Contradictions and the Colonial Impact*, ed. M. Jolly and M. MacIntyre (Cambridge: Cambridge University Press), pp. 45–64.

Ram, K., 1994. 'Militarism and market mania in Fiji,' in *Sustainable Development or Malignant Growth: Perspectives of Pacific Islands Women*, ed. A. Emberson-Bain (Suva: Marama Publications), pp. 237–50.

Randall, V. and R. Theobald, 1998. *Political Change and Underdevelopment: A Critical Introduction to Third World Politics* (London: Macmillan).

Randell, S., 1983. 'The participation of women in the evaluation of church-funded development projects,' in *Women, Aid and Development*, ed. L. Melville, (Canberra: Women and Development Network of Australia), pp. 103–7.

Rankin, K., 2002. 'Social capital, microfinance and the politics of development,' *Feminist Economics*, 8(1): 1–24.

Rao, S., 2002. Interview with author, Suva, 15 March.

Rasmussen, J., 1980. *Notes on Sub-Regional Follow-Up Meeting For Pacific Women on the World Conference of the United Nations Decade for Women, 29 October–3 November 1980, Suva* (Washington, DC: Overseas Education Fund of the League of Women Voters).

Reid, E., 1984. 'Since Mexico '75, a decade of progress?,' *Development: Seeds of Change*, 4: 76–9.

Reilly, B., 2000. 'The Africanisation of the South Pacific,' *Australian Journal of International Affairs*, 54(3): 261–8.

_____ and K. Graham, 2004. 'Conflict through Asia and the Pacific: causes and trends,' in *Searching for peace in Asia Pacfic: An Overview of Conflict Prevention and Peacebuilding Activities*, ed. A. Hejimans, N. Simmonds and H. van de Veen (Boulder: Lynne Rienner Publishers), pp. 9–22.

Reilly, N., 2009. *Women's Human Rights: Seeking Gender Justice in a Globalising Age* (London: Polity Press).

Ricketts, J., 1997. 'Our lives will never be the same,' in *With Heart and Nerve and Sinew: Post-coup Writing from Fiji*, ed. A. Griffen (Suva: Christmas Club), pp. 146–64.

Riles, A., 2001. *The Network Inside Out* (Ann Arbor: University of Michigan Press).

Robertson, R., 1961. 'Fiji women find new interests,' *South Pacific Bulletin*, October: 54–55, 62.

Robertson, R.T., 1986. 'Making new histories of Fiji: the choice between materialist political economy and neocolonial orthodoxy,' *Journal of Pacific Studies*, 12: 33–58.

—— and W. Sutherland, 2001. *Government by the Gun: The Unfinished Business of Fiji's 2000 Coup* (Melbourne: Pluto Press).

Rokotuivuna, A., 1975. 'Are planners human?,' in *The Pacific Way: Social Issues in National Development*, ed. S. Tupouniua, R. Crocombe and C. Slatter (Suva: South Pacific Social Sciences Association), pp. 7–9.

—— 1997. 'Reflections of an activist,' in *With Heart and Nerve and Sinew: Post-coup Writing from Fiji*, ed. A. Griffen (Suva: Christmas Club), pp. 136–45.

—— 2002a. Interview with author, Suva, 20 March.

—— 2002b. Interview with author, Suva, 22 November.

—— *et al.*, 1973. *Fiji: A Developing Australian Colony* (North Fitzroy, VIC: International Development Action).

Rongokea, L., 2008. 'How can one talk about sisterhood and solidarity when we cannot openly address our own differences?,' paper presented at AWID's 11th International Forum on Women's Rights and Development, Cape Town, South Africa, November 2008.

RRRT (Regional Rights Resource Team), 2001. *All About CEDAW in 10 Questions and Answers: A Basic Information Guide to CEDAW* (Suva: RRRT).

—— 2002a. *Report on the Presentation of the first PIC Country Report to UN CEDAW* (Government of Fiji Is.) DFID (Pacific) RRRT.

—— 2002b. *Right Hia: A Regional Rights Resource Team Newsletter*, 1 (January–March).

—— 2003. *CEDAW Roadmap: Reporting Before the Committee* (Suva: RRRT).

Ruppert, U., 2002. 'Global women's politics: towards the 'globalising' of women's human rights,' in *Common Ground or Mutual Exclusion: Women's Movements and International Relations*, ed. M. Braig and S. Wölte (London: Zed Books), pp. 147–59.

Ryle, J., 2005. 'Roots of the land and church: the Christian state debate in Fiji,' *International Journal for the Study of the Christian Church*, 5(1): 58–78.

SCF (Save the Children Fiji), 2001. *A River Divides: Participatory Impact Assessment, Pilot Project Report* (Suva: SCF).

Scheyvens, R., 2003. 'Church women's groups and the empowerment of women in Solomon Islands,' *Oceania*, 74(1/2): 24–43.

Schild, V., 2002. 'New social citizenship in Chile: NGOs and social provisioning under neo-liberalism,' in *Gender Justice, Development and Rights*, ed. M. Molyneux and S. Razavi (Oxford: Oxford University Press), pp. 170–203.

Schoeffel, P., 1979. 'The ladies row of thatch: women and rural development in Western Saṃoa,' *Pacific Perspective*, 8(2): 1–11.

—— 1982. 'Women's associations and rural development: Western Samoa and East New Britian,' *Pacific Perspective*, 11(2): 56–61.

—— 1983. 'Involving women in project design, implementation and evaluation,' in *Women, Aid and Development*, ed. L. Melville (Canberra: Women and Development Network of Australia), pp. 96–102.

—— 1986. 'The rice pudding syndrome: women's advancement and home economics training in the South Pacific,' in *Australian Council for Overseas Aid, Development in the Pacific: What Women Say*, Development Dossier 18 (Canberra: Australian Council for Overseas Aid), pp. 36–44.

—— 1988. *Women in Development: Fiji*, Country Briefing Paper (Manila: Asian Development Bank, Programs Department (East), December).

—— and E. Kikau, 1980. 'Women's work in Fiji: an historical perspective,' *Review*, 1(2): 21–6.

Scollay, R., 2001. 'New developments in trade and economic cooperation among Pacific Islands forum members,' presented to 'Pacific Update' at the Foundation for Development Cooperation, 18 July.

Sen, G., 2002. 'Subordination and sexual control: a comparative view of the control of women,' in *The Women, Gender, and Development Reader*, ed. N. Visvanathan, L. Duggan, L. Nisonoff and N. Wiegersma (London: Zed Books, 4th ed.), pp. 142–9.

Sen, G. and C. Grown, 1987. *Development, Crises and Alternative Visions: Third World Women's Perspectives* (New York: Monthly Review Press).

Shameem, S., 2007. 'The Assumption of Executive Authority on December 5th by Commodore J.V. Bainimarama, Commander of the Republic of Fiji Military Forces: Legal, Constitutional and Human Rights Issues,' statement issued by the Director of the Fiji Human Rights Commission, 3 January 2007. Originally posted to Fijilive website (later withdrawn).

Shibuya, E., 2003. 'The problems and potential of the Pacific Islands forum,' in *The Asia Pacific: A Region in Transition*, ed. J. Rolfe (Honolulu: Asia-Pacific Center for Security Studies), pp. 102–15.

Singh, P., 1994. 'The Pacific aid regime: continuity and change,' in *Sustainable Development or Malignant Growth: Perspectives of Pacific Islands Women*, ed. A. Emberson-Bain (Suva: Marama Publications), pp. 51–62.

Siwatibau, S., 1985. 'Women's access to aid-sponsored training in the South Pacific,' in *Women in Development in the South Pacific: Barriers and Opportunities: Papers Presented at a Conference held in Vanuatu from 11 to 14 August 1984*, ed. Development Studies Centre (Canberra: Development Studies Centre, Australian National University), pp. 88–101.

—— 2002. Interview with author, 26 November.

—— and B.D. Williams, 1982. *A Call to a New Exodus: An Anti-Nuclear Primer for Pacific People* (Suva: Pacific Council of Churches)

Slatter, C., 1973. 'The tourist industry in Fiji,' in *Fiji: A Developing Australian Colony*, ed. A. Rokotuivuna (North Fitzroy, VIC: International Development Action), pp.18–25.

—— 1976. *Women Together: Report of the 3rd National Convention of the YWCA of Fiji 10–13th September 1976, Suva* (Suva: YWCA).

—— 1980. *The World Conference of the United Nations Decade for Women: Equality, Development and Peace, July 14–30 1980, Bella Centre, Copenhagen, Denmark* (Suva: Centre for Applied Studies in Development, University of the South Pacific).

—— 1987. 'Women factory workers in Fiji: the 'half a loaf' syndrome, *Journal of Pacific Studies*, 13: 47–59.

—— 1991. 'Economic recovery on the backs of women workers: women and tax free enterprises in Fiji,' *Review: Diversity in Development*, 12(19): 18–28.

—— 1994. 'Banking on the growth model? The World Bank and market policies in the Pacific,' in *Sustainable Development or Malignant Growth: Perspectives of Pacific Islands Women*, ed. A. Emberson-Bain (Suva: Marama Publications), pp. 17–36.

—— 2001. 'Tensions in activism: navigating in global spaces at the intersections of state/civil society and gender/economic justice,' paper presented to the Workshop on Gender and Globalisation in Asia and the Pacific: Feminist Revisions of the International, Australian National University, Canberra, November.

—— 2001. Personal communication with author, Suva, 21November.

—— 2002. Interview with author, Suva, 6 November.

—— 2005. Electronic Communication with author 21 July.

—— 2006, 'Treading water in rapids? Non-governmental organisations and resistance to neoliberalism in Pacific Islands States' in *Globalisation and Governance in the Pacific Islands*, ed. S. Firth (ANU E Press, Canberra), pp.23–42.

Smales, A., 1980. 'Politics without protest emerge from South Pacific conference,' *Pacific Islands Monthly*, December: 11–15.

SPC (South Pacific Commission), 1976. *Regional Workshop on Future Trends in the Development of Women's Programmes in the South Pacific Region, Suva, Fiji, 8–19 December 1975* (Noumea: South Pacific Commission).

—— 1980a. 'The role of women in development in the Pacific region: paper presented by French Polynesia,' *Twentieth South Pacific Conference, Port Moresby, Papua New Guinea, 18–24 October 1980*, SPConf.20/WP.12 (Noumea: SPC).

—— 1980b. *Draft Resolutions Adopted by the Twentieth South Pacific Conference, Port Moresby, Papua New Guinea, 18–24 October 1980* (Noumea: SPC).

—— 1985. *Report/Regional Meeting of Pacific Islands Women's Non-Government Organisations; Rarotonga, Cook Islands, 19–23 March 1985* (Noumea: SPC).

—— 1994a. *Sixth Triennial Regional Conference of Pacific Women, Noumea, New Caledonia, 2–4 May 1994* (Noumea: SPC).

—— 1994b. *Ministerial Meeting on Women and Sustainable Development, Noumea, New Caledonia, 5–6 May, 1994* (Noumea: SPC).

—— 1995. *Pacific Platform for Action: Rethinking Sustainable Development for Pacific Women Towards the Year 2000* (Noumea: SPC).

—— 1997. *Seventh Triennial Conference of Pacific Women, Noumea, New Caledonia, 16–20 June 1997* (Noumea: SPC).

—— 2001. *Eight Triennial Conference of Pacific Women, Noumea, New Caledonia, 10–14 September 2001* (Noumea: SPC).

—— 2008. 'Pacific turnout to CSW improves,' [Press Release, 7 March]. Online: http://lists.spc.int/pipermail/press-releases_lists.spc.int/2008-March/000396.html Accessed 8 March 2009.

—— 2009. 'Pacific voices heard on financial and climate change crises,' [Press Release, 18 March]. Online: http://lists.spc.int/pipermail/press-releases_lists.spc.int/2009-March/000482.html Accessed 19 March 2009.

Spivak, G., 1996. '"Woman" as theatre: United Nations Conference on Women, Beijing 1995,' *Radical Philosophy*, 75(Jan/Feb): 250.

Steans, J., 2003. 'Engaging from the margins: feminist encounters with the 'mainstream' of international relations,' *British Journal of Politics and International Relations* 5(3): 428–54.

—— and A. Ahmadi, 2005. 'Negotiating the politics of gender and rights: some reflections on the status of women's human rights at "Beijing Plus Ten",' *Global Society*, 19(3): 227–45.

—— and L. Pettiford, 2001. *International Relations: Perspectives and Themes* (New York: Longman).

Steinem, G., 1976. 'Gloria Steinem and Elizabeth Reid talk about revolution,' *Ms*, 5(7): 65–7, 84.

Stephenson, C.M., 1995. 'Women's international nongovernmental organizations at the United Nations,' in *Women, Politics and the United Nations*, ed. A. Winslow (Westport, Conn.: Greenwood Press), pp. 135–54.

Stewart, M., 1960a, 'Training women for leadership in Fiji,' *South Pacific Bulletin*, July: 44–5.

—— 1960b, 'Fiji women enthusiastic about club work,' *South Pacific Bulletin*, October: 54–5, 70.

—— 1962. 'Women in home and community,' *South Pacific Bulletin*, October: 42–4.

Stienstra D., 1994. *Women's Movements and International Organizations* (New York: St. Martin's Press).

—— 1995. 'Organizing for change: international women's movements and world politics,' in *Women in World Politics: An Introduction*, ed. F. D'Amico and P. R. Beckman (Westport, Conn.: Bergin and Garvey), pp. 143–54.

Stivens, M., 2000. 'Introduction: gender politics and the reimagining of human rights in the Asia Pacific,' in *Human Rights and Gender Politics: Asia-Pacific Perspectives*, ed. A-M Hilsdon, M. MacIntyre, V. Mackie and M. Stivens (New York: Routledge), pp. 1–36.

Sue, M.K., 1982. 'Community education training centre (CETC),' *Pacific Perspectives*, 11(2): 63–4.

Sutherland, H., *et al.*, 1986. 'Crisis intervention,' Presentation to National Women in Development Conference/Workshop, University of the South Pacific, Suva, 14 July.

Sutherland, W., 1992. *Beyond the Politics of Race: An Alternative History of Fiji to 1992*, Political and Social Change Monograph No. 15 (Canberra: Department of Political and Social Change, Australian National University).

—— 2000. 'The problematics of reform and the "Fijian" question,' in *Confronting Fiji Futures*, ed. A.H. Akram-Lodhi (Canberra: Asia Pacific Press, Australian National University), pp. 205–25.

Syrkin, M., 1980. 'Suttee at the women's conference,' *Midstream*, 26(8): 34–6.

Tariseisei, J., 2000. 'Today is not the same as yesterday, and tomorrow it will be different again: *kastom* in Ambae, Vanuatu,' in 'Women and governance from the grassroots in Melanesia,' *State, Society and Governance in Melanesia Discussion Paper 00/2*, ed. B. Douglas (Canberra: SSGM Project, Australian National University), pp. 14–16.

Tarte, S., 2001. 'Melanesia in review: issues and events: Fiji,' *Contemporary Pacific*, 13(2): 529–41.

Teaiwa, T., 2001. 'Lo(o)sing the edge,' *Contemporary Pacific*, 13(2): 343–57.

Tinker, I., 1986. 'Reflections on Forum '85 in Nairobi, Kenya: voices from the international women's studies community,' *Signs: Journal of Women in Culture and Society*, 10(3): 586–9.

—— 1997. 'The making of a field: advocates, practitioners and scholars,' in *The Women, Gender and Development Reader*, ed. N. Visvanathan, L. Duggan, L. Nisonoff and N. Wiegersma (London: Zed Books), pp. 33–42.

—— 1999. 'NGOs: an alternative power base for women?' in *Gender, Politics and Global Governance*, ed. M.K. Meyer and E. Prugl (New York: Rowman and Littlefield), pp. 88–106.

—— and J. Jaquette, 1987. 'UN decade for women: its impact and legacy,' *World Development*, 15(3): 419–27.

Tobar, M.R., 2003. 'Chilean feminism(s) in the 1990s: paradoxes of an unfinished transition,' *International Feminist Journal of Politics*, 5(2): 256–80.

Tomlinson, M., 2009. *In God's Image: The Metaculture of Fijian Christianity* (University of California Press, Berkeley).

Toren, C., 1999. *Mind Materiality and History: Explorations in Fijian Ethnography* (New York: Routledge).

Tripp, A.M., 2003. 'Women in movement: transformations in African political landscapes,' *International Feminist Journal of Politics*, 5(2): 233–55.

—— 2006. 'Challenges in transnational feminist mobilization,' in *Global Feminism: Transnational Women's Activism, Organizing, and Human Rights*, ed. M. Marx-Ferree and A.M. Tripp (New York: New York University Press), pp 296–312.

True, J. and M. Mintrom, 2001. 'Transnational networks and policy diffusion: the case of gender mainstreaming,' *International Studies Quarterly*, 45(1): 27–57.

Tupouniua, S., R. Crocombe and C. Slatter, 1975, *The Pacific Way: Social Issues in National Development* (Suva: South Pacific Social Sciences Association).

Tuwere, I.S., 1997. 'The church, state relation in Fiji,' in *Fiji in Transition: Research Papers of the Fiji Constitution Review Commission, 1*, ed. B.V. Lal and T. Vakatora (Suva: School of Social and Economic Development, University of the South Pacific), pp. 53–79.

—— 2002. Vanua: Towards a Fijian Theology of Place (Suva: Institute of Pacific Studies).

UN CEDAW (UN Convention on the Elimination of All Forms of Discrimination), 2000. Consideration of Reports submitted by States Parties Under Article 18 of the Convention on the Elimination of All Forms of Discrimination Against Women – Initial Reports of States Parties – Fiji Islands, CEDAW/C/FJI/1, 14 March.

—— 2002. 'Completing consideration of Fiji report, committee told convention is "a living reality": in Fiji,' Press Release, 22 January.

UNDP-RRRT, *Poverty Reduction and Access and Justice for All Project*. Online: www.undp.org.fj/RRRT Accessed 18 January 2006.

UNDP (UN Development Programme) with Government of Fiji, 1997. *Fiji Poverty Report: A Summary* (Suva: UNDP/UNOPS).

UNESCAP (UN Economic and Social Commission for Asia and the Pacific), 1980. *Draft Report of the Subregional Follow-up Meeting for Pacific Women on the World Conference of the United Nations Decade for Women, Suva, Fiji 29 October to 3 November 1980* (Suva: UNESCAP).

—— 1994. *Pacific Women NGO Programme for Action for the Beijing United Nations Conference 1995* (Suva and Philippines)

UNIFEM Pacific, 2000. *Women, Men, Globalisation and Trade Liberalisation* (Suva: United Nations Development Fund for Women).

UN Commission on the Status of Women, 1967. *United Nations Assistance for the Advancement of Women*, E/CN.6/467 (New York: United Nations).

—— 1970. *Participation of Women in the Economic and Social Development of their Countries*, E/CN.6/513/Rev.1 (New York: United Nations).

—— 1972. *Participation of Women in Community Development*, E/CN.6/514/ Rev.1 (New York: United Nations).

—— 1995. *Fourth World Conference on Women: Platform for Action*. Online: http://www.un.org/womenwatch/daw/bejing/plat1.htm Accessed 6 December 2002.

UN Security Council, 2000. *Security Council resolution 1325 [on women and peace and security]*, 31 October 2000, S/RES/1325 (2000). Online: http://www. unhcr.org/refworld/docid/3b00f4672e.html Accessed 27 February 2008.

United Nations, 1986 . *Report of the World Conference to Review and Appraise the Achievements of the United Nations Decade for Women: Equality, Development and Peace, Nairobi, 15–26 July 1985*, UN New York. Online: http://www. un.org/esa/gopher-data/conf/fwcw/nfls/nfls.en Accessed 20 June 2009.

United Nations Food and Agriculture Organization, 1975. *The Missing Half: Woman 1975* (New York: United Nations).

United States Centre for International Women's Year, 1975. *Kaleidoscope: Tribune of International Women's Year* (Washington, DC: US Center for IWY '75).

UNIWY (United Nations International Women's Year) *Secretariat, 1975. Meeting in Mexico: World Conference of the International Women's Year, 1975* (New York: Center for Economic and Social Information/OPI).

Unknown, 2006. 'Monitoring framework of the violation of the freedom from arbitrary arrest and detention and freedom from cruel or degrading treatment by the Republic of Fiji Military Forces (RFMF) since its Coup d'etat of 5th December 2006.' Online: http://www.defendingwomen-defendingrights. org/pdf2007/Updated260107Monitoring_FijiCoup2006_Shortversion.pdf Accessed 1 July 2007.

Vakalomoloma, J., 2002. Interview with author, Suva, 21 March.

Vakatale, T., 2002. Interview with author, Suva, 18 November.

Van Rooy, A., 1998. *Civil Society and the Aid Industry* (London: Earthscan).

Varani-Norton, E., 2005. 'The church versus women's push for change: the case of Fiji'. *Fijian Studies*, 3(2): 223–47.

Vasakula, R., 2002. 'Fiji law commission's review of rape laws,' paper delivered at FWCC Panel Discussion on Sexual Assault and Marital Rape, Australian High Commission, Suva, 8 March.

Vasisht, M., 2000. Electronic communication to FWRM, 24 March.

Vere, T., 2002a. Interview with author, Suva, 9 April.

—— 2002b. Interview with author, Suva, 22 November.

'Vice President Ratu Joni opens new Family Law Court,' *Fiji Government Online Portal*, 2 November 2005. Online: http://www.fiji.gov.fj/publisher/ printer_5678.shtml Accessed 12 June 2009.

Villabos, D.P., 1980. 'A woman who will be heard,' *Forum'80*, July 24.

Visvanathan, N., 1997. 'General introduction,' in *The Women, Gender and Development Reader*, ed. N. Visvanathan, L. Duggan, L. Nisonoff and N. Wiegersma (London: Zed Books), pp. 1–6.

von Strokirch, K., 2003. 'The region in review: international issues and events,' *Contemporary Pacific*, 16(2): 370–81.

WAC (Women's Action for Change), 1999. *Women's Action for Change* (WAC: Annual Report January – December 1999 (Suva: WAC).

—— 2000. *Women's Action for Change: Annual Report for 2000* (Suva: WAC).

—— 2001. *Women's Action for Change: Annual Report for 2001* (Suva: WAC).

—— 2009. *Wacky: Peacebuilding Newsletter of Women's Action for Change* (WAC), Suva, May.

WAC/SM, 1999. *Women's Action for Change (WAC) Sexual Minorities Project: Annual Report,* January–December 1999 (Suva: WAC).

Wainwright, E., 2003. 'Responding to state failure: the case of Australia and Solomon Islands,' *Australian Journal of International Affairs,* 57(3): 485–98.

Walker, A., 1984. 'Networking for women by women,' *Development: Seeds of Change,* 4: 104–5.

Waqovonovono, M., 1980. 'The Pacific women's resource center,' in *Case Studies on Women in the Pacific* (Kuala Lumpur: Asian and Pacific Center for Women and Development, April).

Wells, B.L., 2002. 'Context, strategy, ground: rural women organizing to confront local/global economic issues,' in *Women's Activism and Globalization: Linking Local Struggles and Transnational Politics,* ed. N. Naples and M. Desai (New York: Routledge), pp. 139–51.

West, L., 1999. 'The United Nations women's conferences and feminist politics,' in *Gender Politics in Global Governance,* ed. E. Prügl and M.K. Meyer (Lanham, MD: Rowman and Littlefield), pp. 177–93.

Willetts, P., 1996. *The Conscience of the World: The Influence of Non-Governmental Organizations in the United Nations System* (London: Hurst).

—— ed., 2000. 'From "consultative arrangements" to "partnership": the changing status of NGOs in diplomacy at the UN,' *Global Governance,* 6(2): 191–212.

Windybank, S., and M. Manning, 2003. 'Papua New Guinea on the brink,' *Issue Analysis,* IA30, The Centre for Independent Studies, 12 March.

Wing, S., 2002. 'Women activists in Mali: the global discourse on human rights,' in *Women's Activism and Globalization: Linking Local Struggles and Transnational Politics,* ed. N. Naples and M. Desai (New York: Routledge), pp. 172–85.

Winston, F., 1985. 'For genuine equality: appraising the results of the UN Decade for Women,' *World Marxist Review*, 28(8): 95–100.

World Bank, 1975. *Integrating Women into Development* (New York: World Bank, August).

World YWCA, 1995. World YWCA Statements of Policy: 100 Years of Forward with Vision (Geneva: YWCA).

Yabaki, A., 2004. 'The Fiji coup and constitutional challenges,' paper presented at the ECSIEP Seminar on The Cotonou Agreement and the Conflicts in the Pacific, Suva, 14 December.

—— 2002. Electronic communication with author, May 16.

Yuval-Davis, N., 2006. 'Human/women's rights and feminist transversal politics,' in *GlobalFeminism: Transnational Women's Activism, Organizing, and Human Rights*, ed. M. Marx-Ferree and A.M. Tripp (New York: New York University Press), pp. 275–95.